BURMA'S FOREIGN RELATIONS

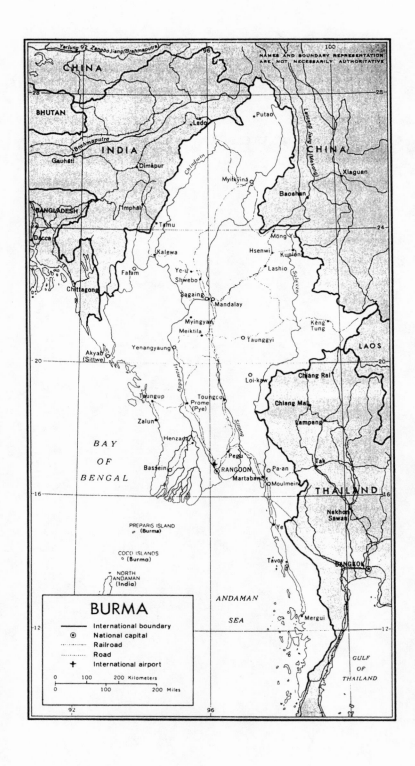

BURMA

— International boundary
⊙ National capital
---- Railroad
········ Road
+ International airport

| 0 | 100 | 200 Kilometers |
| 0 | 100 | 200 Miles |

Burma's Foreign Relations

NEUTRALISM IN THEORY AND PRACTICE

Chi-shad Liang

FOREWORD BY Robert A. Scalapino

PRAEGER

New York
Westport, Connecticut
London

Library of Congress Cataloging-in-Publication Data

Liang, Chi-shad.
    Burma's foreign relations : neutralism in theory and practice /
Chi-shad Liang ; foreword by Robert A. Scalapino.
    p. cm.
    Includes bibliographical references.
    ISBN 0-275-93455-1 (alk. paper)
    1. Burma—Foreign relations. 2. Burma—Nonalignment. I. Title.
DS530.4.L52   1990   90-31953

Library of Congress Catalog Card Number: 90-31953
ISBN: 0-275-93455-1

First published in 1990

Praeger Publishers, One Madison Avenue, New York, NY 10010
An imprint of Greenwood Publishing Group, Inc.

Printed in the United States of America

The paper used in this book complies with the
Permanent Paper Standard issued by the National
Information Standards Organization (Z39.48-1984).

10 9 8 7 6 5 4 3 2 1

CONTENTS

FOREWORD

Burma remains largely territory incognito, even to scholars of the Pacific-Asian region. This society—whose leaders now want their country to be known as Myanmar—has acquired the reputation in recent years not only of being mysterious in its ways but of having military governors who are oppressive toward their citizens at home and xenophobic in their attitudes toward the external world. For years it appeared that the military had consciously adopted a policy of economic stagnation as a strategy for stability. But perhaps we were only witnessing yet another failure of socialism, in this case "socialism with Burmese characteristics."

It is surprising that in the midst of the technological-informational revolution that is sweeping over the world, Burma's governors have still managed to keep their society largely cut off from external developments and controlled by a very traditional military dictatorship. To be sure, the nation's recent rulers could summon the Burmese traditions of monarchy, aloofness, and militancy. The deep ethnic divisions that have marked Burma's modern politics also play a critical role in shaping policies, domestic and foreign. In addition, geopolitics must be considered. Wedged between India to the west and China to the north, with a dynamic, modernizing Thailand—a traditional enemy—to the east, Burma has always had to display an element of caution in dealing with foreigners.

While the internal politics of contemporary Burma contain many mysteries and uncertainties, there is ample circumstantial evidence that General Ne Win remains a powerful figure despite his official retirement. Critical decisions probably must bear his imprimatur. Yet with his age and health bringing the time of succession closer, factionalism within military-political ranks and the politics of intrigue play an increasingly important role. And while repression remains the most prominent feature of the Burmese political landscape insofar as the citizenry is concerned, the recent evidences of student revolution and the emergence of articulate spokesmen for reform suggest that the old order cannot remain intact indefinitely.

No doubt Burma's future politics will be strongly influenced by economic decisions, and both will be decisive in shaping the nation's future foreign policies. In the past, Burma's autarkic economic policies have enabled it to remain one of the very few truly nonaligned states. Indeed, in the fall of 1979, Burma announced its withdrawal from the Nonaligned Movement, proclaiming that the movement had ceased to adhere to its original purposes. Such an allegation has considerable substance. As economic interdependence has grown, most so-called "nonaligned" states have gravitated toward the market economies, with growing influence upon their political and strategic policies as well. Others, smaller in number, have drawn closer to the socialist orbit, headed by the U.S.S.R., although the crises that have recently befallen the Leninist world raise questions about the future of Soviet-led alliances, economic as well as strategic.

In this setting, Dr. Chi-shad Liang has presented us with a comprehensive, detailed account of Burma's foreign policies since its independence on January 4, 1948. After a survey of the historical background and an account of the evolutionary development of Burma's current political institutions, Dr. Liang makes use of a wide range of sources to analyze Rangoon's relations with its Asian neighbors, more distant states in the Pacific-Asian region, the principal Western nations, the old Soviet bloc countries, and the so-called Third World. He also provides a highly informative chapter on Burma's interaction with key regional and international organizations.

In bringing together data that has previous been available only in a great diversity of sources, and in providing an objective, balanced analysis of this data, Dr. Liang has performed a significant service for all students of Asian affairs.

Robert A. Scalapino

PREFACE

Burma became a sovereign state on January 4, 1948, after nearly one hundred years of British rule. Burma's leaders initially contemplated alliance with and sought military and financial assistance from Great Britain and the United States to bolster national security, consolidate political unity, and promote economic rehabilitation and development of their newly independent country, but neither London nor Washington was inclined to give Rangoon any such commitment. Subsequently, internal and external circumstances and events, particularly the Communist victory in the Chinese civil war, prompted them to take a neutral course in foreign relations. The neutralist policy has since been consistently followed by the Burmese government without fundamental change. While the foreign relations of the U Nu government were characterized by positive neutralism, the government under U Ne Win's direct or indirect leadership since 1962 has cautiously taken a semiactive approach after more than a decade of pursuing negative neutralism. However, no government of Burma has ever observed true neutralism in practice, but rather leaned to the People's Republic of China. Sharing a long border with China, which historically was its invader and suzerain state and presently has close ideological ties with the Burmese Community Party, one of the largest and most heavily armed insurgent groups in the country, Burma must cultivate a peaceful and cooperative relationship with this giant neighbor for survival, and this has become Burma's top foreign relations priority.

The neutralist policy has preserved Burma's independence, principally as a result of outside circumstances and the policies of other nations. Its negative and selective approach, however, has turned a country with extraordinary economic potential into one of the least developed nations in the world. Recent widespread protests, originally fueled by public discontent over rampant inflation, food shortages, and other economic hardships, have shaken the leadership of the ruling party and state apparatus and forced the Burmese authorities to schedule a shift from one-party rule to multiparty democracy. Whatever the results of the elections and no matter what faction takes power in the future, it seems most likely that Burma will be opened up for active diplomatic intercourse with other countries in order to rescue its failing economy and promote national modernization while still adhering to neutralism.

The purpose of this book is to study Burma's foreign relations in theory and practice. It analyzes the development of Burma's foreign policy and the factors or circumstances that influenced the adoption of neutralism as the cornerstone of Burma's foreign relations, following a general description of Burma's history and modern politics to help understand some roots of Burma's foreign policy. Then it traces the record of Burma's foreign relations from the time of the country's independence to the present and covers Burma's relations with most of the countries in the world as well as its relations with international and regional organizations. Diplomatic events are presented in chronological sequence. Special attention is paid to Burma's relations with major contestants in international and regional politics to point out the differences between the theory and practice of neutralism. The conclusion reviews Burma's foreign relations in theory and practice, discusses the factors that make for their success or failure, and foresees their future development.

My interest in Burma's affairs began in 1975 when I, for family reasons, gave up my professorship at an American university and took another teaching assignment at Nanyang University in Singapore, which lasted about four years. It is very difficult to gather primary sources of information, due to the exclusionist policies of the Burmese government. For most factual events I have relied on Asian and Western newspaper and magazine reports as well as the published sources quoted in the text. In the fall of 1986, I made a visit to Southeast Asia, including Burma, in connection with this study.

I am particularly indebted to the staff of South/Southeast Asia Library of the University of California at Berkeley, Libraries of Stanford University, Hoover Institution, Echols Collection on Southeast Asia of Cornell University, the Institute of Southeast Asian Studies (Singapore), the Economic and Social Commission for Asia and the Pacific (Bangkok), *Far Eastern Economic Review* (Hong Kong), *Asiaweek* (Hong Kong), *The Straits Times* (Singapore), *The Bangkok Post* (Bangkok), as well as the Information Center of Chulalongkorn University (Bangkok) and Burma's National Library (Rangoon). Thanks are also due to Information Officer Mya Mya Win and Senior Administrative Assistant Soe Tint of the United Nations Information Centre at Rangoon; Rita Tin Aung, Reference Librarian of the United States Information Service at Rangoon; and Dr. Jaswinder S. Brara, Technical Cooperation Officer of the Colombo Plan Bureau at Colombo, for providing me with helpful information in response to my requests. For permission to use copyrighted material in this book, grateful acknowledgment is made to the Federal Research Division of the Library of Congress and the Cornell University Press. I express my deep gratitude to Dr. Robert A. Scalapino, who is Robson Research Professor of Government and Director of the Institute of East Asian Studies at the University of California at Berkeley, and a leading authority on Asian affairs, for writing a penetrating foreword during his exhausting schedule. My appreciation goes as well to Professor John H. Badgley, Curator of Echols Collection on Southeast Asia, Olin Library of Cornell University, and a noted Burma expert, for reading through the entire manuscript and offering valuable comments and suggestions. Finally, I am grateful to my children, Frank, Jenny, and Linda, for their understanding and encouragement. For this study's imperfections, needless to say, I am alone responsible.

BURMA'S FOREIGN RELATIONS

THE HISTORICAL BACKGROUND

Historically, Burma was isolated from the outside world and troubled by its relations with its immediate neighbors, which were frequently at war with one another. These factors doubtless have had great influence on its foreign policy of neutralism and friendship with all nations. A brief description of Burma's historical background is therefore necessary in this study.

Burma lies east of India and Bangladesh, southwest of China, and west of Thailand and Laos. An area of 678,576 sq. km., it is the largest country in mainland Southeast Asia. The population of Burma today is estimated at 38 million. The dominant ethnic group—the Burmans—number more than 30 million; there are more than 2 million Karens and about 2 million Shans. Other major indigenous groups are the Rakhines, Chins, and Kachins, totaling more than 1 million. Most of these peoples live apart from one another and keep their own culture. In addition, large groupings of ethnic Chinese, Indian, and Bangladeshi minorities live in Burma, as well as a small number of Europeans.

Burmese is spoken by most of the people and is the official national language. Educated and official elements of society speak English, which is the recognized second language. About 85 percent of the population are Buddhists, while the rest are Christians, Muslims, Hindus, or Animists.

Burma's economy is based on agriculture with rice as the chief crop; there is some industry, mainly related to timber and minerals.

THE RISE AND FALL OF BURMESE EMPIRES

The early inhabitants of what is now Burma formed city kingdoms and small states. The Pyu state was established in upper Burma prior to the sixth century. The Pyus were succeeded by the Mons, a Mongoloid people who settled throughout southern Burma and Thailand. The Burmans gradually subjugated the Mons, but they assimilated Mon culture.

In 1044, Burman Anawrahta founded the first united kingdom, whose ruling house was known as the Pagan dynasty after its place of origin. King Anawrahta was a military leader, an able administrator, and a zealous reformer. He made the court a center of religious life, being himself a converted Hinayana Buddhist. King Anawrahta died in 1077. King Kyansittha (1084–1112) carried on the work of Anawrahta, reunifying the empire after a series of revolts and holding off foreign invaders. During its heyday the Pagan empire encompassed the areas of present-day Burma and the entire Menam valley in Thailand. It lasted for over two centuries, until the Mongols sacked the capital in 1287.

From the late thirteenth century through the sixteenth century, three centers of power emerged in Burma: North-central Burma was dominated by the Shan dynasties with their capital at Ava. In the south the Mons regained their autonomy with a seaport, Pegu, as their capital. In the foothills of east central Burma, the ethnic Burmese maintained a little kingdom around Toungoo.

In 1531 Tabinshwehti (1431–51) established the second unified Burmese empire known as the Toungoo dynasty. A Mon rebellion cost him this throne and his life. King Bayinnaung, Tabinshwehti's successor, crushed the revolt and subjugated the Shans, conquering Ava and extending Burmese suzerainty over the great block of principalities forming the Shan state in modern Burma. The Toungoo dynasty declined as a result of internal rebellions and Thai and Arakanese invasions in the seventeenth century. Binnya Dala, a Shan, captured the royal capital of Ava and deposed the last king of the Toungoo Dynasty in 1752.

Maung Aung Zeya, a Burman leader later defeated Binnya Dala and proclaimed himself king of Burma in 1752, assuming the title of Alaungpaya. King Alaungpaya died in 1760 from an accidental wound sustained while directing the siege of Ayuthia.

Alaungpaya's second successor, Hsinbyushin (1763–76), and subsequent rulers continued to follow his policy of expansionism. In 1785 King Bodawpaya (1782–1819) conquered the kingdom of Arakan, which brought Burma for the first time into direct contact with the Chittagong coastal district of British India. Frontier incidents began to irritate both sides, which finally led to the First Anglo-Burmese War in 1824–26. Defeated by the British forces, the Burmese had to accept the Treaty of Yandabo, which provided for the surrender of all Burmese claims to previously occupied Indian territories and to Burma's own provinces of Arakan and Tenasserim, plus an indemnity of 10 million rupees.

Relations with the British deteriorated again during the reign of Pagan Min (1846–53). The Second Anglo-Burmese War broke out in spring 1852, following the arrest of two British sea captains by Burmese authorities. British forces attacked and captured Rangoon and several other Burmese cities. On December 20 the Governor-General boldly proclaimed that Pegu was now the third province of British Burma. Faced with the immediate task of ending anarchy in upper Burma, King Mindon (1853–78) acquiesced in this occupation.

King Thibaw (1878–85) decided to play the French off the British. In August 1885 the Burmese government served the Bombay Burmah Trading Corporation (BBTC) with a large fine for defrauding it in the shipment of logs to lower Burma. This pretext would enable the Burmese government to withdraw the concession from the BBTC so that it might give the contract to a French syndicate. The British government at once asked the Burmese government to submit the matter to arbitration. Refused, the British started the Third Anglo-Burmese War. On November 28, after an almost bloodless campaign, Mandalay was occupied and Thibaw surrendered. Following this victory the British, on January 1, 1886, proclaimed the annexation of the remainder of Burma, and the Konbaung dynasty finally came to an end.

BRITISH COLONIAL RULE

After the annexation, spontaneous uprisings occurred all over the country against foreign rule. The British campaigned for four hard years to subdue the country.

When Arakan and Tenasserim were annexed in 1826 they were separately administered under the direct supervision of the government of India. When Pegu was annexed in 1852 it also became a separate commissionership under the governor-general. In 1862 they were amalgamated to form the province of British Burma, headed by a chief commissioner, of which Rangoon was the capital. In 1897 the chief commissioner was promoted to the rank of lieutenant governor and Burma for the first time was granted legislative autonomy.

On January 1, 1923, the British introduced dyarchy, a system that transferred certain subjects to ministers responsible to the Legislative Council and reserved others to the governor. In addition, Burma was given five seats in the new Indian legislature at New Delhi that dealt with what were known as "central subjects." A great increase in self-governing local bodies was also provided for.

In 1935, the British Parliament passed an act providing for the separation of Burma from India to take effect on April 1, 1937. The Burma government came directly under the British Parliament. The governor became solely responsible for external and internal defense, monetary policy, currency, foreign affairs, and the excluded areas of the Shan states, Karenni, and the Tribal Hills. General administration was entrusted to a cabinet of ten ministers under the leadership of a prime minister and responsible to the legislature, which was bicameral. During four prewar years in which the system was operative, four Burmese prime ministers held office.

Under British rule the economy of Burma was prosperous largely due to the increase in demand for Burmese rice in India and Europe as well as the opening of the Suez Canal in 1869 and the improvement in sea transportation. However, Burma's economic expansion brought profits to the British firms and Indian moneylenders and laborers, putting a financial hardship on Burmese cultivators, who were deeply in debt or lost their proprietorships. Increased imports also brought marked disadvantages to the Burmese people through a rise in the cost of living, and caused a dangerous dependence of Burmese economy on a single type of rice.

The disappearance of the royal court, which functioned as the inspirational center for literature and learning, religion, music, dance, and all forms of art expression, led to the decline of indigenous Burmese culture under British rule. Destruction of the court also meant a decline in Buddhist religion. The Sangha lost traditional authority and there was no coordinating or controlling nucleus in Burmese Buddhism. With the decline of monastic schools, the monastery also lost its social importance.

The British government kept the racial groups further apart by denying military services to the Burmans, whom they could not trust, and giving that privilege only to the Karens, Chins, and Kachins. The large-scale immigration of foreign Asians, especially Indians and Chinese during the colonial period, also increased ethnic diversity which inevitably led to communal discord.

Burmese nationalism died down after Britain's ruthless pacification, but later began to grow gradually and unwittingly out of religious associations. Modeled on the Young Men's Christian Association of the West, the Young Men's Buddhist Association (YMBA) was organized in 1906. The YMBA originally concerned itself with education and social affairs; subsequently it became an anti-British political organization. In 1921 the Burmese leaders formed the General Council of Burmese Association (GCBA) by merging with various patriotic organizations. In 1922 the Buddhist monks also formed a political association within the order known as the General Council of Sangha Samagyis Association (GCSS). Before long the nationalist movement spread into the villages by the efforts of the GCBA and the preaching of the monks. Now political nationalism became a popular movement, not confined to the coterie of Western-educated intellectuals. Burma was thus in ferment when the Second World War began.

JAPANESE CONQUEST AND OCCUPATION

The Japanese military became interested in Burma not only because of its strategic resources such as oil, but also because the Burma Road provided a route through which the Allies could supply the Chinese government in Chungking. By blocking the road, Japan could secure a victory over China. Japan began invading Burma in the third week of January 1942 with two thrusts from Siamese territory into Tenasserim. By June the Japanese defeated the British forces and the Chinese forces, which were sent in to help the British defend Burma. The British government of Burma withdrew to India and the nucleus of a civil administration for Burma was established in Simla.

With the invading Japanese armies marched the Burma Independence Army (BIA) commanded by Thakin Aung San, who was promised an independent Burma by the Japanese if he cooperated with their war efforts. After receiving six months' training in Japanese-occupied Hainan Island, Aung San and twenty-nine other Burmans he chose (the "thirty comrades") were sent to Thailand to recruit young soldiers among expatriate Burmese. New recruits later joined this army as it progressed in Burma.

After the Japanese captured Rangoon, the Japanese military administration was established, and Thakin Tun Oke was installed as the chief administrator of the so-called Burma Baho government. On July 24, the BIA, a motley crowd of 30,000 men whose conduct eventually made them unpopular, was finally dissolved. One month later the Burmese Defense Army (BDA) was organized with Aung San in command under strict Japanese control.

On August 1, 1942, the Central Executive Administration was appointed to displace the demoralized Baho regime, and Dr. Ba Maw became chief administrator. Final authority remained firmly in the hands of the Japanese military administration. Faced with Allied harassment tactics and threat of reinvasion, Japanese premier Tojo, in order to enlist the support of the Burmese, announced in January 1943 that Burma would be given independence within a year. On May 8, the Burma Independence Preparatory Committee was formed under the chairmanship of Dr. Ba Maw. On August 1, the Japanese military administration for Burma was formally dissolved and Burma's independence was solemnly proclaimed. Independent Burma's first act was to declare war on the United Kingdom and the United States and to sign the Treaty of Alliance with Japan. This treaty pledged Burma's cooperation with Japan in the war effort and in building the Great East Asia Co-Prosperity Sphere. These two concessions were part of the price of independence. The independence government was also headed by Dr. Ba Maw. Included in the cabinet were Thakin Nu as foreign minister and Aung San as minister of defense; Ne Win was appointed as commander-in-chief. Dr. Gotara Ogawa, formerly minister of commerce and railways in Tokyo, assumed real control as "Supreme Adviser" to the independence government. With the change of government the Burma Defense Army was also renamed the Burma National Army (BNA) on September 16, thus declaring it an army to fight all national enemies.

At the beginning of the war, the Japanese were warmly welcomed by most Burmans who believed their propaganda that "Burma is for Burmese" and the promise of Burma's independence. But what the Japanese had done after some time of occupation clearly indicated that they were only concerned with their personal and their country's interests. The most serious offenders were the infamous political police (Kempetai), who employed brutal tactics to elicit desired information and summarily executed those who refused to cooperate. Coupled with a depressed and exploited economy, the Japanese behaviors inevitably aroused public resentment toward them.

Steadily the anti-Japanese sentiment grew until, in August 1944, an all-party underground resistance movement under the leadership of Thakins Aung San and Than Tun came into existence, known at first as the Anti-Fascist Organization (AFO) and later as the Anti-Fascist Peoples' Freedom League (AFPFL). Working closely with the BNA, the league and the army became the two aspects, political and military, of one movement, that now cooperated with the Allied forces in order to drive the Japanese out of the country. Emissaries traveled back and forth between British India and Burma, and some arms were secretly sent into Burma in late 1944 and early 1945 with the approval of Admiral Mountbatten, Supreme Allied Commander of this theater of war.

The tide of the military struggle began to turn in late 1944. Finally, Japan surrendered on August 12, 1945. Earlier on March 27 the Burma National Army officially deserted the Japanese and came over to the Allies. The BNA helped mopping-up operations against the retreating Japanese.

EARLY CONTACTS WITH THE EAST

Burma and China

Burma had established relations with imperial China even before Burma became a unified country in 1044. In 792, 802, 806, and 862 ambassadors from some of the individual states in Burma went to the Tang capital through Nanchao. During the Pagan kingdom (1044–1287), formal diplomatic relations were maintained. King Kyansittha sent his first mission to the Northern Sung at their capital, Kai-feng, in 1103, followed by his second mission in 1106, when Burma received the honors of a sovereign state.[1]

In 1271 Emperor Kublai Khan of the Yuan dynasty instructed his viceroy in Yunnan to claim tribute from the Pagan kingdom, but the king refused to pay. The demand was renewed in 1273, and on this occasion the Burmese king emphasized his rejection of the demand by putting the Mongol ambassadors to death. Kublai Khan, with many irons in the fire, had to postpone action. In 1283 a Mongol army invaded Burma; it captured Pagan in 1287 and dissolved the kingdom.

King Narapati (1443–69) accepted the overlordship of the Ming king. The Chinese later assisted him to subdue the rebellious chief of Yamethin. In 1451 he received from China a gold seal of appointment as "Comforter of Ava."[2] In 1662 the Manchu Viceroy of Yunnan marched into Burma and demanded the surrender of Yung-li, the last prince of the Ming dynasty who took refuge in Bhamo. The demand was accepted on the condition that the Chinese army leave the country. In 1766 when a dispute arose over the murder of a Chinese merchant at Keng Tung, a Shan state loyal to Burma, the Chinese sent several punitive expeditions, all unsuccessful. At the request of the Chinese commander, a peace treaty was signed at Kaungton in 1770, allowing for the withdrawal of Chinese forces, the restoration of trade between the countries, and the sending of tribute missions by Burma to Peking every ten years.[3]

After the annexation the British signed an agreement with China on July 24, 1886, by which China recognized the British conquest of upper Burma, and which provided for the resumption of trade and established a joint commission to define the boundaries. The demarcation of the border proceeded episodically after the creation of a boundary commission following the adoption of the 1897 convention. After the clash in 1935 China took the case to the League of Nations, and a boundary commission was appointed under Colonel Frederic Iselin, a neutral chairman from Switzerland. This neutral commission later presented its reports setting a border line (the so-called Iselin line), which was recognized by Britain and China in 1941.

The Sino-Japanese War caused Burma to assume considerable importance as a military supply route to China. At the end of 1937 the Chinese government began to construct the famous Burma Road, which linked Kunming precariously with Lashio.

Burma and India

Due to geographical proximity, historically India exercised great influence upon Burma through trade and religion as well as through immigration. The earliest dynasty of kings in Burma was said to be Indian in origin. According to Burmese chronicles, the first Burmese kingdom was at Tagaung in norther Burma, and it was founded by an Indian prince who had lost his kingdom in India.[4]

Trade relations between India and Burma developed from ancient times. According to Chinese chronicles, at least as early as the second century B.C., there was a regular trade route by land between Bengal and China through upper Burma and Yunnan. Through this route the Indians came and established their colonies in Burma. In the third century B.C. Emperor Asoka of India sent Buddhist missionaries to Suvarnabhumi—perhaps the present lower Burma. Also some devout Buddhists, fleeing from persecution in India, came to Pagan, for its fame as a religious center was growing. Eight Indian monks were entertained for three months by King Kyansittha who fed them with his own hands and listened to their tales. In 1090 the king built the Ananta Temple in imitation of the temple in India.

In upper Burma Indian immigrants came overland through Assam; in

lower Burma they came by sea from Madras. In some localities, such as
Thaton, Prome, Pegu, Rangoon, and many a town in Arakan, Indian
immigrants formed a large proportion of the population. In coming to
Burma the Indians brought their literature and arts. Writing probably
arrived about A.D. 300 from South India to the Pyus as part of the great
Hindu expansion overseas. Both the architecture of the Pyus and the art
of the Mons flowed in from India.

King Anawrahta visited "the Indian land of Bengal," perhaps
Chittagong, and planted magical images of men there after his conquest
of north Arakan. King Kyansittha sent a mission with a treasure-laden ship
to Goya in Bengal. King Alaungsithu (1112–67) also journeyed to Bengal,
where he found the images placed by Anawrahta.[5]

Burma and Ceylon (Sri Lanka)

Burma established close contacts with Ceylon, primarily in religious
affairs. As early as in the fifth century A.D., a Theravada Buddhist com-
mentator, Buddhagosa, crossed over to Ceylon, studied the scriptures
there, and wrote a series of commentaries. King Anawrahta made Pagan
the center of Theravadian learning by inviting scholars from the Mon
lands, Ceylon, and India. King Kyansittha continued Anawrahta's policy
of friendship with Ceylon and encouraged pilgrims and merchants to travel
freely between the two countries. King Alaungsithu traveled to Ceylon
where he was well received by the king of Ceylon, who gave him his
daughter in marriage, and he left an Indian there as his envoy.

After many long years of friendship and regard, Burma and Ceylon
quarreled over the rigid control exercised by the Burmese over the portage
routes. King Narathu interfered with Ceylon's trade with Cambodia via
the Malay Peninsula, seized a Sinhalese princess on her way to Cambodia,
and placed an embargo upon the Burmese elephant trade with Ceylon. A
Sinhalese force invaded Burma, took the city of Pagan by surprise, and
killed the king.

During the reign of Narathihapati (1254–87) there were exchanges of
pilgrims, monks, and religious missions between Burma and Ceylon. In
1456 King Narapati bought land there for the maintenance of Burmese
monks visiting the Temple of the Tooth. The fifteenth-century kings of
Pegu also sent missions to Ceylon.

During foreign domination of Ceylon, Burma sent no missions to that
country. Subsequently a Sinhalese abbot arrived in Amarepura to seek
reordination and to study. Before the monk returned to Ceylon after a stay

of some three years, Bodawpaya (1782–1819) conferred the title of Royal Teacher on him. This monk later founded the Amarapura sect in Ceylon, still held in the highest regard by the people of Ceylon because of its austerity.[6]

Burma and Siam (Thailand)

Burma's relations with Siam were frequently strained and hostile. In 1294 King Wareru of Martahan received from Sukhotai royal recognition. When Wareru was assassinated the Tais of Sukhotai attacked Martahan. In 1356 Ayuthia attacked the Mons of lower Burma. In 1548 King Tabinshwehti of Toungoo invaded Siam from Martahan, and captured the king's son, brother, and son-in-law, which forced Siam to sue for peace. King Bayinnaung took Ayuthia in 1563 and made it a vassal state of Burma. Bayinnaung staged a second invasion of Siam in 1568 when Ayuthia revolted. Ayuthia fell to Burmese forces in August 1569, and Siam remained under Burmese control for the next fifteen years.

Then Pra Naret, the young prince of the Siamese king and governor of Pitsanulok, declared independence and became King Naresuen of Siam. In an attempt to recover Siam, King Nandabayin of Burma led five unsuccessful expeditions into Siam between 1585 and 1592. The war between Burma and Siam later continued intermittently. After Tharlun Min ascended the Burmese throne in 1629, he sent a mission to the king of Siam, thus assuring him that the Burmese had no territorial ambitions and in turn making certain that the Siamese would not incite the Shans to rebellion. Anyway, a period of peace followed between Burma and Siam, the latter of which faced difficulties in the struggle for supremacy between the English and the French.

Alaungpaya invaded Siam at the end of 1759. His force laid siege of Ayuthia in April 1760. The king was later mortally wounded by the explosion of a carelessly handled siege gun, and his army began a hurried retreat homeward. Hsinbyushin attacked Ayuthia again early in 1766. After a long and stubborn resistance, it fell in March 1767. The capture was accompanied by an orgy of looting and physical destruction, which left the place in complete ruins.[7]

The Siamese under leader Phya Taksin strived for a rapid recovery. By the end of 1768 he had regained Ayuthia. In 1775 Hsinbyushin ordered a fresh invasion of Siam. Singu, who succeeded Hsinbyushin, decided to bring the war to an end and ordered the Burmese forces to evacuate Siamese territory. Following his easy conquest of Arakan in 1785, King

Bodawpaya launched a full-scale invasion of Siam but failed. The Burmese staged two fairly large-scale offensives—one in 1787 and the other in 1797—but both also failed. The Siamese made great efforts to regain the Tavoy and Mergui regions, and their raids into the area continued until after the British occupation of Tenasserim in 1824.

On December 21, 1941, Thailand and Japan signed an alliance, allowing Japanese troops to move through the country. In 1943 Japan gave Thailand control over two Shan states in Burma: Kengtung and Mongpan. The two provinces were returned to Burma after the war.

Burma and Laos and Cambodia (Khmer)

Burma's early relations with the kingdom of Laos were generally hostile. In 1558 Lao forces from Luang Prabang attacked Chiengmai, but Bayinnaung appeared on the scene and drove them out. In 1564, Bayinnaung attacked Vien Chang where the fugitive Mekuti, king of Chiengmai, took refuge. Vien Chang's king Settatirat fled, and the Burmese occupied the city, capturing the queen and the *Oupahat* as well as Mekuti. In 1566 the allied forces of Settatirat and Siamese prince Mahin attacked Pitsanulok, but the arrival of a Burmese army forced them to abandon the enterprise. Bayinnaung then attacked Vien Chang again, but failed.

After Settatirat died in 1571, Bayinnaung played the role of Vien Chang's king maker. Following his death, anarchy in Laos reigned supreme for several years and no solution could be found. Finally King Nandabayin (1581–99) permitted the release of Settatirat's only son, Nokeo Koumane, who had been taken as a hostage to Burma when Bayinnaung placed the *Oupahat* on the throne in 1575. In 1592 Nokeo Koumane gained possession of Luang Prabang and was accepted as king. His first act after establishing control over Laos was to proclaim publicly its independence of Burma.

In 1707 the Lao kingdom split: Luang Prabang and Vientiane became capitals of two separate and mutually hostile states. The king of Vientiane saved his kingdom from invasion by assisting the Burmese against Luang Prabang.

Burma was frequently at war with Cambodia for the Mon territories. King Suryavarman I (1002–50) of the Khmer empire conquered the Mon kingdom of Dvaravati and was defeated by the armies of Anawrahta, king of Pagan, when he attacked other Mon states of Burma. During the reign of Udayadityavarman II (1950–66), King Anawrahta extended his conquests as far as Lopburi and Dvaravati. The Khmers had to recognize Burmese suzerainty over the conquered territories as the price of receiving back Lopburi. Mon monks introduced Theravada Buddhism into Cambodia from Burma at the end of the twelfth century.

EARLY CONTACTS WITH THE WEST

Burma and Italy

Burma was introduced to the West at the end of the fourteenth century by Marco Polo, who described Kublai Khan's war against the king of Mien (Burma) and Bangola (Bengal). Before that time Burma was practically unknown to Europeans. Beginning in the fifteenth century, Burma attracted from the West curious explorers, zealous Christian missionaries, and ambition traders who were lured by the tales of the treasure bowls of the Orient. The first recorded European visitor to Burma was a Venetian merchant, Nicolo di Conti, who came to Arakan in 1435. He traveled overland to Ava, and stayed four months in Pegu. King Binnya Ran II (1492–1526) received two more Italians. Hieronomo de Santo Stefano visited Pegu in 1496 to sell the king a valuable stock of merchandise. Later came Ludovico de Verthema.

Caesar Frederick, a Venetian prospector, visited Pegu in 1569. In 1583 the Venetian Casparo Balbi also visited Pegu and had a conversation with King Nandabayin. In 1743 an Italian Barnabite priest, Father Gallizia, who had received papal consecration as first Bishop of Burma, arrived at Syriam en route to Ava with a small band of assistant clergy. Two Italian priests, Father Domingo Tarolly and Father Albone, had been imprisoned with other Europeans at the capital during the first year of the First Anglo-Burmese war and released in 1853 after Mindon ascended the throne. They were later sent by the king to meet the British commander-in-chief and inform him that envoys would be sent soon to discuss peace.

In 1982, a Burmese mission headed by Kinwun Mingyi visited Italy en route to Britain and was accorded high honors by the Italian government. The Burmese envoys signed a treaty with Italy that merely contained expressions of goodwill and friendship, promising closer commercial relations between Italy and Burma at a later date.

Burma and Portugal

After the Portuguese captured Goa on the western coast of India in 1510 and conquered Malacca in 1511, their admiral Don Alfonso de Albuquerque sent Ray Nunez d'Acunha to report on conditions at Tenasserim, Martaban, and Pegu. The envoy was received by King Binnya Ran II in 1512. As a result of his visit a Portuguese trading station was opened in 1519 at Martaban.

Portuguese also came to Burma as mercenaries. King Tabinshwehti captured the port of Martaban in 1541 with an army comprised of a contingent of Portuguese mercenaries. Portuguese captain Diogo Soares de Mello, Tabinshwehti's follower and his companion-at-arms, helped Bayinnaung to capture Toungoo. Philip de Brito y Nicote, one of the Portuguese mercenaries who had risen to the rank of commander, became the governor of Syriam in 1599. The king of Arakan was so worried over the possibility of de Brito's joining hands with the Portuguese pirates that he sent the expedition to Dianga and in a surprise attack massacred 600 Portuguese residing there. One of the Portuguese pirates, Sebastian Gonzales Tibao, escaped and took over another island, declaring himself king. In 1613 Anaukpetlun laid siege to Syriam and took it. De Brito was impaled and left to die and most of his officers were executed. The remainder of his Portuguese followers were sent north to be settled in villages between the Chindwin and Mu rivers, where for centuries afterward their descendants formed a Catholic community with its own priests. They enrolled in the royal guard as musketeers and gunners. The Arakanese king, encouraged by the defeat of de Brito, destroyed the island kingdom of Sebastian Gonzales Tibao, in spite of efforts made by Goa to save it.

Burma and the Netherlands

In 1608 the Dutch East India Company sent Pieter Willemsz van Elbing to Arakan to examine the prospects of trade with Burma. He advised against opening a factory at Mrohaung when he discovered that the king of Arakan really wanted naval and military assistance rather than trade. It was not until Thalun's reign in 1635 that the Dutch established their first factory in Burma at Syriam. In 1679 the Dutch withdrew their factories, having finally decided that trade with Burma was not profitable.

Burma and France

In his 1727 memoirs on the subject of the French position in the Indian Ocean, General Joseph Dupleix, the French governor of Pondicherry, told of Burma's supplies of teak and crude oil and recommended using Burmese ports for shipbuilding. Two years later, as a result of his efforts, a French shipyard was founded at Syriam, but the Mon revolt caused the French to abandon it in 1742. In July 1751, Dupleix sent Sieur de Bruno to Burma and negotiated a treaty by which, in return for commercial concessions, the Mons were to receive substantial French aid. Bruno, as the resident representative of the French, became in effect the political and military advisor to the Mons in 1752.

The French decided to cultivate good relations with Alaungpaya after he had finally established himself in upper Burma. Dupleix sent a present of arms to Alaungpaya, who accepted them but continued to view the French as enemies. In 1756 Alaungpaya stormed Syriam. Bruno, directing Syriam's defensive forces, sent message after message to Pondicherry for reinforcements. After Alaungpaya captured Syriam, Bruno and a few of his senior officers were executed, and the rest of the French contingent were either pressed into royal service or resettled at the Roman Catholic villages in upper Burma.

In 1783 France requested facilities for its shipping from the king. King Mindon was friendly toward the French in order to counterbalance British power in Burma. In 1872 Mindon sent Kinwun Mingyi, his chief minister, on a visit to England, and on his way he negotiated a treaty with France which contained definite commercial arrangements.

In May 1883 King Thibaw sought and later reached an agreement with France for the import of arms. The British were alarmed by this negotiation, for France at the time was trying to conquer Tongking and was suspected of harboring even wider territorial ambitions in that region. After Jules Ferry, the French premier, was no longer in power, and France faced trouble in Tongking and wars with China and Madagascar, France denied the existence of any ambitious agreement with Burma, as it would not risk a showdown with Britain.

Burma and Britain

Burma became of political and strategic importance to the British when they were competing with France for influence in India. Burma, rich in natural resources, also provided potential advantages for British trade. The first recorded Englishman to set foot in Burma was the merchant Ralph Fitch, who arrived at Bassein from Bengal in 1587 looking for commercial opportunities. afterward, Thomas Samuel of the British East India Company's factory in Ayuthia, who had been sent up to Chiengmai with Indian goods for sale, was taken prisoner by Anaukpetlun's forces when they conquered the city. Samuel died after his arrival in Pegu. In 1617,

Henry Forrest and John Stavely were sent by the company to claim the dead man's estate.

The English established their first factory in Burma at Syriam in 1648. When the First Anglo-Dutch War broke out in 1652, the Dutch literally cleared the Bay of Bengal of English shipping and doomed their factories. The English withdrew in 1657 but reopened in 1709. The factory was later destroyed by the Mons. Thomas Saunders, governor of Madras, was alarmed at the influence Bruno had over the Mons and at the rumors of a French plan to intervene in Burma by occupying the island of Negrais. He therefore ordered a strong expedition to take Negrais by force and build a factory there. Afterward, Alaungpaya ordered troops to take back Negrais, burn down the factory, and massacre all its employees. The Calcutta authorities sent Captain Walter Alves to demand punishment of the perpetrators of the Negrais massacre. The king refused to consider making any reparation but was anxious for the East India Company to resume trade relations. The company had decided that trade with Burma was not profitable, and, with a French for the time being reduced to impotence in India, there was no fear of French influence in Burma.

The annexation of Arakan by Bodewpaya resulted in the Burmese sharing a long frontier with the British in India. Since then the British had made close contacts with Burma. In order to eliminate France's influence in Burma, the British, in 1885, launched a third war against Burma and annexed the entire country. In J. S. Furniwall's view, the annexation must be regarded as an episode in the rivalry of Britain and France for supremacy in Southeast Asia.[8]

Burma and the United States

In 1813 an American missionary, Adoniran Judson, landed in Rangoon. Soon he founded the American Baptist Mission there. During the first year of the First Anglo-Burmese War, Judson, who was then in Ava, was jailed along with other English-speaking foreigners and captive India soldiers. He was released in November 1825. Later at the request of the Ava government he became interpreter and translator in the negotiation of the Yandabo treaty with the British. The American medical missionary, Dr. Price, was also caught in Ava during the war period and suffered imprisonment along with Judson. Price later returned to Ava to serve as physician to the royal court.

In 1826 Judson extended Baptist missionary activities to British-annexed Tenasserim. Under the protective encouragement of British colonial rule in Tenasserim, the American Baptist missions began to make substantial progress. With more and more Karens to respond affirmatively to the missionary call, U.S. missionaries set up schools to promote literacy. An American Baptist college was also established in Rangoon. It was later renamed Judson College in honor of the missionary and became a constituent college of Rangoon University in 1920.

Although there were no direct contacts between the U.S. government and the Burma court, King Mindon made an unsuccessful attempt to establish a treaty between the United States and Burma by sending a letter to U.S. President Franklin Pierce through an American Baptist missionary, the Reverend Mr. Kindaird.[9]

POLITICAL DEVELOPMENTS
OF MODERN BURMA

Needless to say, a nation's internal politics influence its external policy.
Hence, it is essential to understand Burma's political developments in the
study of its foreign relations. Political developments of modern Burma
may be divided into six periods: (1) the struggle for independence, (2) the
first parliamentary democracy, (3) the caretaker government, (4) the second
parliamentary democracy, (5) the military rule, and (6) the constitutional
dictatorship.

THE STRUGGLE FOR INDEPENDENCE, 1945–47

When the war ended in August 1945, the Burmese saw the opportunity
for national independence, but the British, again in charge, not only denied
Burmese demands for independence but also resisted returning Burma to
the degree of self-government granted by the 1937 constitution. On
May 17, 1945, the Churchill government issued a White Paper for the
future Burma which would suspend the 1937 constitution with its elective
prime minister, and the London-appointed governor would retain all
authority. Following a brief period of the British military administration, the
Burmese government-in-exile in India returned and took charge of the administration in October 1945. The British governor, Reginald Dorman-Smith,

who had headed the prewar colonial government, refused to recognize the AFPFL and appointed to his executive and legislative councils men of the old generation and others who had no standing among the nationalists. The AFPFL then denounced the White Paper and the Smith government, and it called for an immediate election, a constitutional convention, and self-government. To give his AFPFL bargaining power in dealing with the British administration, Aung San organized more demonstrations and labor strikes. He also formed the People's Volunteer Organization (PVO), a paramilitary force to engage in armed struggle for independence if necessary. Faced with AFPFL hostility, the government was unable to implement its policies.

The situation forced Governor Smith to take leave, on grounds of ill health, in June 1946, and Hubert Rance was appointed in his place. The new governor, a former chief of the Civil Affairs Service in Burma, had established cordial relations with Aung San in the last year of the war. Rance got permission from London to come to terms with Aung San. A new executive council was formed that made Aung San its deputy chairman—in actuality, prime minister—and with six adherents of the AFPFL among its eleven members the strike was quickly called off. Soon Aung San demanded immediate independence under the threat of an AFPFL rebellion by Communist elements. He and some other political leaders were later invited to London by Prime Minister Clement Attlee to discuss Burma's political future. In January 1947 the London conference resulted in an agreement with several provisions: that Burma was to become independent within a year and could decide whether or not to remain within the British Commonwealth; that a constitutional assembly was to be elected in April 1947; that, in the interim period, Aung San and the other Burmese on the governor's executive council would function as an interim Burmese government; and that the border areas, should their inhabitants desire it, would be included within the boundaries of the new nation.[1]

In April the elections for constituent assemblymen gave an overwhelming majority to the AFPFL and U Nu was elected as its president when the assembly met on June 9. On July 19, 1947, Prime Minster Aung San and six other ministers were assassinated in the Secretariat Building by the hired gunmen of U Saw, a prewar prime minister ignored in the postwar power distribution. Governor Rance then invited U Nu to form a cabinet. In September the new constitution was approved by the Constituent Assembly, and in October U Nu and Clement Attlee signed a treaty granting Burma full independence. The British Parliament ratified the treaty in December, thus ending British rule over Burma. In the words of the Burmese Department of Information and Broadcasting: "Freedom has been won without a fight, a fact which testifies to Britain's wisdom and Burma's unity."[2]

THE FIRST PARLIAMENTARY DEMOCRACY, 1948–57

The independent Union of Burma was inaugurated on January 4, 1948. U Nu was chosen prime minister and the Constituent Assembly served as a provisional parliament until general elections were held. Under the Constitution of 1947 the newly independent nation was a quasi-federal state with a system of parliamentary democracy. The central government (see Figure 2.1) included a bicameral legislature consisting of a Chamber of Nationalities and a Chamber of Deputies—the former represented the states and the latter represented the people; a cabinet headed by a prime minister responsible to the Chamber of Deputies; a titular president elected by the legislature; and an independent judiciary. Burma proper was ruled directly by the central government in Rangoon. The border states existed as semiautonomous units of the Burmese Union. Shan and Karenni states had the option of seceding from the Union after ten years. State legislatures were not separately elected but were composed of members of the Union legislature from their representative states. The Union prime minister, in consultation with the state legislatures, chose state governors, who served as ministers in the Union cabinet. The Supreme Court had jurisdiction over disputes between the Union and state governments and between the states. The states could pass laws as long as they did not conflict with Union law, but the states lacked the power of taxation.[3]

When U Nu became prime minister in 1948, general elections were scheduled to be held within eighteen months. But his government soon faced a variety of insurrections: The Burma Communist Party (White Flag Communists); the Communist Party of Burma (Red Flag Communists); the White Band PVO; the Karen National Defense Organization (KNDO); the Mon National Defense Organization (MNDO); and the Mujahids (Muslims of Pakistani and Burmese origin) all rebelled against the government. The minorities demanded greater autonomy for their ethnic groups, while the Communists fought to win total power. By the spring of 1949 insurgents controlled most of the countryside, and even parts of Rangoon were at times in rebel hands. Subsequently, however, the tide began to turn in favor of the government. In Frank N. Trager's view, five

Figure 2.1
Governmental Structure in Burma under the Constitution of 1947

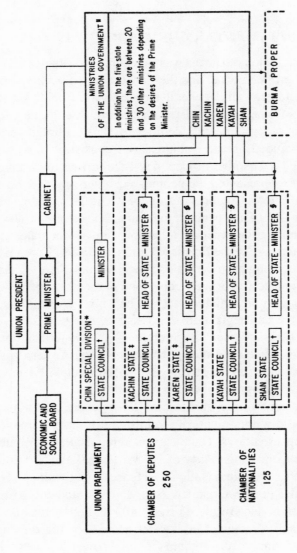

* The Chin Special Division is an appendage of Burma proper with only a few of the rights accorded to other states.
† Members of the Union parliament from the states other than Burma proper automatically hold all seats in the state councils.
‡ Although the constitution recognizes the right of secession, it denies this right to the Kachin and Karen states.
§ A member of parliament appointed as minister for his state becomes thereby the head of his state.
‖ The Union government is also the government of Burma proper.

Source: Reprinted from George McTurnan Kahin, ed., *Governments and Politics of Southeast Asia*, 1st ed. © 1959 by Cornell University. Used by permission of the publisher, Cornell University Press.

factors mitigated against the dissidents: (1) personal rivalry among the leaders and ideological differences among the insurgent groups; (2) the charismatic leadership of Prime Minister U Nu; (3) the Buddhist revival; (4) the stressful unity of the three leadership groups within the government—the political elite, the armed forces, and the bureaucracy or civil service; and (5) popular support for the government.[4]

As a result of the widespread insurgency the first national election had to be postponed four times. It was finally held in 1951–52 over a seven-month period during which government troops moved around the country to guard the ballot boxes. The AFPFL easily captured both houses of Parliament. In the Chamber of Deputies it won 85 percent of the seats and 60 percent of the votes cast. As expected, U Nu continued to serve as prime minister. U Nu and other AFPFL leaders were committed to building a socialist welfare state, and they put priorities on land reform, nationalization, and socialist industrial planning. National unity remained one of the major concerns of the government.

In the 1956 election, the Burma Workers and Peasants Party (Red Socialists), other cryptocommunists, and the Justice Party allied to form the National Unity Front (NUF) in opposition to the AFPFL. The AFPFL took 173 seats in the Chamber of Deputies with 56 percent of the popular vote while the NUF won 48 seats with 37 percent of the popular vote. Alarmed by his party's declining popularity, U Nu voluntarily stepped down as prime minister in June 1956 in order to devote his full attention to revitalizing and reunifying the party. When U Nu resumed the office in March 1957, however, the AFPFL was even less unified than before. Conflicting interests, organizational rivalries, and suspicious personalities finally caused it to split into two bitterly hostile factions in April 1958. The "Clean" AFPFL was headed by U Nu and Deputy Prime Minister Thakin Tin, while Deputy Prime Minsters Ba Swe and Kyaw Nyein led the "Stable" AFPFL. In a special session of Parliament U Nu won a vote of confidence by a slim majority of eight votes only after making concessions to the NUF and the minorities in exchange for their support. The uncertain conditions had brought the country to the verge of civil war. On September 26, U Nu, sensing his government's difficulties, invited General Ne Win to govern the nation. Ne Win had been commander-in-chief since 1948 and was one of the original "Thirty Comrades" trained by the Japanese to lead the Burmese fight against the British. U Nu hoped his leadership could restore internal security and create conditions under which a fair election could be held. Parliament agreed and accepted U Nu's arrangement.

THE CARETAKER GOVERNMENT, 1958–60

Ne Win formally took over the government in October 1958. The government was composed of former civil servants and other notable people without strong political affiliations. Senior army officers were appointed to all the major government departments and boards, from which those who had been inefficient, guilty of corruption, or merely political appointees were removed. The caretaker government gave the highest priority to reestablishing law and order, and it undertook vigorous military offensives against the insurgents.

In order to improve business and economic conditions in the country, the Defense Service Institute, headed by Brigadier Aung Gyi, took control of the state-owned industrial and commercial enterprises. As a result the Institute operated a large economic complex that included banks, factories, shopping and numerous other commercial enterprises. Some were taken from private control, and others were newly established by the Institute. In the spring of 1959 nonpolitical National Solidarity Associations were formed in towns and villages throughout the country facilitating the cooperation of military and civilian personnel in security and social welfare projects. The administration of the border states was brought into closer conformity with that of the rest of the Union. By amendment of the Constitution the feudal chiefs in the Shan and Kayah states were stripped of their previously rightful seats in the Chamber of Nationalities, and they surrendered their hereditary political and revenue powers in their states in exchange for large sums of money.

Not being an elected member of Parliament, General Ne Win could only serve as prime minister for a limited period of six months under Section 116 of the Constitution. Hence, the Constitution was amended to extend his tenure of office to twelve months, giving him sufficient time to create the conditions necessary for free and fair elections. The elections were finally held in February 1960. The results of the elections gave the "Clean" AFPFL an overwhelming parliamentary majority and reduced the "Stable" AFPFL to a minor party, as most of its national leaders suffered personal defeats in their respective constituencies. The NUF was all but wiped out. The "Clean" AFPFL's victory, however, was largely because of U Nu's personal charisma rather than because of support for his party. The caretaker government, replaced by the newly elected government, was generally considered to have successfully accomplished what it set out to do, according to the *Far Eastern Economic Review*.[5]

THE SECOND PARLIAMENTARY DEMOCRACY, 1960–62

U Nu who was elected by the new parliament as prime minister took office on April 3, 1960, and was soon faced with serious problems of party unity and economic reforms as well as with the task of carrying out various campaign promises he had made to special interest groups. The prime minister reorganized his party and renamed it the *Pyidaungsu* ("Union Party"). But before long an intraparty power struggle developed, splitting the party into a district, town-based, "uneducated" faction and a more urban, Rangoon-based "educated" faction. The former was headed by Kyaw Tun; U Win led the latter. There were two causes for this split: disagreement among the chief members of the Pyidaungsu over the leadership of the party and conflicting views on the future development of socialism in Burma.[6]

In his first speech to the Parliament two days after resuming the premiership U Nu promised to limit state participation in the economy and pledged that no existing private enterprise would be nationalized during his four-year term of office. For a while he was able to keep his promises, but eventually, under pressure of the dominant "uneducated" faction of his party that wanted profitable government jobs, U Nu nationalized the private sector of the import trade in January 1962. This decision did draw attention to the corrupt and inefficient practices within the licensed importers and the state agencies, but it alienated the business community.

The prime minister, making good another campaign promise, sponsored a constitutional amendment to make Buddhism the state religion. The Muslims, Christians, and Animists all expressed their dissatisfaction at this enactment, resulting in a second amendment that affirmed protection of religious freedom and toleration of all faiths. This in turn drew opposition from the Buddhists, thereby intensifying religious antagonism.

During the campaign for the 1960 parliamentary elections, U Nu promised separate states within the Union to both the Arakanese and Mon minorities and was proceeding to fulfill this promise. In addition, he declared an altered federal relationship with the Shans. In February 1962 the prime minister called leaders of the semiautonomous states to Rangoon to discuss minority problems. They considered the possibility of replacing the present Constitution with one that provided for "pure federation."

On March 2, 1962, the armed forces led by General Ne Win staged a coup d'état. U Nu, his cabinet ministers, the Union president, the chief justice of the Supreme Court, and certain Shan and Kayah leaders in Rangoon were all arrested and imprisoned. Later the military government announced that the coup had been made necessary by the breakdown in the political party process, by the decline in the economy, by the demands for a loosely organized federal structure and for the state religion, and by the continuing phenomenon of insurgency.[7] By and large five factors may have contributed to the military takeover: (1) the weakening leadership of Prime Minister U Nu and his Union Party; (2) the increasing importance of the militant and distrusted "uneducated" faction of the Union Party; (3) the deteriorating state of the economy; (4) the threat to the Union's very existence by the demands of some minority leaders for "pure federation" and by the animosities among the religious groups resulting from the quarrel about making Buddhism the state religion; and (5) the confidence in military governing ability based on the successful experiences during the caretaker government.[8]

MILITARY RULE, 1962–74

Following the coup, the Revolutionary Council, consisting of seventeen military leaders and headed by General Ne Win, was established and given the responsibility for administering the state. An eight-man cabinet was formed with Ne Win as prime minister. U Thi Han, a former director of military supplies, was the only civilian in the cabinet. It was also announced that the Constitution was suspended and Parliament was dissolved, that a Court of Final Appeal (later called Chief Court) replaced the existing Supreme and High Courts, and that General Ne Win retained the powers of the former president as well as "supreme legislative, executive, and judicial authority."

THE MILITARY GOVERNMENT
(March 1962)[9]

The Revolutionary Council

Chairman:	General Ne Win
Members:	Brigadier Aung Gyi
	Commodore Than Pe
	Air Brigadier Clift
	Brigadier Tin Pe
	Brigadier San Yu
	Brigadier Sein Win
	Colonels:
	Thaung Kyi
	Kyi Maung

Aung Shwe

Than Sein

Kyaw Soe

Saw Myint

Chit Myaing

Khin Nyo

Hla Han

Tan Yu Saing

The Cabinet

General Ne Win: Prime Minister, Defense, Finance, Revenue, Judiciary, and National Planning

Brigadier Aung Gyi: Trade Development, Industry, and Supplies

Brigadier Tin Pe: Agriculture and Forests, Cooperatives, Commodity Distribution, and Land Nationalization

U Thi Han: Foreign Affairs, Labor, Housing, Mines, Public Works, and Rehabilitation

Colonel Kyaw Soe: Home Affairs, Immigration, Democratization of Local Administration, Religious Affairs, and National Registration

Colonel Saw Myint: Information, Culture, Relief, Resettlement, National Solidarity, and Social Welfare

Commodore Than Pe: Education and Health

Lt. Colonel Ba Ni: Communications and Transport

On April 30, 1962, the Revolutionary Council declared a national ideology and plan of action termed "The Burmese Way to Socialism" in which it emphasized that a system different from parliamentary democracy could achieve the nation's socialist aims:

Burma's parliamentary democracy has not only failed to serve our socialist development but also . . . lost sight of and deviated from the socialist aims. The Revolutionary Council therefore firmly believes that it must develop, in conformity with existing conditions and environment and ever-changing circumstances, only such a form of democracy as will promote and safeguard the socialist development.[10]

After the coup, local and regional administration was also brought under military control through the creation of the Security and Administration Committees (SAC). The Central Security Administration Committee, responsible to the Revolutionary Council, administered laws and directives, coordinated government projects, and was responsible for maintain-

Figure 2.2
Organization of the Revolutionary Government of the Union of Burma, December 1971

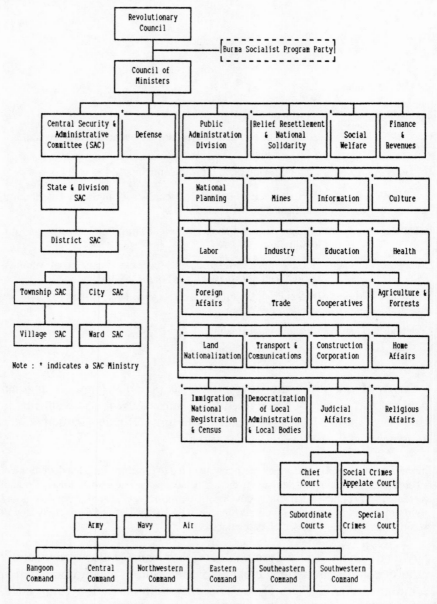

Source: John W. Henderson et al. (eds.), *Area Handbook for Burma* (Washington: GPO for The American University, 1971).

ing public discipline. Below it, there was a four-tiered hierarchy of state or division, district, township, and village SAC; on all levels their chairmen were military officers (see Figure 2.2). All public policies were determined by the Revolutionary Council and minority autonomy was limited to languages, literature, culture, and religious beliefs and customs.[11]

The military regime recognized that a political party was essential to guide the state toward socialism. In May 1962 General Ne Win invited all principal political parties—the AFPFL, the Union Party, and the United Workers Party (formerly NUF) to discuss the matter of forming a single united party. Unable to reach an agreement, on July 4 the Revolutionary Council established its own party, the Burma Socialist Programme Party (BSPP). In March 1964 the law to protect national solidarity banned all political parties except BSPP, and Burma became a one-party state.

The BSPP was the alter ego of the Revolutionary Council (see Figure 2.3). The party was composed of three committees: central organizing (nine members), party discipline (five members), and socialist economic planning (ten members). The members of the first two committees had to be drawn from the Revolutionary Council. Although the third could have included non-Council members, they were subject to the approval of the Council.[12] Beginning as a cadre party with twenty members, of which seventeen served in the Revolutionary Council, the BSPP was transferred in 1971 to a mass party (also called the Lanzin Party) whose members had reached 73,369. The First Party Congress was held in July 1971 after the party constitution was adopted. The Central Committee and Central Executive Committee were established as party policy-making organs. The party Central Committee also chose the members of the Revolutionary Council. General Ne Win was elected by the Central Committee as party chairman as well as chairman of the Central Committee and the Central Executive Committee. Brigadier General San Yu and Colonel Thaung Kyi were chosen as general secretary and joint general secretary of the party, of the Central Committee and the Central Executive Committee, respectively. The party followed an East European model of "democratic socialism." Subordinate to the party, workers and peasants councils provided mass support for party activities.

The military government established a socialist economic system, in which the state took over production, distribution, import, and export. The development of heavy industry was emphasized over agriculture, forestry, fisheries, and mining, elements in which Burma was naturally endowed. This policy resulted in economic stagnation. The first congress of the

Figure 2.3
Organization of the Burma Socialist Programme Party, February 1971

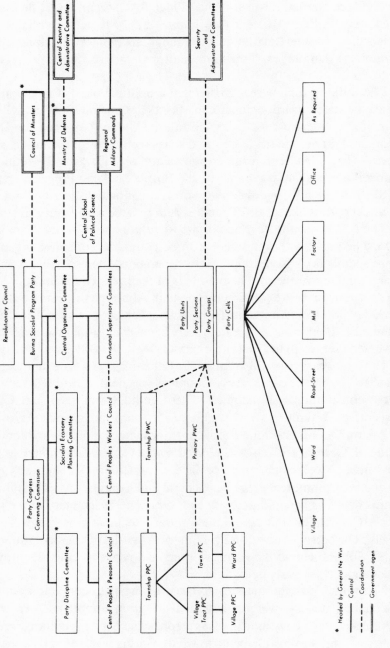

* Headed by General Ne Win

——— Control

- - - - Coordination

═══ Government agen

Source: John W. Henderson et al. (eds.), *Area Handbook for Burma* (Washington: GPO for The American University, 1971).

BSPP in 1971 changed the doctrinaire socialist approach. It retained the national goal of an industrialized socialist state, but recommended delaying this goal until 1993–94 and mandated a series of four-year plans under the overall guidance of a twenty-year plan. This plan reversed priorities and restressed agriculture, forestry, fisheries, and mining. The private sector was assured of a role, and foreign assistance was recognized as necessary.[13]

Politically, the military leaders wanted to end internal strife and peacefully achieve unity. In April 1963 a general amnesty was declared, and in June all insurgent groups were invited to come to Rangoon for peace negotiations. The talks failed because of the insurgents' unacceptable demands, and national unity remained a troubled problem for the government.

The Revolutionary Council permitted freedom of the press, public assembly, and free speech as long as these privileges were not used to undermine the government. In September 1962, nevertheless, the government passed the Printers and Publishers Regulation Act, requiring all publications to apply for an annual government license. In December 1965 all private newspapers were banned. The government also attempted to extend control over the political activities of monks; in April 1964 it ordered all sangha groups to register with the government. But by organizing massive demonstrations, the sangha successfully resisted the official decision.

On April 20, 1972, General Ne Win retired from the military services, together with twenty of his top aides. The newly constituted "civilian" cabinet included the retired general as premier, ten newly retired and three active-duty military leaders, and only two "real" civilians.[14]

Earlier, in 1971, General Ne Win had moved to draft a new constitution to return power to the people. A ninety-seven–member Constitution Drafting Commission, headed by BSPP General Secretary General San Yu, was formed by the BSPP Central Committee in September. The commission was instructed to state clearly in the draft constitution that Burma's goal was to become a socialist state, that its political and economic organizations would be based on socialist democracy and socialist economy, that all nationalities in Burma would live and work together "through weal and woe on the basis of equality," and that the people's civil rights would be matched with duties to work for socialism.[15] The third draft was finally overwhelmingly adopted by a referendum lasting from December 15–31, 1973. Out of an electorate of about 14.76 million, 13.3 million, or 90.1 percent voted in favor of the new fundamental law.[16]

THE CONSTITUTIONAL DICTATORSHIP,
1974 TO THE PRESENT

The new constitution came into force on January 4, 1974, on the twenty-fifth anniversary of Burma's independence from Britain. The Union of Burma was renamed "The Socialist Republic of the Union of Burma," a "socialist state of the working people." On March 2, the twelfth anniversary of the military coup, the Revolutionary Council dissolved itself and transferred power to the newly elected *Pyithu Hluttaw* ("People's Assembly"), thus placing Burma under a constitutional dictatorship.

CURRENT POLITICAL SYSTEM

CONSTITUTIONAL FRAMEWORK

The 1974 Constitution[1] establishes a socialist democracy as the basis of the state structure, along with a socialist economic system and a socialist society. The sovereign powers of the nation reside in the people of all races whose strength is based on peasants and workers. All citizens are equal before the law, regardless of race, religion, status, or sex.

The Pyithu Hluttlaw ("People's Assembly") is the highest organ of state power, popularly elected for a term of four years. Under the constitutional amendment adopted in March 1981, the term may be shortened or extended. The Assembly convenes at least twice a year and when not in session, its powers are exercised by the Council of State.

The Council of State is empowered to direct, supervise, and coordinate the operations of the various organs of state power and the public services. It stands above the cabinet and judiciary. The Council consists of twenty-nine members, fourteen of which are elected by each state and division from among members of the People's Assembly of the state or division concerned; fourteen are elected by the members of the People's Assembly from among themselves; and one ex officio member who is the prime minister. The elected members of the Council elect among themselves a chairman of the Council, who becomes the president of the Republic and

Figure 3.1
Governmental Organization of the Socialist Republic of the Union of Burma, 1983

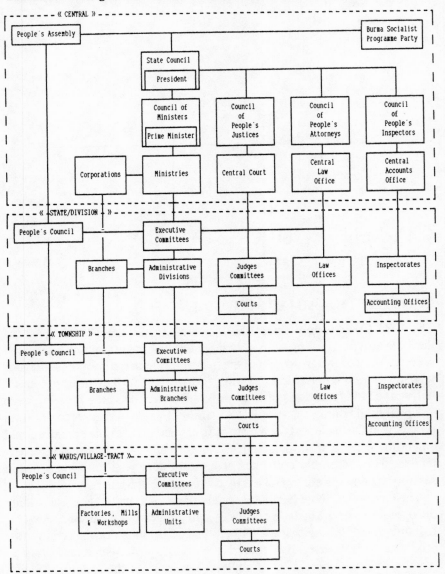

Source: Frederic M. Bunge (ed.), *Burma: A Country Study* (Washington: GPO for The American University, 1983).

head of state, and a vice chairman who becomes the vice president of the Republic and serves as acting president when the chairman is temporarily unable to discharge his duties. A secretary is also chosen in the same manner by the Council from among its members. The Council of State is responsible to the People's Assembly and its term of office is concurrent with that of the People's Assembly.

The Council of Ministers or Cabinet is the highest executive organ of the state. The members of the Cabinet are elected by the People's Assembly from among its members collectively nominated by the elected members of the State Council. The Cabinet elects a prime minister from among its members and deputy prime ministers from among the ministers nominated by the prime minister. The State Council appoints deputy ministers from among the members of the People's Assembly nominated by the Cabinet. The Cabinet is responsible to the People's Assembly or to the State Council when the People's Assembly is not in session. All Cabinet members serve the same term as that of the People's Assembly, and they may concurrently serve on the State Council.

The Council of People's Justices is the highest judicial organ of the state. There are two additional central organs of state power, the Council of People's Attorneys, responsible for law enforcement, and the Council of People's Inspectors, responsible for the inspection of public undertakings. Members of the three Councils, like members of the Cabinet, are elected by the People's Assembly from among its members collectively nominated by the elected members of the State Council. All are responsible to the People's Assembly or to the State Council when the People's Assembly is not in session and serve a concurrent term with the People's Assembly.

There are four levels of administrative areas: ward or village tract, township, state or division, and the nation. Various organs of state power are formed at each local level to discharge legislative, executive, judicial, law enforcement, and inspection functions, and these are organized much as are their counterparts in the central government. The organs of state power at different levels must function according to socialist democratic practices, which include respecting given advice and wishes, collective leadership, collective decision making, and abiding by collective decisions (see Figure 3.1).

The Constitution stipulates a single-party system. The Burma Socialist Programme Party (BSPP) or the Lanzin Party, established by the former Revolutionary Council, is mandated as the sole political party to lead the state. The supremacy of the BSPP is also safe-guarded by the law; the State

Figure 3.2
Organization of the Burma Socialist Program Party, 1981

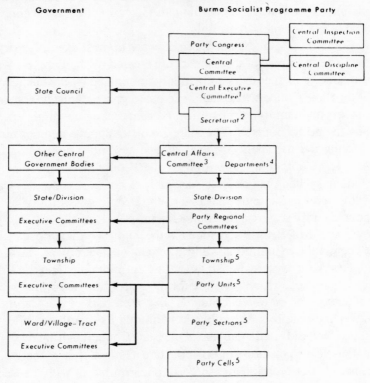

Government   Burma Socialist Programme Party

NOTE-Based on Fourth Congress, August 1981

[1]The head of this committee is party chairman

[2]Consists of general secretary, joint general secretary, and four secretaries

[3]Its six functions are-concerned with organization management, education, publications, research, and Central Institute of Political Science

[4]Responsible for 11 committee functions

[5]Formed in village-tracts, wards, townships, mills, factories, state enterprises, government bodies, universities, armed forces, and other places depending on size of membership

——▶ Control

Source: Frederic M. Bunge (ed.), *Burma: A Country Study* (Washington: GPO for The American University, 1983).

Party Protection Law enacted in October 1974 bans agitation, conspiracy, collaboration, or any organized or individual attempt to weaken or destroy the BSPP—offenses punishable by three to fourteen years imprisonment or 5,000 kyats fine, or both. Later the Violation of Party Discipline Law requires three to fourteen years imprisonment for all members of the BSPP who conspire or collaborate to destroy the party through any organization, instruction, or publication opposing party principles and directives or leakage of party secrets; another law provides finance to the party from state coffers to keep it solvent.[2]

The organization of the BSPP is both territorial and functions (see Figure 3.2). The territorial organization is roughly parallel to the administrative subdivision of the country. On the lowest tier are the party cells, each consisting of three to fifteen members. Three to nine cells constitute a section. Above the party sections are party units at the township and state and division levels. The armed forces, government ministries, and state enterprises are included in the functional organizations. The supreme organ of the party is the Party Congress. The Congress elects the Central Inspection Committee and the Central Committee which in turn elects the Central Executive Committee, chairman, vice chairman, general secretary, and joint general secretary as well as the Discipline Committee. The most influential of the party organs is the Central Executive Committee, which is responsible for directing and coordinating the work of all party apparatuses, including the fourteen party regional committees at the state and division level. The Central Executive Committee's functions are carried out through the secretariat, several departments, and central affairs committees.

Apart from regular party organizations, the BSPP established mass and class organizations for the purpose of "agitating and organizing the people into appreciating and accepting the party's policies and decisions and to induce wide mass participation in the national development projects." These include the War Veterans' Organization, the Literary Workers' Organization, the Motion Picture Council, the Theatrical Council, and the Music Council Organizing Committee, and the Lanzin Youth Central Organizing Committee, as well as the Workers' Association and the Peasants' Association.[3]

ELECTIONS AND THE FORMATION OF GOVERNMENT

The first national elections under the new socialist Constitution were held from January 27 to February 10, 1974. Altogether 288,681 deputies were elected, with voting taking place in all except a few suddenly cancelled constituencies because of the rebels' disturbances. Out of 451 constituencies for the People's Assembly, elections were successfully held in 450, while in Paletwa Township one constituency's election had to be cancelled. In the elections to the state and divisional People's Councils, 974 out of 976 were successful, the two unsuccessful constituencies being Paletwa and Thayetchaung. In addition, 22,652 deputies at the township level and 264,602 deputies at the ward or village-tract level were successfully elected.[4]

The People's Assembly elected twenty-eight members of the Council of State, which in turn elected U Ne Win as the chairman who automatically became president of the Republic. General San Yu, secretary of the former Revolutionary Council and Armed Forces chief of staff, was elected Council secretary, who was second in order of precedence and served as acting president when the chairman was temporarily unable to discharge his duties. The People's Assembly also elected an eighteen-member Council of Ministers. U Sein Win, a retired Brigadier of the Army and former Revolutionary Council member, was chosen as prime minister. Most of the other ministers had also served in the former military government, and the political power remained in the hands of the old guardians. Edwin W. Martin described it as "New Constitution, Old Faces,"[5] which in a sense legitimized the previous military rule. The entire membership of the Council of State and the Council of Ministers following the first general elections in 1974 was as follows:[6]

The Council of State

Chairman: U Ne Win (Retired General)

Secretary: General San Yu

Members: U Kyaw Soe (Retired Colonel)

U Kyaw Zaw (Retired Lt. Colonel)

U Kyaw Win (Retired Colonel)

U Ken Za Mung

U Khin Maung

U Soe Hlaing (Retired Colonel)

Sao Ohn Hnga

U Tin Thein (Retired Colonel)

U Tun Myint

U Tun Lin (Retired Lt. Colonel)

U Dingra Tang

U Ba Myein

Colonel Min Thein

Dr. Maung Maung

U Maung Lwin (Retired Colonel)

Mahn San Myat Shwe (Retired Colonel)

U Hla Tun Pru

Colonel Hla Han

U Tha Din

U Thaung Kyi (Retired Colonel)

Commodore Thaung Tin

Brigadier Thaung Dan

U Than Sein (Retired Colonel)

U Than Sein (Arakan)

Dr. Thein Aung (Retired Colonel)

Thakin Aung Min

U Sein Win, Prime Minister, de facto member (Retired Brigadier General)

The Council of Ministers

Prime Minister: U Sein Win (retired Brigadier General)

Deputy Prime Minister and Minister for Planning and Finance: U Lwin (Retired Colonel)

Minister for Home and Religious Affairs: U Ko Ko (Retired Colonel)

Minister for Industry: U Maung Maung Kha (Retired Colonel)

Minister for Mines: Dr. Nyi Nyi

Minister for Transport and Communications: U Tha Kyaw (Retired Lt. Colonel)

Minister for Construction: U Htin Kyaw (Retired Colonel)

Minister for Cooperatives: Colonel Sein Lwin

Minister for Health: Colonel Kyi Maung

Minister for Education: Dr. Khin Maung Win

Minister for Defense: Brigadier Tin Oo

Minister for Agriculture and Forests: U Ye Goung (Retired Lt. Colonel)

Minister for Trade: U San Win (Retired Lt. Colonel)

Minister for Labor: U Tun Tin (Retired Colonel)

Minister for Information: U Chit Khin (Retired Colonel)

Minister for Social Welfare: U Van Kulh (Retired Colonel)

Minister for Culture: U Aye Maung

Minister for Foreign Affairs: U Hla Phone (Retired Colonel)

The second general elections were held between January 1 and 15, 1978. There were 464 deputies elected for the People's Assembly, 976 for state and division People's Councils, 22,846 for township People's Councils, and 154,353 for ward and village tract People's Councils—a total of 178,639 deputies.

In March the People's Assembly chose the Council of State members. Ne Win and San Yu were reelected as chairman and secretary of the Council, respectively. Maung Maung Kha, who replaced Sein Win as prime minister in 1977, won reelection. Tun Tin, deputy prime minister and minister for planning and finance, kept his seat, as did Colonel Than Tin, minister for mines and labor, who had taken over the portfolios, as did Maung Maung Kha, in a 1977 Cabinet reshuffle. Sein Lwin, who had been minister for transport and communications, became minister for home and religious affairs. The entire membership of the Council of State and the Council of Ministers following the second general elections in 1978 was as follows:[7]

The Council of State

Chairman:	U Ne Win (Retired General)
Secretary:	U San Yu (Retired General)
Members:	U Kyaw Sein
	U Khin Maung
	U Saw Di Doo (Retired Lt. Col.)
	U Saw Ohn
	U San Tun
	U Soe Hlaing (Retired Col.)
	U Sein Win (Retired Brig. Gen.)
	U Tin Thein (Retired Col.)
	U Tin Aye (Retired Lt. Col.)
	U Van Kulh (Retired Col.)
	Dr. Maung Maung
	Dr. Maung Lwin (Retired Col.)
	U Min Thein (Retired Col.)
	U L. Kwang Nawng (Retired Col.)
	U Lwin (Retired Col.)
	U Hla Maung (Retired Col.)
	Dr. Hla Han (Retired Col.)
	U Tha Gyaw (Retired Lt. Col.)
	U Thaung Kyi (Retired Col.)
	U Thaung Tin (Retired Commodore, Navy)
	U Thaing Than Tin

Thakin Aung Min

Brigadier Ba Thaw

U Hla Maung

U Khin Aye (Retired Lt. Col.)

U Tin Aung

U Maung Maung Kha, Prime Minister, de facto member (Retired Col.)

The Council of Ministers

Prime Minister: U Maung Maung Kha (Retired Col.)

Deputy Prime Minister, Minister for Planning and Finance: Thura U Tun Tin (Retired Col.)

Minister for Defense: General Kyaw Htin

Minister for Home and Religious Affairs: Brigadier General Sein Lwin

Minister for Agriculture and Forests: U Ye Goung (Retired Lt. Col.)

Minister for Industry I: Brigadier General Tint Swe

Minister for Education: Dr. Khin Maung Win

Minister for Industry II: Colonel Maung Cho

Minister for Cooperatives: Colonel Sein Tun

Minister for Health: Colonel Win Maung

Minister for Foreign Affairs: U Myint Maung (Retired Col.)

Minister for Labor and Social Welfare: U Mya Maung (Retired Col.)

Minister for Construction: Brigadier General Hla Tun

Minister for Transport and Communications: Brigadier General Khin Ohn

Minister for Mines: Brigadier General Than Tin

Minister for Trade: Colonel Khin Maung Gyi

Minister for Information and Culture: U Mahn San Myat Shwe (Retired Col.)

In the third general elections held from October 4 to 10, 1981, more than 178,000 deputies were elected: 474 to the People's Assembly; 976 to state and divisional People's Councils; 22,850 to township People's Councils; and about 154,300 to ward and village-trace People's Councils. After having been elected by the People's Assembly, the Council of State on November 9 picked U San Yu, the secretary of the Council and retired army general, as chairman of the Council and president of Burma to succeed U Ne Win, who voluntarily stepped down on account of old age, ill health, and assurance of a smooth transition of power.[8] Aye Ko, retired lieutenant general, was chosen to replace San Yu as secretary of the State Council. The Cabinet reelected Maung Maung Kha as prime minister. Tun Tin remained deputy prime minister and minister for planning and finance. Defense Minister General Kyaw Htin became deputy prime minister and minister for defense. There were seven new members: Colonel Bo Ni, minister for home and religious affairs; Kyaw Nyein, minister for education; Ohn Gyaw, minister for social services and labor; Chit Hlaing, minister for foreign affairs; Aung Kyaw Myint, minister for information and culture; Saw Pru, minister for transport and communications; and Tun Wai, minister for health. The entire membership of the Council of State and the Council of Ministers following the third general election in 1981 was as follows:[9]

The Council of State

Chairman: U San Yu (Retired General)

Secretary: U Aye Ko (Retired Lt. General)

Members: U Kyaw Sein
              Thakin Khin Zaw
              U Khin Maung
              U Khin Aye (Retired Lt. Col.)
              U Saw Ohn
              U Soe Hlaing (Retired Col.)
              U San Kyi (Retired Brigadier General)
              U Sein Lwin (Retired Brigadier General)
              U Sein Win (Retired Brigadier General)
              U Zaw Win (Retired Col.)
              Brigadier General Tin Oo
              U Hpauyu Hka (Retired Col.)
              U Van Kulh (Retired Col.)
              U Ba Thaw (Retired Brigadier General)
              Thura U Min Thein (Retired Col.)
              Dr. Maung Maung
              Dr. Maung Lwin
              U Mahn San Myat Shwe (Retired Col.)
              U Hla Maung (Retired Col.)
              Dr. Hla Han (Retired Col.)
              U Tha Kyaw (Retired Lt. Col.)
              U Thaing Than Tin
              U Thaung Tin (Retired Commodore, Navy)
              U Than Sein (Retired Col.)
              Thura U Aung Pe (Retired Col.)
              Thakin Aung Min
              U Maung Maung Kha, Prime Minister, de facto member (Retired Col.)

The Council of Ministers

Prime Minister: U Maung Maung Kha (Retired Col.)

Deputy Prime Minister, Minister for Planning and Finance: Thura U Tun Tin (Retired Col.)

Deputy Prime Minister, Minister for Defense: General Thura Kyaw Htin

Minister for Agriculture and Forests: U Ye Goung (Retired Lt. Col.)

Minister for Cooperatives: U Sein Tun (Retired Col.)

Minister for Transport and Communications: Thura U Saw Pru (Retired Major General)

Minister for Foreign Affairs: U Chit Hlaing (Retired Commodore, Navy)

Minister for Industry I: U Tint Swe (Retired Brigadier General)

Minister for Industry II: U Maung Cho (Retired Col.)

Minister for Construction: U Hla Tun (Retired Brigadier General)

Minister for Mines: U Than Tin (Retired Brigadier General)

Minister for Trade: U Khin Maung Gyi (Retired Col.)

Minister for Education: U Kyaw Nyein

Minister for Information and Culture: U Aung Kyaw Myint (Retired Lt. Col.)

Minister for Home and Religious Affairs: Col. Bo Ni

Minister for Social Welfare and Labor: U Ohn Kyaw (Retired Col.)

Minister for Health: U Tun Wai

The fourth general elections were held from October 6 to 20, 1985, for Council Members at all four levels of the Burmese government. With no opposition permitted, virtually all the 200,000 BSPP candidates received the necessary majority of votes cast. In the new People's Assembly a majority were holdovers of the 469 members of the old People's Assembly; only about 140 were newcomers. All outgoing ministers and all but six outgoing deputy ministers were renominated and reelected.

The new national legislature met on November 4 and it substantially recreated the outgoing governmental institutions. San Yu remained chairman of the Council of State and president of the Republic. Aye Ko moved up to the new vice chairman position of the Council, and Sein Lwin, who became joint general secretary of BSPP after Tin Oo resigned from the office in 1983, replaced Aye Ko as secretary of the Council. The Council had twelve new members and one of them was outgoing Foreign Minister Chit Hlaing. Many of the other new faces on the Council were, like their predecessors, token representatives of ethnic minorities.

The new Cabinet also resembled the old, with only four new faces. Prime Minister Maung Maung Kha and Deputy Prime Ministers Tun Tin and Kyaw Htin remained in place as did most other ministers, including Min Gaung, minister for home and religious affairs, who took over the portfolio from Bo Ni, close associate of the disgraced Tin Oo, in 1983. Ye Goung, who as agriculture and forests minister had dealt extensively with foreign aid delegations, replaced Chit Hlaing as foreign minister. Sein Tun, who had been minister for cooperatives, headed the new ministry of energy (created in April 1985), with responsibility for Burma's critical petroleum sector, while Maung Cho continued as head of the ministry of industry II (for heavy industry).[10] The entire membership of the Council of State and the Council of Ministers following the fourth general elections in 1985 was as follows:[11]

The Council of State

Chairman:	San Yu (Retired General)
Vice Chairman:	Aye Ko (Retired Lt. General)
Secretary:	Sein Lwin (Retired Brigadier General)
Members:	U Khin Aye (Retired Col.)
	U Chit Hlaing (Retired Commodore, Navy)
	U Jap Tu
	U Soe
	U Sai Aung Tun
	U San Maung
	U Zaw Win (Retired Col.)
	U Tin Aung (Retired Lt Col.)
	U Tun Tin (Retired Col.)
	U Tun Yi (Retired Major General)
	U Tun Yin Law
	U Van Kulh (Retired Col.)
	U Ba Hla
	U Ba Thaw (Retired Brig. General)
	U Bu Ral
	Dr. Maung Maung
	U Mahn San Myat Shwe (Retired Col.)
	U Hla Tun (Retired Brig. General)
	U Vamthu Hashim
	U Tha Kyaw (Retired Lt. Col.)
	U Thaung Tin (Retired Commodore, Navy)
	U Than Sein (Retired Col.)
	U Aung Sint
	Thura U Aung Pe (Retired Col.)

U Ohn Kyi (Retired Col.)

Maung Maung Kha, Prime Minister, de factor member (Retired Col.)

Council of Ministers

Prime Minister: U Maung Maung Kha (Retired Col.)

Deputy Prime Minister, Minister for Planning and Finance: Thura U Tun Tin (Retired Col.)

Deputy Prime Minister, Minister for Defense: General Thura Kyaw Htin

Minster for Foreign Affairs: U Ye Goung (Retired Lt. Col.)

Minister for Energy: U Sein Tun (Retired Col)

Minister for Transport and Communications: Thura U Saw Pru (Retired Major General)

Minister for Industry I: U Tint Swe (Retired Brigadier General)

Minister for Mines: U Than Tin (Retired Brigadier General)

Minister for Home and Religious Affairs: U Min Gaung (Retired Major General)

Minister for Industry II: U Maung Cho (Retired Col.)

Minister for Trade: U Khin Maung Gyi (Retired Col.)

Minister for Education: U Kyaw Nyein

Minister for Information and Culture: U Aung Kyaw Myint (Retired Lt. Col.)

Minister for Social Welfare and Labor: U Ohn Kyaw (Retired Col.)

Minister for Health: U Tun Wai

Minister for Cooperatives: U Than Hlaing (Retired Col.)

Minister for Livestock and Fisheries: Rear Admiral Maung Maung Win

Minister for Construction: Major General Myint Lwin

Minister for Agriculture and Forests: Brigadier General Than Myunt

THE FEATURES OF THE CURRENT POLITICAL SYSTEM

The government formed under the new Constitution still commits itself to the "Burmese Way to Socialism" with the same people at the helm. The difference between the previous and present governments is that the former was ruled by decree of the Revolutionary Council while the latter is ruled by law of an elected legislature. In fact, however, it represents only the transformation of a military dictatorship into a constitutional dictatorship. As in the past, the current political system is characterized by (1) the fusion of governmental powers, (2) a unitary state, (3) a sole and self-perpetuating ruling party, (4) the predominance of the military, (5) the absolute leadership of U Ne Win, and (6) a totalitarian and closed society.

The Fusion of Governmental Powers

In form, legislative, executive, and judicial powers are separately performed by different organizations, but in fact there is a fusion of powers.
The People's Assembly is the highest organ of state power, exercising the
sovereign powers of the nation on behalf of the people. Though the
People's Assembly only exercises the legislative power, it is entrusted by
the Constitution with all the legislative, executive, and judicial powers.
The powers performed by all the other organs of state power are delegated
by the People's Assembly and in performing the delegated powers all the
other organs of state power are responsible to the People's Assembly.
There are no checks and balances between the People's Assembly and any
of the other organs of state power. Furthermore, members of all the other
organs of state power are also concurrently members of the People's
Assembly. In power and in personnel, all the other organs are virtually
parts of the People's Assembly. This unity in the central government is
also true of the local governments, where there are similar patterns of
power distributions and relationships among various organs of state power.

A Unitary State

Under the Constitution Burma is a unitary state. For purposes of
administration the nation is subdivided into seven states and seven divisions. Below state or division level are townships and wards for urban
areas, and village-tracts for rural areas. The activities of local governments
are strictly under the direction and supervision of the central government.
All local governing bodies serve as administrative arms of the central
government and ultimately are accountable to the People's Assembly in
Rangoon. Any People's Council or People's Councils, for example, may
be dissolved by the People's Assembly for (1) violating any provision of
the Constitution, (2) undermining national unity, (3) endangering the stability of the state, (4) contravening any resolution adopted by the People's
Assembly, or (5) insufficiently discharging duties. The validity of the acts
of local governments is determined by the People's Assembly.

The Constitution stipulates that local autonomy under central leadership
is the system of the state and that local affairs should be solved as far as
possible at the local level. These provisions, however, simply recognize
the multiethnic and multicultural character of Burmese society.

A Sole and Self-Perpetuating Ruling Party

The Constitution mandates the Burma Socialist Programme Party as the
sole political party of the state which leads the state with its ideology, the

Burmese Way to Socialism, as the guiding principle for national development. The BSPP was created early in the Ne Win regime, but it was not until 1974 when the basic law was constituted that gave the party a legal role in the Burmese political system.

The BSPP is authorized to nominate candidates for national and local legislatures in consultation with mass and class organizations formed under its leadership and with the electorate of the constituency concerned. Popular participation in the nominating process is permitted in theory, but has little effect in practice. For each election a single slate of party-nominated candidates is presented to the electorate, usually unchallenged. In 1974, the population of Taze township, Sagaing Division, put up their own slate of candidates, opposed to the BSPP's, for the People's Assembly and the township council. All non-BSPP candidates were arrested, held for eighteen months, then tried and acquitted.[12] An election is actually more or less a formality, and the party's will prevails nationwide. In the general elections of 1985, successful candidates for the People's Assembly included 265 of the 280 party Central Committee members—leaving out, by plan, only Ne Win himself and the chairman of the fourteen state and division People's Councils.[13]

The BSPP is actually an integral element in the structure of the government, which carries out the resolutions of the party, functioning as its executive organ. Furthermore, the members of all organs of state power are in fact designated by the party and routinely selected by the representative bodies concerned. Consequently, members of the government and of the party are identical; top party officials concurrently occupy high positions in the government. Given a monopoly of political power with prohibition of existence of other political parties, the BSPP has become a sole and self-perpetuating ruling party in Burma.

The Predominance of the Military

From the coup in March 1962 until early 1974 the soldiers employed the Burma Socialist Programme Party to govern Burma. As the 1974 Constitution gives the BSPP a leadership role in the nation, the military rule has still been perpetuated through its continued control over the party because the military itself is the backbone of the party. In 1977 BSPP regular membership was 181,617 in addition to 885,460 candidate members. About 60 percent of all members were either active or retired military and police.[14] Military control over the BSPP is further strengthened by the practice of filling almost all party positions with active or retired officers, especially the Central Committee and the Central Executive Committee. In the 280-member Central Committee of August 1985, quite aside from large numbers of retired military personnel, there were 68 serving officers. The seventeen members of the Central Executive Committee were all military.[15]

With its total dominance of the Lanzin Party—the unique legal source of political power—the military is assured control of the government. Some 80 percent of 450 delegates elected to the People's Assembly in 1974 were military or ex-military.[16] In the Council of Ministers, there were three serving and twelve retired officers out of eighteen members following the first general elections in 1974; ten serving and six retired officers out of seventeen members following the second general elections in 1978; two serving and thirteen retired officers out of seventeen members following the third general elections in 1981; and four serving and thirteen retired officers out of eighteen members following the fourth general elections in 1985.[17]

The Absolute Leadership of Ne Win

While the Burmese administration is controlled by the BSPP which is in turn dominated by the armed forces, these three branches—the administration, the party, and the army—are all under the direction and leadership of U Ne Win. One of Southeast Asia's most enigmatic rulers, Ne Win has held absolute power ever since he toppled the U Nu regime in 1962. No real rival has challenged his authority. Over the years, he has successfully kept all armed insurrections, including the one initially led by U Nu, at bay. A planned coup against him by some junior military officers in 1976 was quickly squelched. The party functionaries who attempted to downgrade him by giving him fewer votes than San Yu and Kyaw Soe in the Central Committee election at the Third Party Congress in 1977 were soon purged.

In 1981, Ne Win voluntarily relinquished the presidency of the Republic and held only the chairmanship of the BSPP. However, as head of the ruling party and former chief of the armed forces with actual control of the military—the core of real power—Ne Win retained a firm grip on power. Burmese public opinion after his announcement to retire from the government also recognized that "he is giving up the job, but not power."[18] In July 1988, Ne Win also voluntarily stepped down as head of the BSPP. But the newly installed leaders of the party and the government, including party chairman and Burma's president Maung Maung, are virtually hand-picked by Ne Win. Though holding no official position, his stature in Burmese society is still strong enough to remain not far removed from major policy decisions. One diplomatic source commented, "When the smoke has cleared again, we'll probably find that Ne Win is still there, powerful as ever, but ruling from behind the scenes."[19]

Acting much like an autocratic king in precolonial Burma, Ne Win ruled the nation largely by personal whim. the Burmese government has been imprinted with his personal qualities since 1962.

A Totalitarian and Closed Society

The Constitution of 1974 elaborates in considerable detail the rights of the citizens. However, it also stipulates all rights to be exercised with limits, and forbids any citizen to undermine the sovereignty and security of the state, the essence of the socialist system, the unity and solidarity of the national races, public peace and tranquility, or public morality.

The government has enacted laws to prescribe the restrictions. In mid-January 1975, the People's Assembly approved an Anti-State Activities Law. It empowered the Council of State to declare a state of emergency over the whole country or part of it for sixty days whenever it considered the prevailing situation a threat to national sovereignty, peace, and security. New legislation also gave the Council powers to detain people without trial for up to six months and restrict their fundamental rights of free movement, speech, and action for a period of one year following the declaration of a state of emergency.[20]

Citizens are grouped into mass organizations of workers, peasants, or youth. All political expression outside that framework is not tolerated. Efficient intelligence and internal security forces operate virtually free of legal restraints. Burmese and foreigners alike are subject to travel restrictions. Foreign travel is very difficult and a Burmese needs approval of the full cabinet in order to get a passport. Until August 1969, no foreign tourist was allowed to stay in Burma for more than twenty-four hours. From August 1969 to June 1970, a three-day visa was granted to foreign tourists, extended to seven days in June 1970.[21] Control of the press and mass media imposed after the coup in 1962 continues more strictly today. When the September 1984 issue of *Cherry* magazine featured a cover picture of a teenage film actress dressed in jeans and a low-necked blouse, the authorities immediately clamped down on the magazine and said it was not faithful to Burma's cultural values since she wore neither traditional nor national costume.[22]

IMPORTANT POLITICAL EVENTS

Reconciliation with Former Politicians

In 1980, in addition to offering amnesty for political foes, the government initiated the State Medal of Honor, called *maing ngant gon-yi*, to be awarded to former and present politicians in recognition of their contributions to the nation. Along with the medal, the recipient also received a life pension. The recipients included ousted Prime Minister U Nu and former Red Flag Communist Chief Thakin Soe, who was sentenced to death after his capture but was reprieved under an amnesty proclaimed some years ago. As a gesture to heal old wounds, Ne Win held private talks in 1980 with U Ba Swe, Kyaw Nyein, and other prominent ex-politicians and hosted a luncheon at Rangoon's President House honoring "my colleagues of the freedom and revolutionary struggles." Among the guests were U Nu, Thakin Soe, and ex-rebels Bohmu Aung (once defense minister under U Nu) and Saw Kya Doe (a Sandhurst-trained brigadier).[23]

U Nu was expected to play a significant role in Burmese society. At the invitation of Ne Win, Nu returned to Rangoon from exile in India in July 1980 "to devote himself to the promotion of religion at home and abroad." He was subsequently appointed president of the Pali Buddhist Texts Translation Society, heading an effort to translate the Pitakas, or "Baskets of the Laws," into English. Ne Win supported this endeavor. Worried about Burma's isolation from the world and continuing opposition to his regime from rebellious ethnic and communist groups, Ne Win said religion could be the force to bind the country together.[24] Furthermore, Nu, the only surviving founding father of the nonalignment movement with the death of Nehru, Sukarno, Nasser, and Tito, may help the Burmese government strengthen its nonalignment credentials. As Burma withdrew from the movement in September 1979, irritated by Cuba's pro-Soviet stand, Nu's presence in Rangoon, let alone his statements on this matter, could help Burma's nonalignment cause.

Labor and Student Unrest

In May 1974, two months after the establishment of Ne Win's constitutional government, the first worker's strike took place at the state-run Railway Corporation's main workshop at Myitinge. Soon strikes spread to other state-owned factories, mills, and workshops in central and upper Burma. Though the basic grievance of the workers was the unavailability of rice at the government stores and the high cost of living, the strikers also carried antigovernment posters demanding the abolition of the People's Assembly and a return to the old parliament before the coup. The government finally quelled the strikes at a cost of twenty-two people killed and seventy-three others wounded.[25]

In December 1974, students at Rangoon University, ostensibly protesting against the funeral arrangements provided by the government for the former United Nations' Secretary-General U Thant, staged an antigovernment riot.The students, after seizing U Thant's body, declared the university campus "a liberated area" and regarded themselves "a rival government." Following the removal of U Thant's body from the campus by government forces on December 11, mob violence spread to various sections of the city. The government immediately proclaimed martial law, imposed a dusk-to-dawn curfew, and ordered assemblies of more than five persons off the streets. The curfew and the ban on assemblies were subsequently withdrawn when the situation returned to normal, but martial law remained in force until September 1, 1976. The rioters damaged property worth over £718,000. Government repression resulted in 15 deaths, 81 injuries, and 2,887 arrests.[26]

Student unrest broke out again in June 1975. Starting at the Natural Science College in Rangoon's northern suburbs, 3,000 rioters marched to the city center and demanded, among other things, a halt to rocketing prices and mounting unemployment among educated people and an end to military rule. In March 1976 some 200 students seized the Rangoon University convocation hall,made it their headquarters, and started making fiery antigovernment speeches. The universities and educational institutions in Burma were closed for about one-fourth of their operating time between 1962 and 1978 on account of student troubles.

Since the late 1970s campus unrest had not resurfaced for many years, largely because the government decentralized the university system and dispersed the traditionally Rangoon-centered student population. In September 1987 the government's currency demonetization was so unpopular that it triggered student demonstrations again in Rangoon and other major cities. However, the effective control of the police and the closure of all schools quickly defused the situation and within a few days all was back to normal.[27]

On March 12, 1988, a teahouse brawl between students of the Rangoon Institute of Technology and the ruling party faithful at the edge of Rangoon resulted in student-army battles at Rangoon University and several other campuses and culminated in violent antigovernment riots on March 18. Universities and schools were ordered closed. When classes resumed in

June, students started protesting again, demanding the release of students imprisoned since the March demonstrations and the right to form a student union. The student riots during March and June were swiftly and ruthlessly stamped out with mass arrests.[28]

Violent protests flared again in July and spread through Burma's major cities. Continuing disturbances caused a series of shake-ups of the party and government leadership and government's promise to hold multiparty elections. But the students remained unsatisfied and called for an immediate end to authoritarian rule and creation of an interim administration. They moved toward a more public stance by forming an All-Burma Student Union in late August 1988, with establishment of a temporary fourteen-member executive committee chaired by student leader Min Ko Naing, in defiance of the law. It was given implicit recognition by the authorities on September 1 when President Maung Maung said that "he welcomed the formation this week of a student union that revived an organization banned in the early 1960s."[29] Students, traditionally the vanguard of opposition, are becoming again a major threat to the government.

Abortive Coup Plot

In July 1976 a group of junior staff officers plotted to seize power by assassinating President Ne Win, his second in command, General San Yu, and his intelligence chief, Colonel Tin Oo, the first coup attempt since the military rule in 1962. The conspirators intended to restore to power General Tin U, who was removed as defense minister and chief of staff in March, dissolve the BSPP, and run the country on more liberal lines under Tin U's leadership.[30] The coup attempt, though unsuccessful, signaled the first crack in the armed forces' facade of monolithic unity under Ne Win's leadership.

Purges in Party and Government

A major shake-up in the ruling Burma Socialist Programme Party occurred in November 1976 when about 54,193 members, including some leaders, were expelled from the party for being found "unworthy of continued party membership." Prior to that time, about 100,000 members had been dismissed since the Second Party Congress in October 1973. At the Third Party Congress, convened in February 1977, there was also a purge of the Central Committee and about forty committee members were forced to resign. Another major purge came at the BSPP extraordinary congress in November 1977, at which 113 former members of the Central Committee branded as "antiparty" and "antipeople" elements were denied reelection. Apparently the rapid transition from a cadre party with twenty regular members in 1962 to a mass party beginning in 1971 brought in members less committed to its ideology and more keen on gaining favors or positions of influence.

In March 1977, immediately following the conclusion of the Third Party Congress, a Cabinet reshuffle resulted in a number of "official resignations." Prime Minister Sein Win and Deputy Prime Minister and Minister for Planning and Finance U Lwin were dismissed for their capitalist leanings. During the Third Party Congress, the cabinet was blamed for failure to implement the Second Congress's directives, especially those in economics. In September 1977, Tun Lin, minister of transport and communications, and Thar Sein, deputy prime minister and minister of planning and finance, were dismissed without reason. Around the same time another fifty or so high-ranking government officials were dismissed.

Brigadier General Tin Oo, who had long been presumed Ne Win's heir presumptive, fell suddenly into disgrace in mid-May 1983. Tin Oo, former head of the National Intelligence Bureau, a joint secretary general of BSPP, and a member of the powerful State Council, was first "permitted" to resign from the party post, and then was arrested, tried, and sentence to life in prison for corruption. Specifically, the brigadier-general was accused of building structures on his private property with public funds and setting up a separate fund out of which he paid his wife's medical expenses. But diplomats in Rangoon believed that Tin Oo's enemies had convinced Ne Win that Tin Oo was grabbing too much power.[31]

Tin Oo's downfall was followed by successive dismissals of his proteges. Among them were Colonel Bo Ni, minister of home and religious affairs and former head of the Military Intelligence Service (MIS); Colonel Kan Nyunt, head of MIS; Brigadier General Myo Aung, army quartermaster general and former chief of the Rangoon Military Command; and Major-General Tin Sein, minister for livestock and fisheries. It was speculated that as many as 1,500 individuals may in some manner have been involved in the purges.[32]

Shift in Economic Policy

In the economic field, the government admitted that the Second Four-Year Plan (1974–78) was a complete failure. In early October 1976, Ne Win had seen cause to quote the constitution of the BSPP in what seemed to be a prelude to a new economic policy. The Burmese Socialist Programme Party, he said, did "not hold that any mundane idea or social system is complete and final."[33] On September 10, 1977, the Private Enterprise Rights Law was passed. The law, whose proclaimed purpose was "to further promote production through private enterprise on lines which could not yet be taken up by state-owned economic organization, guaranteed that manufacturing and transporting enterprises would not be nationalized before 1994—the end of Burma's current Twenty-Year Plan—and held out the promise of tax relief for some industrial sectors."[34] The government has coupled the new policy with an increased role for foreign capital in economic growth. In 1976, government leaders stated the importance of securing foreign capital, and in setting up a consultative group led by the World Bank that year, the Burmese government made a significant step toward gaining more foreign funds for development projects.

The Third Four-Year Plan (1978–82) showed significant success with 6.7 percent of growth, a rate reportedly exceeding the target, though less in fact. Beginning in 1983, the Burmese economy again began to falter. In addition to some economic factors reaching their natural limits, the economy suffered from both consumer shortage of gasoline and kerosene and a significant decline in some development projects. Furthermore, the black market, which provided most consumer goods beyond domestic industry's limited range, significantly drained capital. In 1985 Burma's export earnings dropped by more than 10 percent because of a poor rice crop and low world price of rice, teak, and minerals. And 1986–87 export earnings of $148.5 million, seven months into the first year, was far short of the target of $535 million. Imports in 1985 remained substantially below the 1982 level, and Burmese foreign exchange reserves had dropped from a high of $253.7 million in 1980 to $27.1 million in December 1987. In early 1988 the external debt was estimated at $4 billion.[35]

On August 10, 1987, Ne Win called for a reappraisal of the country's progress in his address to the coordination meeting held between Lanzin Party CEC and Council of State and Central Organs of Power Party factions. He said, "We cannot assert that the conditions of '62 or of '74 are identical with the conditions of today . . . changes will have to be made to keep in harmony with the times."[36] Afterward Ne Win announced new measures that lifted government controls from most aspects of production, transportation, and the distribution of rice and staple crops, including the rice trade to the private sector.[37] Following a series of riots that began in March 1988, originally fueled by public discontent over deteriorating economic conditions, the Burmese government in July promised to open virtually all areas of the nation's economic life to private enterprises, excluding only oil production, armaments, jade, and gems. After Sein Lwin was ousted by massive protests on August 12, the authorities pledged further economic reforms to address people's grievances.[38]

On November 4, 1985, Burma devalued all 100-, 25-, and 20-kyat notes and replaced them with a newly issued 75-kyat note. According to *Working People's Daily*, this second demonetization since 1964 was intended

to uncover black money in the hands of money hoarders who are hindering socialist economic construction, to strengthen, through this action, the value of state money, to stop economic activities which cause the rise in prices of commodities day by day through price manipulation with black money and to recover the taxes from those who are evading in various ways.[39]

The Demonetization Law authorized an immediate refund to be paid in legal tender upon the return of old notes, up to the value of 5,000 kyats. On September 5, 1987, Burma went through its third currency demonetization: all 75-, 35-, and 25-kyat notes were removed from circulation, and new 45- and 90-kyat denominations entered the money supply. Unlike the 1985 demonetization, the old banknotes this time were not accepted for conversion. In John B. Haseman's view, one purpose of this move was to weaken inflation by reducing the amount of money in circulation. Another was to destroy the value of huge holdings in the designated notes by insurgent groups, black-marketeers in Burma and Thailand, and wealthy merchants who, it was feared, would attempt to gain control of the newly free rice market.[40] However, the demonetization, estimated to have made worthless 60 to 80 percent of the money then in circulation, also hit small traders and ordinary Burmese.

Continued Fighting Against Insurgency

Communist and ethnic rebellions against the Burmese government continue to trouble Rangoon. To combat the insurgency, the government employs various tactics in addition to military operation. To mobilize the population against the rebels, it has organized anti-insurgency rallies and demonstrations and characterized the rebels as drug dealers, bandits, and perpetrators of heinous crimes against the society. The People's Militia, established throughout the country, is regularly enlisted in internal security campaigns. In order to win the allegiance of minority peoples in contested areas, in 1980 the government declared a general amnesty, the fourth of the kind since independence. The government also held peace negotiations between 1980 and 1981 with representatives of the BCP and the Kachin Independence Organization, but both talks broke off with no resolution because of these organizations' unacceptable demands. The BCP insisted that it be allowed continued existence as a political party, that its armed forces be allowed to remain intact, and that frontier areas where the BCP had its hideouts be treated as its base area. The Kachins asked for, among other things, an autonomous Kachin state in Burma.[41]

Rangoon has long tried through diplomatic means to urge the People's Republic of China to stop supporting the BCP, Burma's largest and most heavily armed insurgent force with as many as 15,000 men. But it was not until Peking felt a need for better ties with Rangoon in the face of perceived Vietnamese-Soviet expansion following Hanoi's late-1978 invasion of Cambodia that the Chinese began to cut financial aid to their Burmese Communist comrades in 1979. There has been a comparative lull in fighting between the Burmese army and the BCP after the latter's military offensive was defeated in 1980.

The BCP has recently renewed its efforts to woo ethnic opposition to Rangoon in order to strengthen its influence. In October 1980 it forged a new pact with the Christian-led Kachins of the Kachin Independence Army (KIA), and in June 1982 a broken alliance with the Shan State Army, first formed in 1975, was patched up. In March 1986 a meeting was held at the BCP headquarters in Panghsai between the leaders of the BCP and representatives of the National Democratic Front (NDF), which consisted of nine ethnic antigovernment movements,[42] during which both sides agreed to allow one another's safe passage through their individual areas of control and to waive their collection of taxes on goods passing through these areas. Later the Karen National Union (KNU) denounced the alliance with the BCP on the grounds that the latter in fact supported a one-party system of government and was involved in the production and distribution of narcotics.

Today, the BCP controls a 20,000-square-kilometer area in northeastern Shan state and along the Chinese frontier in Kachin state. In addition, its troops move freely in areas the BCP calls "guerrilla zones," located along the Shweti, near Mong Kung and Lai-Hka in central Shan state, and in some isolated areas of Tenasserim division. Lacking dependable supplies from the PRC, the BCP has turned to a profitable narcotics trade for financial support. As the situation stands now, "the BCP is consolidating its hold on the opium trade. They are too busy to take on the Burmese army."[43]

The Karen National Union (KNU) has a Liberation Army (KNLA) with an estimated 4,000 combatants. The Burmese government's "four-cuts" program against the KNU, designed to cut off the rebels' line of provisions, cut contacts between rebels and the Karen masses, cut their financial resources, and cut off the heads of the guerrillas themselves, has weakened the KNU's strength. For the last many years, thousands of government troops have taken the battle almost continuously into the areas controlled by the KNU's Karen National Liberation Army, keeping them in their camps just across from the Thai border and continuing to throttle their lifeblood blackmarket trade.[44]

Having taken up arms in 1961 in pursuit of minority rights, the Kachin Independence Army (KIA) is estimated to field at least 6,000 troops active from Putao in the far north to the Namhkam area of Shan state in the south. The Kachins have suffered repeated military setbacks by the government in recent years and are no longer a serious threat to Rangoon. The lack of any steady source of arms virtually checks their revolt.[45]

The Shan State Army (SSA), armed wing of the Shan State Progressive Party, has been in marked eclipse since the surrender of its commander Hso Lane in June 1983 and the death of his successor Hso Num the same year. Its military strength, once estimated at 4,000, now appears to have dwindled to some 1,500 men operating in the Hsipaw-Kensi Mansam area of northern Shan state in a loose alliance of convenience with the BCP.[46]

Hardly more of a threat is the Shan United Army (SUA) of Khun Sa which, since its 1982 expulsion from Thailand, has established an all but unchallenged preserve on the Burmese side of the northern Thai border. Composed of 4,000 well-organized and heavily armed hill-tribe recruits commanded by ethnic Chinese officers, the SUA became a highly profitable commercial enterprise engaged in the production and sale of heroin, committed to Shan nationalism only in name.[47]

U Nu's Parliamentary Democracy Party (PDP) has now virtually disintegrated; it ceased to be an effective fighting force when U Nu gave up the struggle in the jungles and retreated to an Indian monastery in the mid-1970s. It is now little more than another private army increasingly preoccupied with smuggling profits and local territorial Disputes. Many ranking figures, including U Nu's defense minister, Bohmu Aung, have been induced by Rangoon's amnesty to return from exile in Thailand.[48]

Army Chief of Staff and Minister of Defense General Kyaw Htin declared at Armed Forces Day celebrations on March 27, 1985, "Troops must continue striving for the total annihilation of insurrection in our country,"[49] signaling a shift of Rangoon's policy from containment of the insurgency to extermination. Consequently, government's military operations against Communist and ethnic rebels have been stepped up since late 1986. For a small government army of approximately 185,000 men with inadequate weaponry, however, the goal is hardly achievable. At best, the Burmese troops will keep the insurrectionists at bay as they did in the past, but will never eliminate them. As such, rebellion will continuously drain Rangoon of men and treasure, let alone damaging political unity. According to one report, the insurgents deny the government perhaps 40 percent of the total land area (although a much smaller percentage of the population), and immeasurable resources in the rebel-occupied regions. They also force the government to channel one-third of the national budget into defense spending instead of into development efforts.[50]

The Reshaping of Party and Government

Following violent protests since Marsh 1988, a special congress of the Burma Socialist Programme Party (BSPP) was called on July 23, 1988, to discuss the unrest, at which Ne Win surprisingly announced his resignation as party chairman by citing antigovernment rioting in March and June as well as his age as the major factors in his decision.[51] But probably the real reason for Ne Win's stepping down was to shrug off direct responsibility for further bloody suppression of the riots by removing himself from center stage and ruling from behind the scenes in a way that would preserve his good name for history. Five other party leaders—Vice Chairman and Burma's President San Yu, General Secretary Aye Ko, Joint General Secretary Sein Lwin, members of the Central Executive Committee Kyaw Htin and Tun Tin—also submitted their resignations to the congress. The congress accepted Ne Win's retirement from the party as well as San Yu's resignation but declined to accept four others' resignation. The congress also approved Ne Win's proposal to liberalize the nation's economy but rejected his call for a referendum on one-party rule.

The BSPP central committee named Sein Lwin as party chairman and Kyaw Htin as joint general secretary with General Secretary Ayo Ko remaining in office. The three vacant seats in the central executive committee, left by the dismissed Prime Minister Maung Maung Kha and the resignation of Ne Win and San Yu, were filled by Khin Maung Gyi, Maung Maung, and Lieutenant General Than Shwe, the new deputy minister for defense.

Sein Lwin was elected chairman of the State Council on July 27, 1988; he also became Burma's president, by an emergency session of the People's Assembly, one day after being named party leader. The People's Assembly also elected Kyan Hitin as secretary of the State Council, Tun

Tin as prime minister and minister for planning and finance, Ye Goung as deputy prime minister and minister for foreign affairs, Than Tin as deputy prime minister and minister for mines, Armed Forces Chief of Staff General Saw Maung as defense minister, and Major General Pe Myaing as minister for home and religious affairs. In addition, Maung Maung was chosen as chairman of the Council of People's Attorneys to succeed Myint Maung who, along with Prime Minister Maung Maung Kha and minister for home and religious affairs Min Gaung, had been dismissed for the charge connected to the March crisis.[52] The reshuffled cabinet is still dominated by the military, with Education Minister Kyaw Sein as the only civilian in it.

The Burmese government under Sein Lwin, a hard-liner known for ruthless suppression of dissent, began to arrest prominent critics, including retired Brigadier General Aung Gyi, who served on Ne Win's Revolutionary Council after the 1962 military coup but a year later broke with Ne Win over economic policies and resigned, and a Burmese journalist working for the Associated Press, Sein Win, in an attempt to head off further troubles. But the protests resumed in earnest in early August and forced Sein Lwin to step down as party head and state chief. Attorney General Maung Maung, a civilian, was then named in his place. According to some diplomats, Maung Maung might have been chosen as a figurehead, with hard-line military men remaining in charge behind the scenes; Ne Win is still the power behind the government.[53]

The new president made statements conciliatory to government opponents after assuming office. He announced that a ten-member commission would be formed to explore grievances and recommend solutions by September 30.[54] By appealing for time to explore economic and political restructuring, the government hoped to address public grievances within the current system. Having sensed a taste of political power by forcing the government's concessions, the protesters, now representing a broad cross-section of the population that comprises students, workers, monks, and even professionals such as physicians, lawyers, writers, and film actors, continued to press further demands. Under intense pressure, the authorities lifted martial law, withdrew soldiers from streets, and promised to propose a referendum on one-party rule at a congress of the ruling party on September 12. Soon afterward, the government also announced the release of nearly 1,700 political detainees, including Aung Gyi and Sein Win. But the mass demonstrations went on and demanded the abolition of the authoritarian rule, establishment of an interim administration, and free elections.[55]

Several opposition organizations emerged in late August amid the chaos and uncertainty. A group of older politicians and retired military men formed a League for Democracy, Peace and Freedom under the titular leadership of U Nu, the former prime minister who was overthrown in the 1962 coup. Students created an All-Burma Student's Union. Aung San Suu Kyi, daughter of Burma's founding father Aung San, and retired Brigadier General Aung Gyi also tried to lead different opposition groups.[56] Demonstrations continued to grow—once estimated at one million demonstrators in Rangoon alone—and to include government employees and several hundred defecting air force personnel and soldiers. Students and Buddhist monks had taken over local administrations in many areas. U Nu also announced formation of a rival government on September 8 and set elections for October 9 though it was not seen as likely to affect events because it was not supported by the demonstrators.

Under such circumstances, a special congress of the BSPP convened on September 10, two days before its announced date, to permit multiparty general elections directly without a referendum. An emergency session of the People's Assembly then decided the elections would be held within three months. It also named a five-member commission of elderly party functionaries to administer the elections and called for changes in the Constitution to allow for political opposition. But the opposition immediately denounced this formula and set an ultimatum for the government to step down or face continued strikes and demonstrations. Three prominent opposition figures, Aung Gyi, Aung San Suu Kyi, and Tin U, a former chief of staff and defense minister who was purged in 1976 and jailed until the 1980 amnesty, visited the government election commission to formally reject any role in elections organized under the present government. They also issued a joint statement demanding that a neutral interim administration be set up to oversee any election.[57] As a result, much of the country has been brought to a standstill by strikes and demonstrations. There are also outbursts of looting and vandalism. Most of the government has virtually ceased to function. There are widespread rumors of a possible military takeover if the situation continues to deteriorate.

The Cornerstone of Burma's Foreign Relations

Burmese leaders have always claimed that Burma has pursued a neutralist foreign policy ever since the time of independence in 1948. In his policy speech to the Chamber of Deputies on April 5, 1960, U Nu, the first prime minister and the principal architect of Burma's foreign policy, stated that "Burma is pledged to the policy, followed since independence, of positive neutrality, nonalignment with any bloc."[1]

As a matter of fact, however, the neutralist policy did not develop until two years later. The newly independent government of Burma faced severe economic difficulties because of war devastation and serious armed revolt by the Communists and ethnic minorities. Small, weak, and lacking huge armed forces, moreover, Rangoon was also apprehensive of outside interventions and armed aggression. Such circumstances required a foreign policy to achieve three urgent objectives: (1) promotion of economic rehabilitation and reconstruction, (2) maintenance of political stability and unity, and (3) safeguarding of national security and independence. For the last objective, Burma's hope and reliance were placed on the United Nations organization. In U Nu's words:

When we joined the United Nations, we were not prompted by considerations of financial aid, medical aid, educational missions to plan our educational program and other such benefits likely to accrue from membership. These things, however desirable, are immaterial. What was foremost in our minds was the expectation of the U.N. assistance when our country is subjected to aggression by a stronger power. We have pinned our faith to the United Nations organization on this score.[2]

For the first and second objectives, Burma sought economic and military assistance from Britain and the United States. To the Burmese, politically, Burma was close to the sphere of Anglo-American influence; Britain had earned Burmese goodwill through its peaceful transfer of power; the United States, a friendly country of Britain and an advocate of colonial independence, was quick to recognize the new Burmese government. Rich and powerful, Britain and the United States could best meet Burma's needs. Nurtured in Marxism, Burmese leaders might have been receptive to close ties with the Soviet Union, but the Kremlin not only offered no help to Rangoon but accused the Burmese government of being a stooge of the imperialists and supported the very factions working to undermine the new regime.

In the summer of 1949, General Ne Win, then deputy prime minister, and E Maung, minister for foreign affairs, went to London and Washington to request assistance. During his visit the Burmese foreign minister also expressed his country's willingness to consider a Pacific area security pact.[3] Prime Minister U Nu had already emphasized the importance of economic development and preserving security through a system of beneficial alliance. In his speech of "Democracy versus the Gun" on June 14, 1949, he said:

Although our independence is over a year old, we have until now no economic or defense treaty on which we can fall back in time of need. It is obvious that we cannot go on in this fashion indefinitely. . . . It is now time that we should enter into mutually beneficial treaties or arrangements, defense and economic, with countries of economic interest. The Union Government is at present counting this question in all its aspects.[4]

While seeking a beneficial alliance, U Nu doubtless had alliance with the West in mind. Arguing against Nu's view in Parliament, U Kyaw Nyein, former foreign minister and leader of the Socialists, quoted Indian Prime Minister Nehru in support of his plea for a neutral foreign policy, and warned his colleagues of the dangers of becoming associated with power blocs. In reply, Nu admitted that "the ideal course would be to remain strictly neutral," but he pointed out that strict neutralism could not meet Burmese needs to develop the nation economically and to pull the country together from the chaos created by the insurrections.[5]

The prime minister did advocate an equal relationship with the East and West when he offered the "Programme of Leftist Unity" on May 25, 1948.

Two of the fifteen points of the program dealt with foreign policy. Point one set the objective of securing for Burma "political and economic relations with the Soviet Union and the democratic countries of Eastern Europe in the same manner as we are now having with Britain and the United States." Point five guaranteed that the government would refuse any foreign aid which would "compromise the political, economic and strategic independence of Burma."[6] However, the program was less an affirmation of long-range policy than a tactical measure by U Nu by which he hoped to resolve the differences among the left-wing factions in his weakening AFPFL coalition. In actuality, U Nu and his less extreme supporters were able to avoid putting the program in practice, and many of the fifteen proposals were later sharply modified or remained inactive.[7]

Burma's relations with Britain and the United States were excellent. Burma's requests for their assistance, however, did not meet with a positive response. The United States concentrated on European affairs, and also regarded military assistance to Burma as the obligation of its former colonial power. Britain, for its part, was less than sympathetic to the policy of the Burmese government on the resolution of internal conflict involving the Karens, whom Britain considered as its traditional friends and anti-Communist. Unable to get Anglo-American support to deal with its domestic problems, coupled with the Communist takeover of Mainland China and the gradual emergence of a neutralist force in Asia, Burma recast its West-leaning policy. In a speech to Parliament on September 28, 1949, U Nu expressed the new position of his government in foreign relations. He said that the government was not interested in either anti-Right or anti-Left pacts, but only in an antiaggression pace, and would not assume "either the Anglo-American or the Soviet attitude of mind." It intended to maintain friendly relations alike with Britain, the United States, and the Soviet Union, although, he added, of the three powers, "the British are closest to us." Emphasizing the Anglo-Burmese relations as "absolutely straightforward," he declared: "Our relations with other countries must be equally straightforward."[8]

On December 11, 1949, one week before recognizing the People's Republic of China, U Nu spoke of an independent course and nonalignment with any power bloc in foreign affairs: "Our circumstances demand that we follow an independent course and no ally ourselves with any power bloc. . . . The only political programme which we should pursue is the one which we genuinely believe to be the most suitable for our Union whatever course the British, the Americans, the Russians and the Chinese Communists might follow."[9]

However, the new nonaligned stance did not exclude Burma from continuously seeking Western aid to fight rebels and promote economic development. On March 2, 1950, U Nu said:

Our declared policy in regard to foreign affairs—of not aligning ourselves with any bloc—does not exclude us from cooperating as closely as possible with the Western democracies in matters relating to economic development . . . it will be our endeavor to obtain aid of various kinds from the West, that is, the United States and Britain. . . . If aid from friendly countries is forthcoming, the anti-insurrection drive can be accelerated and the restoration of peace and stability can be rapid.[10]

Neutralism was finally established as a cornerstone of Burma's foreign relations after the outbreak of the Korean War in June 1950, which brought the Cold War between East and West to a critical stage. Since then U Nu had repeatedly explained this policy of neutralism. On July 19, 1950, he said, "We must find out which country or countries have common interests with us, and if we find any it is up to us to work together with them. However, we do not desire alignment with a particular power bloc antagonistic to another opposing bloc."[11] On September 5, 1950, he stated, "If we consider that a right course of action is being taken by a country we will support that country, be it America, Britain, or Soviet Russia. Although a small country, we will support what is right in the world."[12]

In his speech to Parliament on March 8, 1951, after Burma voted with the Soviet Union and its satellites in the UN General Assembly against a United States-sponsored resolution to brand Communist China as aggressor in Korea, U Nu justified Burma's action within the context of neutralism. He said:

This House is perfectly aware of the existence of the two power blocs led respectively by Anglo-Americans and Soviet Russia. Although our country is a tiny mite compared with these countries, we can consistently pursued an independent line in tackling international problems with the sole purpose of achieving the Union's peace and world peace without any regard for the wishes of these powers. Because of this independent policy, both the Anglo-American bloc and the Soviet bloc suspect our motives. . . . To be candid, we can never be the camp followers or stooges of any power. . . . The sole criterion for all our decisions is our sense of what is right and proper.[13]

In June 1951, the *New York Times* also quoted U Nu as saying that "Burma's foreign policy is not framed on the basis of political ideologies, therefore, Burma has no intention of taking sides in the struggle between Communist and anti-Communist forces."[14] In short, according to U Nu, neutralism contained five basic principles: (1) nonalignment with any power bloc; (2) friendly relations with all countries and enemy of none;

(3) acceptance of no economic aid with strings attached; (4) impartial examination of every foreign policy issue on its merits; and (5) willingness to contribute to building world peace, and to help any national that might need help.[15]

To U Nu, neutralism in foreign relations was essential to national interests and world peace. First, major powers work not for the interests and benefit of anybody else but for their own. Nu said:

As they [Britain, the United States, and the Soviet Union] are building up strength for global control, they are making rival claims and shouting each other down, for the defense of democracy, respect for human dignity, liberation from imperialism and the building of heaven on earth. But whatever ideologies they have, whatever policies they outline, whatever resolutions they pose, whatever slogans they shout, in actual practice, whenever there is a conflict with their interests, they are not ashamed to discard their policies, to shelve their resolutions, and to change their slogans as easily and quickly as a woman of no character changing her lovers. Since these great powers are not acting for the interests of anybody else but their own, do not let yourselves be their stooges . . . never trust them completely to the extent of leaving our all in their hands.[16]

Second, the decisions of major powers are not always right. Nu said:

Once Burma has taken sides with either the Anglo-American bloc or the Soviet bloc she must support the side taken in any and everything, right or wrong. We will have no choice. That is a position we must never fall into. Our conviction is that in this world there is nobody who is always wrong or always right. To err is human. One will be right sometimes, and sometimes wrong. Nobody can say that the Anglo-Americans are never wrong either politically or economically. Similarly, no one can say that Soviet Russia is never wrong. Therefore, we cannot blindly support any country or countries right or wrong. We do not ever want to be in such a position.[17]

Third, alignment with a power bloc increases world tension. Again in Nu's words:

As you all know, our Union is a small country . . . with the internal situation unsettled, economy unstable and military strength poor. Therefore, I cannot say that world war cannot break out by such a tiny mite of a country remaining neutral, but I can say this much, however small a country may be, its alignment with any power bloc will more or less help to increase world tensions.[18]

Fourth, through nonalignment Burma can steer clear of power conflicts and avoid being hurt or destroyed in the quarrels of others. Finally, nonalignment gives Burma maximum freedom of action in international affairs, freedom to judge each issue on its merits and to take a stand on what its leaders believe to be right at any given time without dictation or pressure from any external source.

A product of outside circumstances and events, the policy of neutralism in foreign relations was further confirmed and solidified by internal politics. Neutralism enabled a compromise between the two ideologically different political forces, in the country of which the Rightists were pro-West and the Leftists were pro-East.[19] Neutralism's popularity also has its roots in the nation's history, geography, and traditional culture. Neutralism appeals to Burmese people, who remember political and military misfortunes caused by ties with Britain and Japan. Neutralism also represents a reaction to the exclusive control of Burma's external affairs by the British during the period of colonial Burma. Cut off geographically from India, China, and Thailand by rough mountainous terrain and dense jungles, Burma has been relatively isolated from the outside world. Sharing a long border with China, nevertheless, neutralism becomes particularly desirable for Burma, which must act impartially to avoid offending this giant neighbor. Burmese culture, nourished by Buddhism, emphasizes personal responsibility rather than reliance on others: If one sins, one suffers; if one is or does good, one benefits. Buddhism also considers all human situations impermanent. In foreign relations, therefore, the government should make its own decisions and employ flexibility to handle each problem in changing circumstances rather than following foreign ideology.

It is hence only natural that the neutralist foreign policy, initiated by Burma's first administration, has been consistently followed by successive administrations. In his first speech to Parliament as prime minister on June 13, 1956, U Ba Swe asserted that the government "will continue to pursue a policy of independent neutrality" and that "ours is an active, dynamic neutrality primarily concerned with bringing about understanding and better relations between the two opposing blocs, creation of good will among nations and the inevitableness of coexistence."[20] U Nu continued the same policy after he reassumed the premiership in March 1957 and headed the government again in 1960. General Ne Win made no change in the neutralist policy when he led the caretaker government during 1958–60. After taking over the government in October 1958, he stated, "My Government does not entertain any notion to introduce any changes whatsoever in the foreign policy being pursued. I wish to announce that my Government intends to continue in the practice of strict neutrality free from any entanglements."[21]

The Revolutionary government reaffirmed the neutralist foreign policy as best serving the larger interests both of Burma and of the world in a declaration right after the coup.[22] The neutral policy remains unchanged under the constitutional government since 1974. Article 26 of the 1974 Constitution of the Socialist Republic of the Union of Burma especially specifies that the state consistently practices an independent foreign policy, aimed at international peace and friendly relations among nations, and upholds the principles of peaceful coexistence.[23]

Over the years this popular foreign policy has been interpreted or named with various phrases by Burmese leaders, such as "independent neutrality," "active neutrality," "positive neutrality," "strict neutrality," "policy of nonalignment," or "neutralism." Whatever its phrase, this policy, general enough and vague enough, provides considerable flexibility for government action in foreign relations.

BURMA AND THE PEOPLE'S REPUBLIC OF CHINA

As Burma shares a 1,500-mile border with China, which historically was its suzerain state and repeatedly invaded its territory, good relations with China are imperative. In analyzing the objectives of Burma's future foreign policy in 1947, General Aung San, the father of modern Burma, emphatically said: "Burma must strive to attain a union with other countries of Southeast Asia. We must endeavor to establish friendly relations with the two great nations of India and China."[1] No international concern has been so important to Burma as its relations with China. A historian once estimated that the Burmese foreign office spent more than 50 percent of its time on the China problem.[2]

Burma was on friendly terms with the Republic of China, which had encouraged the Burmese nationalists, quickly extended recognition to the independent Burma, and sponsored its entry into the United Nations. In the summer of 1949, however, it became increasingly clear that the Chinese Communists were going to win the civil war in China, which might have prompted Burmese Deputy Prime Minister General Ne Win and Foreign Minister E. Maung to visit London and Washington. Upon their return to Rangoon on August 25, 1949, Maung reported a U.S.–Great Britain–Burma agreement to consult on the advance of communism in

China. After the Republic of China was forced to evacuate to Taiwan, and the Chinese Communists took control of mainland China and established the People's Republic of China (P.R.C.) on October 1, 1949, Burma became the first non-Communist and Asian nation to recognize the new Chinese government, an act apparently based on reality and fear. Two weeks before Burma's action on December 17, 1949, the Burma foreign minister stated in London: "We shall have to recognize the new government of China soon. Nothing has been decided yet, but it is a question of recognizing facts."[3] Later in his report to Parliament, Premier U Nu said simple reality changed Burma's policy toward China. He said:

When we regained our independence, the Kuomintang Government was still in control of China. . . . Our relations with the then Government of China were cordial. . . . In fact, the Kuomintang Government was one of the governments which sponsored Burma's admission to the United Nations. . . . But things moved fast in the Chinese Civil War, and by the end of 1949 the Chinese Communists had obtained control over the whole of China except the island of Formosa on which Chiang Kai Shek took refuge. Faced with this reality, we recognized the new Government of China as the legal government at the end of 1949, and immediately took steps to reestablish our Embassy there.[4]

According to a noted Burmese scholar, nevertheless, "the fear of aggression was at the back of the Union Government's mind when it decided to be the first to recognize the new Communist regime in China" in December 1949.[5] In truth, the Burmese have always had deep fear about China, as a Burmese put it, "when China spits we swim down the Irrawaddy." Burma has since made every effort to court China's friendship and to avoid antagonizing it. In U Nu's words, "Our tiny nation cannot have the effrontery to quarrel with any power. And least, among these, could Burma afford to quarrel with the new China."[6] Michael Leifer calls the policy "a non-offensive foreign policy."[7] As a result, Burma's relations with China have been generally characterized by Burma's accommodation to China's policies rather than the other way around. Based on this observation, the development of Burmese-Chinese relations since 1949 may be classified into seven periods: 1949–53, 1954–57, 1957–59, 1960–67, 1967–69, 1970–78, and 1979 to the present time.

1949–53

From 1949 to 1953 the relations between Burma and the P.R.C. were neither friendly nor hostile. During this period China adopted a militant foreign policy and incited "wars of liberation" in Asia. Liu Shao-chi, a leading figure in Communist China, signaled the Chinese design at the Australasian Trade Union Conference in Peking in November 1949.[8] At the same conference Liu also condemned U Nu along with Sukarno of Indonesia and Nehru of India as "stooges of the imperialists." Though Burma was quick to recognize the Chinese Communist regime, Peking's initial response to Burma's recognition was decidedly cool. In reply to the Burmese government's announcement of recognition of the P.R.C., Premier Chou En-lai declared on December 31, 1949, that Burma must first sever relations with remnant Kuomintang (KMT) reactionaries and then send a representative to Peking to conduct talks on the matter. It was not until June 1950 that the exchange of ambassadors was finally made. China did not take an aggressive policy toward Burma in the early years because it was preoccupied with the consolidation of political power, social reconstruction, economic rehabilitation and development at home as well as the support of Communist armed struggles in Korea, Malaysia, and Indonesia. For these and other specific reasons of their own, several issues which involved China in Burma's national security, had been handled by Peking with considerable moderation.

Indigenous Communists

Two Communist parties in Burma, the Burmese Communist Party (BCP or the White Flag) and the Communist Party of Burma (CPB or the Red Flag) have staged continuous insurrections against the government since independence. After the Chinese Communist victory in 1949, the dominant party, the BCP, led by Thakin Than Tun, came to look increasingly to Peking instead of to the Communist Party of India for ideological guidance and support. Two of the top leaders of the BCP, Ko Aung Gyi and Bo Than Swe, were sent to China to establish regular channels of contact with Peking. They were received in Peking almost as plenipotentiaries from one government to another. Between 1950 and 1953 there were reports of several White Flag missions to Peking and the training of the BCP cadres in China's Yunnan province. Some Burmese Communist leaders had taken up residence in Peking at that time, where they broadcast propaganda in Burmese and developed a deep sympathy for the Chinese Communist system of rule.

Fortunately for the Burmese government, whose survival was seriously threatened by indigenous insurrections in the early years of independence, the Chinese Communist regime gave no more than moral and limited material support to its Burmese comrades. Peking's leaders even denied any connections to the Burmese Communists which U Nu reported on upon returning from China in 1954.[9] Peking seemed to realize that the Burmese Communists had no hope of gaining power by use of force. The Burma Communist movement from its inception was badly torn by factionalism and became very weak and ineffective. The Chinese Communists probably felt an all-out effort to help would be worthless. At the same time, since many a high-ranking official of the Burmese government was Marxist oriented, Peking may have believed that the Burmese Communists would possibly take control of the government by due process.

The Problem of Chinese Refugee Troops or So-Called Chinese Irregular Forces (CIF)

A number of Chinese Nationalist troops had crossed the border fleeing from the Communists in late 1949 and stationed themselves in Burmese territory. The refugee soldiers numbered 4,000 in April 1951 and increased to 16,000 by April 1953. The CIF, named the Yunnan Anti-Communist National Salvation Army (or Kuomintang) and led by General Li Mi, had established base areas and training camps in Burma and made a number of incursions into mainland China. They also exacted provisions from the local population, smuggled and trafficked in arms and opium, and joined forces with Karen insurgents.[10] By March 1953 the Burmese government was forced to concentrate over 80 percent of its defensive forces against these intruders. Most troublesome was the possibility that the Chinese Communists might use it as a pretext to invade Burma.

In December 1949, Peking warned neighboring countries against harboring any CIF members. Much to Burma's relief, China subsequently elected not to regard the Nationalist problem in Burma as an item of dispute with Rangoon. On October 23, 1951, U Nu publicly acknowledged assurance from Peking that the Chinese Communists would not enter Burma in pursuit of the CIF forces. Early in 1953 Peking even offered Burma "assistance" in eliminating these forces, but the Burmese government rejected it for fear of massive Chinese intervention.[11] U Nu told the Chamber of Deputies on March 2, 1953, that he had "made arrangements by which our representatives can meet the representatives of the People's Republic of China to have full and frank discussions of this problem whenever the occasion arises."[12] The P.R.C. wanted to cooperate with Burma on the CIF, which it surely believed posed no real danger to its own security.

The Border Problem

The border problem between Burma and China dated back to 1886, when China and Great Britain first agreed that the common frontier be jointly delimited and demarcated at a later date. Though repeated negotiation occurred between the two countries, this problem had never been finally settled. The People's Republic of China published a map in December 1950 showing all of Burma north of Bhamo as Chinese territory, marking the claimed boundary as undetermined. The map soon came to the attention of the Burmese government and became a topic of discussion between Rangoon and Peking. U Nu told Parliament on March 8, 1951, that he had taken the matter up with Peking and had been assured that it was simply a case of an old (i.e., Nationalist) map having been reproduced without revision, for lack of time. He also quoted Chinese assurance to the Burmese ambassador in Peking as follows:

There are no problems between Asian countries like China, India and Burma which cannot be solved through normal diplomatic channels. The Chinese government had no time to draw a new map and had only reproduced an old map. The Sino-Burmese border has been shown as undemarcated boundary and we see no difficulty in sitting down together and demarcating boundary. China has no territorial ambitions.[13]

Again in 1953 the P.R.C. published an authoritative atlas that showed most of the frontier with Burma as undemarcated and laid claim to everything north of Myitkyina. Burma's efforts to quickly demarcate the boundary with China produced no result. The Chinese Communists did not appear to be in a hurry to solve this problem. Their map could legally justify the free entry of their troops into the "unsettled areas," presumably to hold off any further attacks against Yunnan staged by the Chinese Nationalist Troops located in Burma and to expand Peking's influence among the minority peoples there. According to a report in July 1953, "five units of the Red China People's Army," a little over 200 men, entered Burmese territory and established camps about twenty-five miles inside the northern Wa state. Once when their error was pointed out, the Red troops told local Burmese authorities that they were not in Burmese territory since the frontier was undemarcated.[14] Furthermore, the P.R.C. apparently expects to favorably settle the borderlines with a future Burmese Communist government. The notes to the map of Yunnan published in 1953 said, with reference to the border dispute between Burma and China: "These problems await the establishment of a people's Burma and the final victory of the Asian people's revolution."[15]

The Chinese Minority

The population of overseas Chinese in Burma was estimated at 350,000 in 1949. Though small in comparison to those of Indonesia or Thailand, they provided the P.R.C. with a potential source of foreign agents to conduct a variety of subversive actions. Therefore, the Burmese government was particularly concerned about their movements and Peking's policy toward them. When the Chinese Communists first gained power, they accepted the traditional view that all Chinese, no matter where they resided, were the concern of the P.R.C. Article 98 of the Chinese Constitution at the time stated: "The People's Republic of China protects the property rights and interests of Chinese residents abroad." Soon they adopted a "great patriotic unity" policy toward overseas Chinese. In essence, the patriotic unity policy means that all overseas Chinese should give their allegiance and support to the new Chinese government and not to the Kuomintang. Peking also called on overseas Chinese to help socialist construction in China through investment, purchase of government bonds, and contributions to public works in their home district.[16]

As the policy was applied to overseas Chinese in Burma, Peking encouraged them to support actively the White Flag liberation movement, gave them various forms of aid, and mobilized its adherents to engage in power struggles with those of the Kuomintang for control of the Chinese associations, schools, press, and other public institutions. A second secretary of the Chinese embassy in Rangoon was particularly given the responsibility for manipulating the Chinese community. Nevertheless, the P.R.C. did not make the Chinese minority a serious problem of internal security for Burma, because it was too busy with other matters. In addition, lack of influence among Burma's Chinese and a desire not to provoke open confrontation with the Burmese government may also restrain Peking's actions. The majority of overseas Chinese in Burma, more concerned with making a living and not interested in Marxism, were not loyal to the Chinese Communist regime. The land reform of 1950–52, which subjected their dependents at home to class warfare, further alienated the Chinese in Burma from the new ruler of mainland China.

During the early years after establishing diplomatic relations, contacts between Burma and the P.R.C. were on a very limited scale. By the end of 1951, Peking sent an official cultural mission to Rangoon. In April 1952, Burmese Minister of Culture U Tun Pe made a return visit to China, participated in Peking's May Day celebration, and had an audience with Mao Tse-tung. Later in the same year a Burmese land reform study mission under the minister of land nationalization arrived in Peking for the October 1 celebration of the founding anniversary of the P.R.C. Mao received them personally as well. Sino-Burmese trade was insignificant. According to United Nations' statistics, Burma exported to China during the year ending September 30, 1953, goods worth $1,743,000 and imported from China goods worth $1,449,000.[17]

Burma's reaction to China's policies not directly related to itself were also extremely cautious. In spite of opposing aggression as a principle of its foreign policy, Burma voted against the United National General Assembly resolution of February 1, 1951, that named the P.R.C. an aggressor in Korea, and abstained on the one of May 18 requesting the members of the world organization to embargo strategic items to North Korea and Communist China. For the former action, the Burmese representative explained that the action would only make a peaceful settlement more difficult and that nothing could be gained by calling a country an aggressor when it was extremely doubtful that sanction would halt the aggression; and for the latter the representative said that "the resolution would have no practical effect so far as. . . [his] country . . . [was] concerned," since "Burma's trade with China . . . was not appreciable and none of the materials listed in the . . . resolution . . . [entered] into such trade as . . . existed."[18] As to the invasion of Chinese forces into Tibet in 1950, many countries criticized it but Burma expressed only regret. U Thant, then secretary of the information ministry, said in a radio broadcast on November 5, 1950: "Burma believes in the settlement of differences by peaceful means, and therefore, the Union Government cannot but regret that the Central People's Government of China should have seen fit to take this drastic action on Tibet."[19]

1954–57

Beginning in 1954, the People's Republic of China shifted its foreign policy from anti-noncommunism to peaceful coexistence, and this policy lasted until 1957. Several factors may have contributed to the change in Peking's policy. First, China needed a peaceful and stable international environment to facilitate economic construction. Second, the frustrated "armed struggle" strategy encountered in Korea, Malaya, and the Taiwan Strait, as well as a number of international developments, such as the Geneva Conference ending the armed struggle of North Vietnam against France, demonstrated to Peking that its revolutionary objectives were largely unattainable in the short run. Third, the United States-imposed encirclement of China prompted Peking to cultivate the goodwill of its neighboring states in an attempt to turn them into a "safe" area. Fourth, Peking desired to extend its prestige and influence to the emerging Third World nations. Fifth, Peking followed the policy of peaceful coexistence adopted by the Soviet Union after Stalin's death in 1953. As a result, the relations between Burma and China during this period were close and cordial, called a *Pauk Phaw* ("kinship") relationship.

Chinese Premier and Foreign Minister Chou En-lai made his first visit to Rangoon in late 1954 on his way home from the Geneva Conference on Indochina and a meeting with India's Nehru in New Delhi, which shattered Communist China's largely self-imposed isolation from the non-Communist world. While in Burma, Chou successfully warned U Nu not to join the Manila Pact and SEATO or engage in any kind of military agreement with the United States, his apparent immediate purpose of the journey.[20] A join communique issued by Chou and U Nu on June 29 repeated the Five Principles of Peaceful Co-existence which Chou and Nehru had earlier agreed upon as the guiding principles of relationship between the two countries. It stated:

In regard to the principles agreed upon between China and India to guide relations between the two countries, namely: 1. Mutual respect to each other's territorial integrity and sovereignty; 2. Non-aggression; 3. Non-interference in each other's internal affairs; 4. Equality and mutual benefit; 5. Peaceful co-existence. The Prime Ministers agreed that these should also be the guiding principles for relationship between China and Burma. If these principles are observed by all countries, the peaceful co-existence of countries with different social systems should be ensured and the threat and fear of aggression and interference in internal affairs would give place to a sense of security and mutual confidence.[21]

Chou's visit marked the turning point in Sino-Burmese relations. In U Nu's words:

By June 1950 we had entered into normal diplomatic relations with the new Government of China. But our relations with the new Chinese regime remained uncertain for a number of years . . . and the new Chinese Government seemed inclined to give our Communists their moral support, apparently regarding us as stooges of the West. . . . Premier Chou En-lai's visit to India and Burma in 1954 proved to be the turning point in Sino-Burmese relations, and since then both of us have been guided by the five principles which were embodied in the Joint Statement issued by Premier Chou En-lai and me at the time. Consequent of a firm understanding on a political level, we have developed rapidly expanding economic and cultural relations, which is as it should be between two friendly neighbors.[22]

At Chou's invitation U Nu visited Peking in December 1954 and received the same sort of royal reception that had been accorded Nehru in late October. At a farewell banquet U Nu emphatically assured that Burma would never permit itself to be used as a base for espionage or military operations against China, much to Peking's relief of its most apprehensive problem concerning Burma. Nu also expressed his desire to mediate the conflict between China and the United States. He said: "We want these two countries to be on the friendliest terms . . . I will exert my utmost to bring about an understanding between the People's Republic of China and the United States of America."[23]

During the Bandung Conference held in Indonesia in April 1955, U Nu tried to deepen his friendship with Chou En-lai. According to William C. Johnstone, "U Nu appears to have devoted his greatest efforts toward an avoidance of different issues and of friction between Chou En-lai and the proponents of pro-Western attitudes."[24]

The Sino-Burmese ties were strengthened by frequent contacts between the leaders of the two countries, the so-called personal diplomacy favored by the Chinese premier, who considered "contact between the leaders of different countries . . . a very important measure for enhancing under-standing and trust among nations and easing tension."[25] Undoubtedly, personal diplomacy among world leaders may promote mutual under-standing and friendship. But Chou skillfully used it to influence opinion by virtue of his position as the leader of a big country. Judging from his statement after Chou's visit to Rangoon in June 1954, U Nu appeared to become an admirer of Mao's China. In his Martyr's Day speech on July 19, 1954, Nu said, "The Kuomintang China was plagued with bribery and corruption from top to bottom. Under Mao such practices vanished like the snow of yesteryear. . . . China's new leaders, at great sacrifice to themselves, are building a new world for the masses. As Asians we are delighted at the great strides made there."[26]

With respect to Burmese Communist insurrectionists, the P.R.C. gen-erally refrained from assisting them in order not to damage its friendship with the Burmese government. During his visit to China in 1954 U Nu raised the question of Chinese sanctuary and assistance to Burmese guerrillas, and the Chinese promised to uphold their commitment to noninterference.[27] Though Chou En-lai admitted at Bandung to having granted Chinese sanctuary to the Kachin rebel leader Naw Seng and 200 of his followers allied with the Burmese Communists, it would seem that Peking's contribution to the Burma Communist movement was financial and psychological, not military or logistical. According to John H. Badgley, between 1954 and 1958 all but about 15 percent of the Communist and proto-Communist insurgents surrendered, but none of them was armed with weapons from Communist China.[28]

Peking's new policy of peaceful coexistence also brought a drastic change in policy toward overseas Chinese communities. Chou En-lai asserted in December 1954 that the nationals of one in the territory of the other would be discouraged by the mother country from engaging in political activity, that the rights and interests of such nationals would be protected by the government under which they actively lived, and that negotiations would begin at the earliest opportunity on the subject of dual nationality.[29] At the Bandung Conference in April 1955 Chou reassured the host countries that his government was "ready to solve the problem of dual nationality of overseas Chinese with the governments of the countries concerned."[30] U Nu took the view that a decision on the nationality of overseas Chinese in Burma would have to await the outcome of the Sino-Indonesian negotiations, which later left much to be desired.[31] Therefore, China was unable to conclude a similar treaty with Burma. While visiting Rangoon in December 1956 Chou En-lai gave a detailed exposition of Peking's new position on overseas Chinese policy and did not insist on a formal treaty as the basis for solving the problem. He urged Chinese abroad either to be citizens of the countries where they lived, or, if they retained Chinese citizenship, to refrain from entering local politics. Should they wish to be politically active they should return to China. Obviously, Peking was well aware that its old policy toward overseas Chinese contradicted its present foreign policy. The overseas Chinese, whom the Chinese Communists could not control, had become a liability to them and could create stumbling blocks to friendly relations with Southeast Asian countries.

The border issue seemed to be a good test of Burma's policy toward the Peking government and of the effectiveness of the Five Principles of Peaceful Co-existence. In the joint statement in Peking in December 1954 Chou En-lai and U Nu acknowledged that the issue of the incomplete boundary line delimitation between China and Burma would be settled in a friendly spirit at an appropriate time through normal diplomatic channels.[32]

In late July 1956, a Rangoon newspaper revealed that about 5,000 regular soldiers of the People's Liberation Army had invaded the Kachin state and were moving in the general direction of Myitkyina. The Burmese government denied the report at first but later confirmed it. According to William C. Johnstone, two factors may have influenced Peking's decision for the incursion. First, by sending troops into "disputed territory" Mao Tse-tung and his colleagues could withdraw them behind the traditional frontier as part of their magnanimous gesture of "peace and friendship." Second, there may have been more than a coincidence in the fact that by July 1956, it was public knowledge that the Burmese government was negotiating with the United States for a resumption of economic aid. It is possible that the leaders in Peking believed a border threat and show of force might deter the Burmese government from close U.S. ties.[33] However, there may be a third factor. While the anti-Peking revolt broke out in eastern Tibet early in 1956 and became serious during the spring, armed demonstration in the general direction of Myitkyina may well have been the purpose to prevent the Tibetan rebels from receiving arms or other forms of support via northern Burma.[34]

Peking's action seemed to contradict the Five Principles. U Nu, though not in office, wrote a letter of appeal to Chou En-lai. Chou invited him to visit Peking in late 1956 to discuss the border problem. In his speech before the Political Consultative Conference, Nu pleaded with his hosts to live up to the Five Principles of Peaceful Co-existence: "The two of us have neither the inclination nor the time to quarrel or to fight or to commit aggression on each other's land . . . [but] a mere declaration of acceptance of a principle is not enough. Both our countries must make special endeavors to their utmost that the principles are strictly observed."[35] In the discussions Chou En-lai volunteered to withdraw Chinese troops from the area west of the Iselin Line. And the Burmese should also withdraw their troops from three villages in the Kachin state: Hpimaw, Gaulum, and Kangfang. Later Chou and Nu issued a joint communique stating that the Chinese had put forward a proposal and that the Burmese had agreed to consider it.

Chou En-lai visited Burma in December 1956 and then traveled with Premier U Ba Swe to Mangshih in Yunnan for a border conference. At the conference Ba Swe made a speech with two distinct points: (1) Burma abhorred the principle of larger nations bullying smaller ones, because in relations between countries justice was the most important principle; (2) he reminded the Chinese that the world was watching Burma and China to see whether or not the Five Principles could be successfully practiced to mutual benefit of both countries.[36] But their joint statement on December 20 indicated that they had not arrived at a solution satisfactory to both parties. Soon after U Nu reassumed the Burmese premiership in early 1957, he met Chou in Kunming, capital of Yunnan, to discuss this issue again, but Peking still stalled on a final settlement. Perhaps the P.R.C. still wanted to use the undemarcated border areas as a good bargaining weapon in dealing with the Burmese government.

In April 1954, Burma and the P.R.C. signed a barter trade agreement, calling for the exchange of about 10 percent of Burma's rice exports, 150,000 tons, for Chinese goods and technical assistance.[37] Burma was very grateful to the Chinese Communists for their barter trade at the time when Burma experienced economic difficulties due to the sharp decline of world prices of rice after the Korean War. To dispose of rice, however, Burma had to take reciprocal quantities of Chinese goods and technicians at noncompetitive prices. Moreover, Burma's direction and terms of trade with China necessarily affected the course of its foreign policy. To Burma the difficulties and implications involved in the barter trade with the Chinese and other Communist countries were obvious. As the Burma minister of trade development remarked on February 8, 1956:

Many of our friends keep on reminding us of the difficulties of such arrangements. Some of them even tell us that there are "hidden dangers." We are not unaware of the difficulties and implications involved. Our position is that we have rice to sell and we must sell it if we are to survive.[38]

Apart from economic expediency, Burma may feel that trade with China helped develop close ties with its giant neighbor. As for China, Burmese rice was a negligible addition to the millions of tons of cereal imported from Western countries. In the opinion of U Aung Thu, secretary of the Burmese Chamber of Commerce and a member of the purchasing commission, China was buying Burmese rice for purely political reasons[39]— promoting its policy of peaceful coexistence.

1957–59

Beginning in late 1957, Peking's flexible, moderate line toward under-developed countries gave way to a hard, dogmatic, and generally hostile approach. Domestically, China's internal antirightist movements resulting from the Hundred Flowers campaign, that encouraged the Chinese people to speak out freely about national policies, led to the purge of the bourgeois class. In foreign relations, China hence concluded that the national bour-geoisie ruling the independent states in Asia should not be trusted to fight imperialism. Evidently, the diplomatic coalition with the neutralists in the last few years had not eroded U.S. power in Asia or established the legitimacy of Chinese interests and objectives. In Peking's view these could be accomplished only through mass movements with the Communist parties there, in whose potential Mao Tse-tung seemed to have a great deal of faith. That the Soviet Union successfully launched *Sputnik I* in October 1957 also led Mao to believe that "the East Wind has prevailed over the West Wind." Mao regarded the United States as a real paper tiger, and he thought international movement could be encouraged without fear of U.S. retaliation. Furthermore, Peking needed a favorable external environment for its radical economic "Great Leap Forward" so that the Chinese people would respond more energetically to the call because of riding an historic high tide of some kind.

However, China's support for the national liberation movement, because of its economic and political limitations, was actually quite selective. In Burma Peking aimed less at revolution and more at promoting its interests. There was no drastic intensification of Chinese efforts to manipulate the overseas Chinese in Burma.

The border problem remained unsolved. U Nu, who returned to power early in 1957, declared settling the border controversy "a matter of life and death." He was in favor of the arrangement he made with Chou En-lai when he visited Peking in 1956, but public opinion in Burma would not allow the Burmese government formally to consent to it. On the other hand, the P.R.C. continued to show no hurry for a final settlement. Except for reasons mentioned previously, the deteriorating political situation in Burma may have given Peking hope that it would get better terms by holding out.[40]

The P.R.C. resumed aid and encouragement to the Burmese Communists after adopting the new tough line. It was of no coincidence that Burmese Communists stepped up their guerrilla operations and waged an all-out nuisance campaign against the government. In 1959 the BCP set up the National Democratic United Front in alliance with the Karen National Unity Party, the New Mon State Party, the Kaya Progressive Party, and the Chin Supreme Council. Since Chinese dealings with the BCP and their legal counterpart, the Burma Workers and Peasants Party (BWPP), were covert, in Harold C. Hinton's view, Peking was given a leverage on the Burmese political scene without provoking a major rupture with the Burmese government, which was too much afraid of the P.R.C. to quarrel with it except in extreme situations.[41]

Illegal immigrants from China also raised a minor sore point in relations between the two countries. From late 1957 to 1959 there were constant reports of border crossings into Burma. By 1959 some sources claimed there were more than 2,000 illegal immigrants from Yunnan in the Wa and Shan states on the northern border. Most of the infiltrators were members of tribal groups from both sides of the border, but there were also refugees from Chinese Communist opposition. And some of these refugees, when rounded up, proved to be Communist agents.[42]

In this period, trade between Burma and the P.R.C. reduced considerably. On April 19, 1957, the Burmese government stopped opening any more letters of credit for barter goods from the P.R.C. because Burma had already received about five times more goods from Communist China than it had paid for with rice under the barter agreement. The Chinese aid program was not renewed by the last AFPFL government in 1957 or by the succeeding caretaker military regime because Burma no longer needed the aid after its foreign exchange position had been stabilized. Peking did not offer to renew aid between 1957 and 1960.[43]

1960–67

In the pursuit of hard-line policies, the P.R.C. had aroused suspicion, fear, and hostility in neighboring Asian countries and stirred up a heated controversy with the Soviet Union and its supporters. At the same time the "Great Leap Forward" was a great failure and resulted in serious economic problems at home. The external isolation combined with internal difficulties forced Peking to modify its policies, which began a new era in Sino-Burmese relations.

The new relations between the two countries was first heralded by finally resolving border disputes. When Ne Win headed the caretaker government in late 1958, he was eager to achieve a definitive border agreement with China, but it was not until after the crisis in Tibet and the Sino-Indian border clashes as well as the announcement of Soviet Premier Khrushchev's forthcoming visit to Burma that the P.R.C. invited the general to visit Peking in January 1960 to make an agreement on the border question. Ne Win's keen sense of timing, according to U Maung Maung, also contributed to the success of the negotiations. The general had already announced that general elections would be held early in 1960. After the election a party government would come into office, and however strong it might be, it would still have to face an opposition in Parliament. If the Chinese government wanted to conclude the negotiations with a strong Burmese government that commanded national respect, it had to be done before Ne Win relinquished the premiership.[44]

Under the pact the two premiers agreed that except for the areas of Hpimou, Gawhun, and Kangfang, the entire boundary from the High Conical Peak to the western extremity of the Sino-Burmese boundary would be delimited along the traditional customary line. The three other areas would be given to China. In return, China would give Burma jurisdiction of the Pan Hung and Panloo tribal areas, which were west of the 1941 line. By and large the arrangement resembled that tentatively agreed on by Chou En-lai and U Nu in 1956 with the chief exception that China agreed to cede the Namwan tract to Burma in exchange for some tribal territories farther to the south. However, the Chinese side gave up its earlier claims to a much larger territory, while the Burmese only made some token concessions. The Sino-Burmese Boundary Treaty was officially finalized at Peking by Premier Chou En-lai and U Nu on October 1, 1960.[45] In both Rangoon and Peking the border settlement was publicized as a triumphal application of the Five Principles of Coexistence. Chou declared the year 1961 as the year of China-Burma friendship and assured the Burmese of Peking's abiding friendship. The P.R.C. appeared to have another purpose of signing the treaty: It was a good model for the Sino-Indian border disputes. As an editorial of *Jen-min jih-pao*, a Chinese official paper, said, the boundary agreement provided an "excellent example of Asian countries seeking reasonable settlement of their boundary disputes."[46]

While in Peking General Ne Win also signed a treaty of friendship and nonaggression providing that there "shall be everlasting peace and cordial friendship" between the two countries which

undertake to settle all disputes between them by means of peaceful negotiations without resorting to force [that] each Contracting Party undertakes not to carry out acts of aggression against the other and not to take part in any military alliance directed against the other Contracting Party [and that] the Contracting Parties declare they will develop and strengthen the economic and cultural ties between the two states in a spirit of friendship and cooperation in accordance with the principles of equality and mutual benefit and of mutual noninterference in each other's internal affairs.[47]

Peking apparently took advantage of this treaty with Burma to cultivate friendship with other Asian countries, to minimize Soviet influence in Asia, and to prevent Burma from establishing a military alliance with any country, particularly the United States. The Chinese official press declared that the treaty and the agreement were of great significance "because the Asian countries have all been subject to the plunder and oppression of imperialism and colonialism" and "have the common aim of opposing colonialism and imperialism." So it asked: Why can't such accord as that between China and Burma also be developed between China and other Asian countries?[48] By the treaty of friendship and nonaggression the P.R.C. was also taking out extra insurance against Burma's involvement in SEATO. While Burma felt happy to be guaranteed of friendship and nonaggression by its powerful neighbor, it does open the possibility that China exercise influence over Burmese defense and foreign policy.[49]

In January 1961, Chou En-lai visited Rangoon with a delegation of over 400, including Foreign Minister Chen Yi, and Lo Jui-ching, chief of the general staff of the People's Liberation Army, to exchange ratifications of Sino-Burmese border agreement and friendship treaty as well as to take part in the celebration of the thirteenth anniversary of Burma's independence. The Burmese government awarded Chou the order of "Supreme Upholder of the Glory of Great Love," especially created for the occasion. A joint communique issued by Chou En-lai and U Nu in Rangoon on January 9, 1961, expressed the "profound satisfaction of the two countries at the emergence of a great majority of countries of Asia and Africa from their formal colonial or semi-colonial status" and opposed the "preservation or resurgence of colonialism in any form." It also expressed concern over the civil war in Laos and declared that there should be no outside interference or pressure in that country.[50]

To develop and strengthen the economic ties between the two countries, Chinese Vice Minister for Foreign Trade, Lu Jen-ming, and the Burmese Minister for Trade Development, U Thwin, reached a trade agreement in Rangoon in October 1960. The agreement provided that during 1961 China would purchase from Burma 300,000 to 400,000 long tons of rice of the crop for shipment in the same year, and that Burma would import from China such commodities as Burma required and China was able to supply so as to balance the trade between the two countries.[51] The agreement seemed mutually beneficial; according to Vidya Prakash Dutt, China's import of rice not only assisted Burma in disposing of its produce but also helped China relieve its critical shortage of food grains in 1960.[52]

During his visit to Rangoon in January 1961, Chou En-lai signed an agreement with U Nu on economic and technical cooperation under which Burma would receive an interest-free loan of about $84 million from China. The loan, repayable in ten years from 1971 in installments either with Burmese export goods or with the currency of a third country agreed upon by China, would be in the form of providing complete sets of equipment, sending technical experts, and helping Burma to train technical personnel. This was the largest loan China had ever made to any non-Communist country for purposes of economic development. In William C. Johnstone's view, it may have had the natural consequence of the dwindling economic aid and use of technicians Burma would have enjoyed from other countries.[53]

At the time of U Nu's visit to China in April 1961, the two countries also agreed to cooperate in solving the problem of the remnant Kuomintang troops. Soon afterward the Burmese, aided by 20,000 Communist Chinese troops, finally managed to push the KMT forces out of Burma's Shan state into Thailand.[54] Earlier in March, aircraft of the Republic of China had airlifted some 4,000 "KMT Irregulars" to Taiwan.

The close cultural ties between Burma and the P.R.C. was facilitated by frequent exchange visits of various groups, the so-called people diplomacy. During this period, the P.R.C. maintained only the most limited support for the Burmese Communist movement. In 1963, when the Burmese government offered amnesty talks with the insurgents, Peking supported the talks and arranged for thirty exiled "White Flag" leaders residing in Peking to take part in the negotiations in Rangoon. Peking may have sought a coalition government in Burma in which the White Flags would participate as the Pathet Lao did in Laos in 1962. The negotiations themselves, however, proved futile and quickly broke down. Of the Burmese Communist leaders who had returned to Burma from China, twenty-eight reportedly escaped to remote jungles in Burma where they assumed de facto leadership of the party at home, while two others, including Thakin Ba Thein Tin, the BCP's then vice chairman, returned to Peking.[55] In 1964 Peking Radio broadcast, much to Rangoon's annoyance, a statement by the White Flags blaming the failure of the talks on sabotage by imperialism, internal reactionism, and revisionism.[56]

When General Ne Win seized power in March 1962, Chou En-lai broadcast and cabled this greeting: "I am confident that the intimate relations of friendship and cooperation between China and Burma will be further strengthened and developed."[57] The military government reaffirmed Burma's foreign policy of neutrality and nonalignment but took steps to remove foreign influence through "the Burmese Way to Socialism." This scheme greatly affected Chinese interests in Burma, as the Burmese government curbed the propaganda and information activities of foreign diplomatic missions, disabling the Chinese embassy from continuing its disputes with the United States and the Soviet Union within Burma. In 1966, when the government suspended the publication of all privately owned foreign-language newspapers, it crippled the pro-Peking Chinese-language newspapers. Under the government's nationalization policies two Chinese state-owned banks were nationalized depriving Peking of the means to expand its influence among the overseas Chinese community and in the Burmese economy through loans from these banks. Chinese-run schools were first forbidden to offer indoctrination courses in Marxism-Leninism and the teachings of Mao Tse-tung and ordered to follow a rigid curriculum set down by Burmese educational officials. And soon after, all private schools were taken over by the government.[58]

Burma's xenophobic measures applied to all foreign countries, not just to China only, so Peking had no reason to protest. China continued on good terms with Burma for general national interests, for the rapprochement then had made Burma an open door for the P.R.C. to the world. Burma was the only non-Communist territory through which the Chinese Communists could come and go, and through which delegations and official missions to China from Africa, Latin America, and the rest of Asia could come and go with ease.[59]

Chou En-lai, accompanied by Foreign Minister Chen Yi, arrived in Rangoon on July 10, 1962. His trip seemed to be most concerned with reaffirming the close ties between the P.R.C. and Ne Win's military regime. During his visit Chou and General Ne Win reviewed the progress made by the two countries in developing economic and technical cooperation and trade relations. In order to further strengthen this cooperation, the two leaders agreed to speed up implementing the Sino-Burmese agreement on economic and technical cooperation and to further expand the trade between the two countries. The two leaders also expressed their deep concern over the deteriorating situation in southeast Asia, particularly in South Vietnam and Laos, affirmed their determination to continue to seek peaceful settlement of the situation, and agreed that a conference on the Laotian problem of the fourteen Geneva powers should be convened.[60]

P.R.C. Chairman Liu Shao-chi, accompanied by Foreign Minister Chen Yi, paid a goodwill visit to Burma in 1963. Liu's journey may also have been to seek Burma's support for Peking's stance on Sino-Indian border disputes. The joint communique issued by Liu Shao-chi and Ne Win on April 25 stated that Burma appreciated the measures of ceasefire, withdrawal of Chinese frontier guards, and release of captured Indian personnel taken by the Chinese government on its own initiative as these measures were favorable to the peaceful settlement of the Sino-Indian boundary dispute, and that Burma further expressed its hope and desire for a peaceful settlement of the Sino-Indian boundary question through direct negotiations between China and India.[61]

Chinese Deputy Premier Marshall Ho Lung came to Rangoon in November 1963, followed by Chou En-lai and Chen Yi, who made brief stopovers in Rangoon en route to Africa and also on their way back. Chou and Chen paid an official visit to Burma in February 1964. In this meeting with General Ne Win, Chou brought up the problem of the Sino-Indian dispute. The general had previously expressed deep concern over it but wished the two parties to work out a settlement by themselves. At Chou's suggestion during his visit, Ne Win later called on Nehru in New Delhi and proposed that he and Chou meet once more to discuss the border dispute, but Nehru refused.

The nuclear test ban was another topic of discussion between Chou En-lai and Ne Win during Chou's visit. China had earlier issued a statement condemning the Test Ban Treaty as a plot to prevent China from developing its own nuclear weapons and advocating a conference of all nations to discuss the complete destruction of nuclear weapons. Chou had also sent notes to various African and Asian governments asking for support. Like the vast majority of Asian nations, Burma had already signed the Nuclear Test Ban Treaty.[62] In the joint communique issued by Chou En-lai and Ne Win on February 18, 1964, Ne Win agreed to the ultimate goal of the total prohibition of nuclear weapons, but mention of the Nuclear Test Ban Treaty was deliberately omitted.

Chou En-lai and Chen Yi visited Burma in July 1964, less than a week after Soviet First Deputy Prime Minister Anastas Mikoyan visited Rangoon, probably to offset any possible gains the Soviets might have made from Mikoyan's trip. However, the joint communique of Chou and Ne Win expressed only their deep concern over the deteriorating situation in southeast Asia, particularly in South Vietnam and Laos.[63]

Chou En-lai and Chen Yi visited Burma on April 3, 1965, and made a brief stop in Rangoon on April 16 after attending the tenth anniversary celebration of the Bandung Conference in Jakarta, Indonesia. On April 26 Chou again paid a two-day visit to Rangoon. In June the vice-chairman of the Standing Committee of the National People's Congress of the P.R.C. headed a goodwill delegation to Burma. And in July Ne Win was invited to visit Peking. U.S. intervention in Vietnam, Chinese aid policy toward African countries, and the proposed Second Bandung Conference in Algeria seemed to be major topics of discussions between the Chinese leaders and Ne Win. Peking had sharpened its attack on the United States after the latter sent its combat troops to South Vietnam in February 1965. In Africa, the P.R.C. had set forth eight principles of Chinese aid to counter Soviet and Western aid to compete for influence in the developing countries there. And China had worked hard to convene a Second Bandung Conference of Asian and African nations with the exclusion of Soviet participation in order to combat the increasing isolation China was feeling. In the joint communique issued on August 1, 1965, General Ne Win opposed outside intervention in the internal affairs of any nation though he did not identify the United States by name so as to avoid being drawn into denouncing U.S. Vietnam policy. He expressed his appreciation of the eight principles observed by the Chinese government in providing economic aid to other countries and endorsed the convening of the Second Bandung Conference without making reference to the Soviet Union.[64]

On April 17, 1966, Chinese Chairman Liu Shao-chi, accompanied by Chou En-lai, made his second visit to Rangoon when General Ne Win had scheduled a fall visit to the United States. Liu and Chou urged Ne Win to condemn U.S. aggression against Vietnam and sought to prevent him from making any pro-U.S. commitments during the forthcoming visit to Washington. In his speeches at various banquets and receptions Liu encouraged anti-imperialism and anti-Americanism. He dropped hints that Burma should be more active and intensify its anti-imperialist struggles: "We Afro-Asian countries must heighten our vigilance, unite even more closely, and persevere in the struggle."[65] But Ne Win carefully took an independent position which, his speech hinted, should be respected by the P.R.C. In his speech at the banquet given in honor of Liu Shao-chi, the general said, "Our two countries have strictly observed the five principles of co-existence in their relations with each other. . . . The People's Republic of China has respected and supported our longstanding policy of peace, independence, neutrality and friendship with all countries." He also resisted China's attempt to draw out a Burmese stance on U.S. intervention in Vietnam. As a result, the joint communique issued at the end of Liu and Chou's visit avoided the question of Vietnam.[66]

1967–69

Burma's relations with the P.R.C. took a sudden turn for the worse in the summer of 1967, principally as a result of the radicalist upsurge in Chinese domestic politics. The outbreak of the Great Proletarian Cultural Revolution in late 1966 and early 1967 brought about a radicalization in Chinese foreign policy. Peking, aggressively exporting Mao Tse-tung's though and the principles of the Cultural Revolution, encouraged the local insurgents to carry out armed struggle against the governments of developing countries and to create storm centers of world revolution. Burma became a target of the Chinese new policy. China's hostility toward Burma, according to Robert A. Holms, also resulted from a long series of failures to extend Chinese influence into Burma and to induce Burma to identify with and support Chinese foreign policy.[67]

Upon their return to Burma from consultations in Peking in May 1967,

Chinese embassy personnel encouraged the overseas Chinese community to participate in Cultural Revolution-type activities. The embassy distributed Maoist propaganda and urged Chinese students to form groups patterned after the Red Guard and to wear Mao Tse-tung badges in defiance of a government order. They trampled on Burma's Union flag and destroyed the portraits of Aung San and Ne Win. These actions sparked anti-Chinese riots in Rangoon on June 22. Chinese shops and houses were sacked and burned, and the Chinese embassy was also attacked. In the ensuing riots, a member of the Chinese embassy, Liu Yi, was fatally stabbed. Though the Burma Information Ministry urged the citizenry to exercise restraint, the clashes between Burmese and Chinese students worsened. The Burmese government then sealed off the Chinese sector of the city, closed all the schools, banned public speeches and gatherings, and issued a dusk-to-dawn curfew.

The Chinese government lodged a strong protest with the Burmese government over the anti-Chinese incident in Rangoon. The protest note from the Chinese Foreign Ministry charged that the incident was "instigated and engineered" by the Burmese government.[68] On June 30, the Chinese government issued a stiffly worded statement charging the Burmese government with aggravating the situation to "a grave extent" and informing it that the Chinese ambassador would not be sent back to his post (China's ambassador to Burma had been in Peking for the past several months and the embassy in Rangoon had been run by a charge d'affaires). The statement also put forward a five-point demand to the Burmese government. The five demands were: (1) Severely punish the culprits; (2) Give relief to the families of the victims; (3) Publicly offer apologies; (4) Guarantee the safety of the Chinese embassy in Burma and the Chinese agencies and all their Chinese personnel; and (5) Immediately put an end to the "fascist" atrocities against overseas Chinese.[69] Between June 28 and December 1, 1967, thirty protest notes had been delivered from the Chinese government to Burmese officials in Rangoon.

The Chinese official press, the *New China News Agency*, even made personal attacks on General Ne Win. It stated:

The reactionary Ne Win government has been sabotaging relations between China and Burma under the label of "Burma-China friendship." Now when class contradictions within Burma have become more acute, the reactionary Ne Win government's hostility toward China has become more exposed, and it finally embarked on the path of opposing China in an all-round way. . . . After the fascist chieftain Ne Win visited the United States in September last year [1966], the reactionary Burmese Government . . . outrageously stirred up a nationwide anti-China and anti-Chinese campaign last June [1967].[70]

"Over one million Chinese" demonstrated in front of the Burmese embassy in Peking charging Ne Win and his "clique" with collusion with Washington and Moscow and demanding a public Burmese apology to the "Chinese government and people" and for the repayment of "blood debt."[71] The Chinese technicians helping the joint projects in Burma also quit work. They did so, Radio Peking implied, because Burmese authorities would not allow Burmese workers "to study Chairman Mao's works or wear Mao badges . . . to see Chinese firms . . . to come into contact with the Chinese experts outside working hours."[72]

Following the June rift the Chinese gave open help to the BCP and formally endorsed its aims to overthrow the Ne Win government. A statement issued by the Central Committee of the Chinese Communist Party said:

[We support] the people's revolutionary armed struggle led by the BCP. We regard such support as our bounden proletarian duty. It is our firm conviction that the BCP headed by Comrade Thakin Than Tun, which persists in the revolutionary line "to win the war and seize political power," will assuredly . . . overthrow the reactionary Ne Win Government and win complete victory in the revolutionary war in Burma.[73]

Since the riots in June 1967 until November 1970 there was a steady stream of articles and speeches in the Chinese media praising the Burmese Communist armed struggle. Chinese media also published propaganda statements made by the BCP. Several hundred Chinese advisors reportedly had entered Kachin state after June 1967, and 5,000 Chinese People's Liberation Army members were in northern Burma by 1969. Beginning in 1968 the Burmese Communists moved from central and southern Burma to northern areas bordering China. There the insurgents had the opportunity to regroup, improve their communications and coordination, and to receive Chinese military training and indoctrination. Captured prisoners were said to have turned over Chinese-manufactured weapons, and many reported attending training courses in China.[74]

The BCP intensified its military actions against the government. General Ne Win reported large-scale fighting along the China border and many guerrillas crossing into China, publicly linking insurgent activity with external support. In early November 1969 Ne Win also confirmed that "from January 1, 1969 to the end of August, there were eight major engagements and ten minor ones" and "we have never suffered so many casualties before."[75] In spite of these ominous developments, Ne Win carefully avoided blaming China for insurgent activity within Burma and appealed to the Burmese people to be calm:

The people who are against us have openly declared they are getting external aid. We on our part do not wish to enrage others. I asked the people not to be provoked to anger, to use harsh words, or to take actions because of the clashes in the frontier area.[76]

The Burmese government seemed to maintain an attitude of self-righteousness and indignation, reflected in a *Guardian* editorial:

Whatever the People's Republic of China may have chosen to say, the present trouble between this huge country and Burma is not of Burma's making. . . . Shocked into a cruel disillusionment that her diligent scruples in nurturing neighboring friendship and in pursuing strict neutrality in international power-politics were not being respected as hoped, Burma, nevertheless, cannot be threatened into compromising her sovereignty or her strictly neutral policy.[77]

Officially, Rangoon took a conciliatory stand. Over the death of Liu Yi the Burmese government expressed deep regret, offered comfort to his family, and promised to prevent the occurrence of further disturbances. On learning of the Peking demonstrations against Burma, Rangoon lodged a protest of its own against what it termed an unfortunate development that would adversely affect the sincere effort of the Burmese government to restore a normal situation in Burma and to preserve the friendly relations between the two countries. In response to Chinese accusations that the Burmese government deliberately subverted the 1961 Agreement on Economic and Technical Cooperation and sabotaged the joint projects, Rangoon refused to further support Chinese aid technicians in the country and ordered their withdrawal. By October 31, 1967, China had discontinued the aid program and taken out all 412 personnel.[78] In the same month Burma finally recalled its ambassador to Peking.

China's Cultural Revolution had caused a grave disaster for the BCP itself, as BCP's Peking returnees, inspired by China's Cultural Revolution and supported by its own young Red Guards, launched its own version of the Cultural Revolution. In 1967 three of the eight members of its Politburo—Yebaw Hlay, Than Myaing, and Ba Tin—were executed after being accused of "revisionism," harboring "rightist" tendencies, and betraying the revolution. In 1968 a central committee member, Aye San, was stabbed to death by one of his own troops; and the chairman of the party, Thakin Than Tun, was assassinated by a follower embittered by the executions and fearful of being purged himself. In 1969 another central committee member, Ko Soe, was executed.[79]

Trade between Burma and China also became a casualty of Chinese radical policy. Following the signing of a trade agreement by the two countries in 1961, the amount of their trade reached a combined record of

$57.4 million in that year, representing 11 percent of Burma's exports to China and 10 percent of its imports from that country. After coming to power in 1962, the Revolutionary Council diversified Burma's trade, and trade with China declined to $45.8 and $37.1 millions in 1962–1963, rose to $42.4 and $45.1 million in 1964–1965, and then slumped to $23 million in 1966. After the Rangoon rift of 1967, commercial relations to China declined drastically and were practically nonexistent in 1969.[80]

1970–78

By 1968 the Chinese Cultural Revolution began to fade, and so did Red Guard diplomacy, which seemed primarily motivated by Peking's perception of the Soviet threat. The precedent-setting Soviet intervention in Czechoslovakia in the name of preserving socialism in August 1968 and later armed clashes with the Soviet Union over several small islands in the Ussuri River raised the possibility of Soviet attack on China. China now was anxious to check Soviet influence in Asia and turned to Burma, which was then the only regional country outside Indochina to have a Chinese embassy.

In 1968 the P.R.C. made some gestures of friendship toward Burma: Peking donated $4,000 in relief aid to the Burmese Red Cross for assisting the cyclone and flood victims in the Arakan division; Chinese charge d'affaires placed a wreath on the grave of General Aung San on the anniversary commemorating his assassination; and Chinese propaganda attacks on the Burmese government became less frequent. For Burma's part, Ne Win and other Burmese officials continued to refrain from openly accusing China of supporting the insurgents. The Burmese media also began to tone down its hostile attitude toward Peking. In March of the same year Ne Win made a conciliatory speech before a peasants' seminar in Rangoon by saying: "We have to rely on our own strength in everything. We cannot depend on anybody. We should not try to find fault with anyone. We do not want to quarrel with anyone."[81] At the end of January 1969 the general visited Pakistan to discuss with Chinese officials there the possibility of improving relations between Burma and China. In Pakistan he expressed a readiness to normalize diplomatic ties with Peking in return for a Chinese agreement to stop their support of the Burmese Communists.[82] In November at the Fourth Seminar of the BSPP, Ne Win made a clear plea to Peking to restore the cordial relations that previously existed between the two countries. He said:

Now specifically to mention China with which our present problem is connected we should like to restore the cordial and friendly relations which formerly prevailed between our two countries. We should strive toward that end, but it takes two to make a friendship, and it is up to the other side also to try. We regard what has passed as past, the unhappy incident of 1967, and we only wish to heal its wounds and erase the scars it might have left on our minds. . . . Restoration of friendship is our constant objective.[83]

Apparently, Ne Win feared that the continued deterioration of the relationship between China and Burma would result in Chinese substantial support to the BCP and would endanger Burma's internal stability and security. Former Premier U Nu's 1969 open search for aid from all quarters, including China, in order to recapture power also might have contributed to Ne Win's desire for friendly relations with Peking.

The first sign of a real thaw in Burma-China relations occurred in August 1970, when several high-ranking Burmese military officers attended a reception celebrating the forty-third anniversary of the People's Liberation Army (PLA) given by the Chinese military attache. Then on October 1, 1970, for the first time since 1966, Ne Win sent Premier Chou En-lai a telegram congratulating him on the founding anniversary of the P.R.C. A reception given by the Chinese charge d'affaires in Rangoon on the same occasion was attended by such Burmese dignitaries as acting Foreign Minister Maung Lwin and Vice Foreign Minister Hla Hpone. Finally, following an agreement to exchange ambassadors anew, the new Burmese ambassador arrived in Peking in November 1970, and in March of the next year the new Chinese representative was posted to Rangoon.[84]

The normalized relations between the two countries was solidified by General Ne Win's visit to Peking in August 1971 at Chou En-lai's invitation. A Chinese plane was especially sent to bring his party to the Chinese capital. Ne Win and his wife were given a warm welcome, and Ne Win met with Mao Tse-tung and Chou En-lai. Chou later accompanied him on his tour outside Peking, a compliment reportedly reserved for cherished friends. During his visit, both sides sought to allay mutual misgivings as well as profess friendship. Ne Win wanted Chou En-lai's advice on how to compensate the losses suffered by local Chinese residents in the 1967 riots. Chou replied that Burma was a sovereign state and could deal with the matter in any way it deemed fit. Chou reaffirmed China's earlier attitude toward the overseas Chinese in Burma, saying that overseas Chinese "should obey the law of the countries in which they reside." He added that China opposed the concept of dual nationality and exploitation of overseas Chinese capitalists. Ne Win for his part promised to grant citizenship to those Chinese who applied for it. Chou also offered to restore the Chinese economic aid program.[85]

On October 7, 1971, the 1961 agreement of Sino-Burmese economic aid and technical cooperation was reactivated. Burma was authorized to utilize, until September 1975, the balance of some $56.7 million of the $84 million ten-year interest-free loan granted under the agreement, with repayment in installments to begin only in October 1980.[86] It seems that the P.R.C. used good economic relations with Burma to keep Rangoon close to Peking politically and diplomatically.

In October 1971 Burma was among the seventy-five–member majority in the UN General Assembly to support the P.R.C.'s admission to the United Nations. To solicit Burma's support for its membership in the UN may have been one of the reasons that Chou En-lai invited Ne Win to visit China in August, though Burma had been a persistent supporter of Peking's membership. Perhaps to show its appreciation for Burma's support, China's first delegation to the UN, comprised of forty members and headed by Vice Foreign Minister Chiao Kuan-hua, stopped in Rangoon en route to New York.[87]

In November 1975, President Ne Win paid a five-day visit to China, his first since 1971. The main object of his visit, according to news reports, was to clarify Burma's relationship with China and to discuss China's position on the pro-Chinese Burmese Communist Party. Predictably the visit resulted in a joint communique proclaiming lasting friendship between the two countries, each reaffirming the five principles of peaceful coexistence. It also promised an expansion of trade contacts, political, social and economic cooperation between the two countries. As well, both countries pledged not to join military alliances directed against each other or to carry out aggressive action against each other.[88] The last two points obviously reflected Peking's intention to prevent Burma from joining a Soviet military alliance against China, just as it kept Burma from a U.S. military alliance when it signed the treaty of friendship and mutual nonaggression with Burma in 1960.

In April 1977, Ne Win visited Peking, where at a reception he stressed "Burma's resolve to strengthen the *paukphaw* ('kinship') relationship existing between the two countries since ancient days." Ne Win visited China again in September on the way to a state visit to North Korea. On the eve of his second trip to Peking in 1977, two pro-Soviet Burmese officials, Transport and Communications Minister Tun Lin and Finance and Planning Minister Than Sein, had been relieved of their duties. The purge seemed to be a gesture of goodwill to China to help Ne Win's request for withdrawing Chinese assistance from the insurgents.

On January 26, 1978, Chinese Deputy Premier Teng Hsiao-ping visited

Burma, the first such trip for many years by a Chinese leader of his position and stature. Hinting that Burma should take a pro-Chinese and anti-Vietnamese position in the current border war between Democratic Kampuchea and Vietnam, Teng said at a banquet:

As for the disputes among Asian countries, we have always stood for seeking resolution through friendly consultations on the basis of the principles of peaceful co-existence. We are sure that as long as the people of Asian countries strengthen their unity and persist in the struggle, they certainly will be able to frustrate any plot of imperialism and hegemonism and win greater victories in their struggle to safeguard their national independence and State sovereignty.[89]

Despite steady improvement of Sino-Burmese relations since the end of the Chinese Cultural Revolution, Peking continued to maintain its ties with the BCP. March 1971 saw the opening of anti-Rangoon broadcasts from BCP's clandestine "Voice of the People of Burma." The radio, based somewhere in the Chinese border province of Yunnan and beaming propaganda in Shan, Gingpaw, Burmese, and Chinese, regularly called for the Communist overthrow of Ne Win's government. Shortly before Ne Win's visit to Peking in August 1971, Chou En-lai was photographed with BCP Vice-Chairman Ba Thein Tin and Central Committee member Pe Tint, who were living in Peking. Later the Chinese media published the text of a BCP message to the Central Committee of the Chinese Communist Party (CCP) on the fiftieth anniversary of its founding in which it pledged once again to overthrow the Burmese government.[90] Peking not only gave moral and material support to the Burmese Communists but also sent cadres and technicians to battle with the Burmese army near the Chinese border in 1973.[91] In May 1975, the CCP sent a message to the BCP eulogizing its chairman Thakin Zin and secretary Thakin Chit, who were killed by the Burmese army, and expressing confidence in the eventual BCP victory. The BCP's ties with China were further consolidated by the succession to BCP leadership of Thakin Ba Thein Tin, a long-time resident of Peking. In January 1976, the Chinese leadership received the new BCP chairman and reported "very cordial" talks with him.

China's continued support of the BCP reportedly led to a bitter argument between Ne Win and the Chinese deputy premier during the latter's visit to Burma. In June, Burmese Defense Minister Kyaw Htin headed a delegation to Peking where they met with Hua Kuo-feng, chairman of the CCP and premier of the P.R.C., Hsu Hiang-chien, deputy premier and minister for national defense, and Wu Hsiu-chaung, PLA deputy chief of staff. The stated aim of the meeting was to further "the close *paukphaw* relations between the two countries."[92] However, the BCP insurgency was undoubtedly a prominent issue of discussion.

The P.R.C. has always valued its ties with the Communist parties in non-Communist Southeast Asia countries, particularly the pro-Peking BCP. The reasons for this are very clear. First, China must maintain its ideological credibility both at home and abroad. To do otherwise would run the risk of internal dissension and betraying revolutionary movements. Whenever Ne Win and other Burmese leaders asked Chinese leaders to drop their support for the BCP, always the Chinese replied that while they wanted close relations at the government-to-government level, the Chinese Communist party had a revolutionary responsibility to aid the fraternal BCP. Second, Peking used the Communist rebels as a leverage to keep the non-Communist governments on friendly terms. China would increase its support to that Communist party at the time of strained relations with the non-Communist country concerned and would reduce its support to that Communist party in periods of good relations. Third, China could not cut its ties with these Communist parties and abdicate its revolutionary leadership to the Soviet Union, now its number one enemy.

1979 TO THE PRESENT

In Chinese perception, Vietnamese/Soviet expansionism since Hanoi's 1978 invasion of Cambodia has threatened regional stability and China's national security as well as its magnificent scheme of "Four Modernizations"—agriculture, industry, military, and economy—which requires a peaceful and stable international environment. To forge a united front with all non-Communist countries in Southeast Asia against perceived Vietnamese/Soviet hegemonism hence becomes a top priority in Chinese current foreign policy. Burma's strategic importance as a reliable friend is thus certainly basic to Chinese thinking.

The P.R.C. has taken a significant step by emphasizing state-to-state relations and downgrading party-to-party links with Burma. Probably beginning in 1979, China stopped supplying arms and material assistance to the BCP which has not launched a main offensive since 1980 and in recent years has turned to drug trafficking for financial support. At Chinese initiative the BCP opened talks with the Rangoon government and made its first overture in September 1980, four months after the rebels' scornful rejection of President Ne Win's general amnesty and just one month after its expiration. The peace talks were held in Peking between the Burmese government's delegation led by Aye Ko, then joint general secretary of the BSPP, and the BCP led by its vice chairman Thakin Ba Thein Tin. But the talks broke off in May 1981 because the BCP insisted on three demands unacceptable to the government: the BCP was allowed continued existence as a political party, its armed forces were allowed to remain intact, and frontier areas where the BCP had its hideouts would be treated as the BCP's base area.[93]

In May 1985 the Chinese authorities recognized the BSPP by officially inviting its chairman U Ne Win to visit China. Today they seem to be ignoring the BCP in favor of promoting state-to-state relations with Burma. The BCP is one of their most established progeny, however, and it remains essential to Chinese interests at least as a diplomatic lever in dealing with the Rangoon government. Should its present situations change internally or externally, the P.R.C. will likely reassert its dual diplomacy of the seventies.

China's efforts to improve relations with non-Communist countries in Southeast Asia also include a revised policy on overseas Chinese. As late as 1977, Peking openly declared its intention to enlist the overseas Chinese in world revolution. Recently, however, China changed its tune and now hopes that ethnic Chinese in Asia will play "the role of friendship envoys" in improving government-to-government relations. Peking also eyes the potentially lucrative business with its neighbors and courts overseas Chinese support in providing capital, technology, and entrepreneurial skills for its current "four modernizations" endeavors. The Burmese definitely welcome this new development. They have been well aware of the role of Chinese help for the Communist rebels, and they still remember that some Chinese in the country served as Peking's agents to create disturbances during the period of Red Guard diplomacy.

Sino-Burmese ties have been further strengthened through increased visits between Chinese and Burmese leaders and expansion of cultural and economic cooperation. Most significant were President Ne Win's visit to China in October 1980; China's new Premier Zhao Ziyany's visit to Burma in January 1981; President San Yu's visit to China in October 1984 and Chinese President Li Xiannian's visit to Burma in March 1985, which apart from reciprocating San Yu's visit, was to improve relations to Burma in resisting Vietnamese influence in the region. The implication of official Chinese statements to mark the visit was that Rangoon should join with Thailand in meeting the threat of an overspill from the Cambodian conflict. To underline this, Li immediately went from Burma to Thailand. The visit of Ne Win, chairman of the Burma Socialist Programme Party, to China in May 1985 at the invitation of the P.R.C. signified cordial relations between the two countries beyond government level. At a reception Teng Hsiao-ping praised Ne Win as a "far-sighted and outstanding statesman of Burma" and "one of the most intimate, close and respected old friends of China."[94]

China's aid to Burma has increased in recent years. While visiting Peking in July 1979, Burmese Prime Minister Maung Maung Kha signed with Chinese Prime Minister Hua Kuo-feng an agreement of economic and technical cooperation under which China would provide $64 million to Burma for development projects. In 1984 Peking again furnished Burma with the equivalent of $15 million in aid. When a Chinese delegation headed by Lu Xuejian, vice minister of foreign economic relations and trade, visited Rangoon in November 1987, another agreement was signed that provided an interest-free loan of 80 million yuan from China to Burma for the Rangoon-Syrian bridge project.[95]

Since 1979 Burma's trade with China has also showed tremendous increase. Burma's exports to China alone went from $8.36 million in 1979 to $86.4 million in 1987, while Burma's imports from China increased from $20.49 million in 1979 to $75.54 million in 1987.[96]

6

BURMA AND THE ASEAN STATES

THAILAND

Burma shares a 1,100-mile border with Thailand as well as a common religion, way of life, and culture. Historically, however, Burma and Thailand were often at war, and mutual suspicion persisted even after Burma became independent.[1] Specific problems arising along the border caused further misunderstanding and political tensions between the two countries. Thanks to the determination and efforts of their leaders, however, the two traditional rivals have long managed to maintain good ties. Since the Indochina crisis following the Vietnamese invasion of Cambodia in 1978, both countries recognize the need to improve their relations for domestic and regional security.

Burma established diplomatic relations with Thailand on August 24, 1948. Thailand was invited to send representatives to participate in the Sixth Great Theravada Buddhist Council held in Rangoon from 1954 to 1956, the first such gathering since 1871. As a gesture of goodwill toward Thailand, Burma waived its World War II claims against Thailand and apologized for sacking the ancient Thai capital of Ayuthia about 200 years ago. Burmese Premier U Nu visited Bangkok at the end of 1954, and the two countries signed a treaty of peace and friendship on October 15, 1956. King Bhumibhol Aduluyadej and Queen Sirikit paid a state visit to Burma in early 1960 just before General Ne Win left the prime ministership of the caretaker government.

After Ne Win returned to power following the military coup in March 1962, he was invited by King Bhumibhol Aduluyadej to visit Thailand. The general arrived in Bangkok on December 4. At a banquet, the Thai king said: "It is indeed very gratifying to note that the relationship between our two countries is today becoming increasingly close and cordial and I am confident that your present visit will not fail to strengthen still further the happy relations and mutual good understanding between our two countries." In his reply, General Ne Win said:

Thailand and Burma are neighbors whose people share a common religion and cultural heritage. Built and developed on the firm and enduring basis which this religious and cultural similarity provides, Thai-Burma relations of friendship and understanding, thanks to the efforts of the leaders of both countries, are now attaining new lights [sic] of cordiality. . . . Looking back at the dark periods in the histories of South-East Asian countries, we find how our forefathers had warred against one another for no other purpose than to enhance their prestige through military conquest. . . . Bearing this object lesson of history in mind we shall strive in every way possible to live in peace, friendship and harmony with all countries, especially our neighbors.[2]

During his state visit to Thailand, Revolutionary Council Chairman Ne Win agreed with Thai leaders to establish a joint organization for promoting good understanding and close cooperation between Burma and Thailand. An agreement on border arrangements and cooperation was signed on May 17, 1963, providing for the setting up of a Burmese-Thai High-Level Committee with the foreign ministers of the two countries as joint chairmen. The committee was to meet and confer on strengthening border security and solving such specific border problems as might arise and on devising general measures of economic and cultural cooperation.[3] Despite this agreement, some border problems have not been finally resolved and continue to strain relations between the two countries.

The Chinese Irregular Forces Problem

Burma was troubled by the Chinese irregular forces who fled from the Chinese Communists and intruded into its territory in 1949. Burma accused Thailand of granting the CIF sanctuary in the area of Chiengmai from which they launched attacks against Burma and made contact with agents supplying them with weapons and other equipment.[4] The Thais emphatically denied it. In 1953 a UN resolution designated Thailand to serve in the Four-Nation Commission, along with Burma, the United

States, and the Republic of China, with the responsibility to evacuate the CIF through Thailand to Taiwan. When Thai police refused to permit Burmese observers at the staging points for the evacuation, Burma resumed action against the CIF and accidentally bombed a Thai village. The Thai government condemned what it termed Burma's "general unfriendliness," and when Burma apologized for the bombing and offered 20,000 kyat (about $4,520) for compensation, Thailand refused to accept the money. Then Burma Premier U Nu gave the money to his ambassador to Bangkok for charitable work in Thailand and during his visit to Bangkok in 1954, U Nu again apologized for this incident.[5]

Insurgent Sanctuary

Burmese minority insurgents living just over the Thai border and using Thai sanctuary as a base of military operations against Burmese government troops has become a thorn in Burmese-Thai relations. After the Karen National Defense Organization (KNDO) made trouble along the Thai-Burma borders in 1963, Thailand assured Burma that it would not permit Burmese rebels to set up bases in its territory. During his visit to Burma in November 1966, Thai Premier Thanon Kittikachorn promised to combat the anti-Burmese activities of the Burmese refugees, and Ne Win in turn pledged to prevent anyone from invading Thailand through Burma.

In November 1969 former Burmese Prime Minister U Nu sent to Bangkok and was granted political asylum by the Thai authorities on the condition that he not engage in political activities. But U Nu soon set up a rebel movement to secure his political ends. He publicly sought aid from big powers to overthrow the Ne Win government by force. Burma was displeased with Thailand's handling of the U Nu affair, but withheld criticism to keep Thailand from providing U Nu a base from which to direct his campaign. Thailand, like Burma, recognized the dangerous potential for conflict arising out of this situation during 1973, and the two neighbors also had a common desire to repair diplomatic fences in the wake of the Vietnam cease-fire agreement. After Ne Win's visit to Bangkok in May 1973, the Thai government terminated U Nu's political asylum and forced him to leave the country in July,[7] removing a source of dissension between the two countries.

In 1976 relations between the two neighbors cooled again because of the continued presence in Thailand of Burmese insurgent groups. Political observers pointed to the statement by Burmese Prime Minister Sein Win at the summit of nonaligned nations in Colombo in August that "to develop good neighborly relations, Southeast Asian countries should faithfully undertake not to provide one's territory as a springboard of attack on its neighbors, both covert and overt."[8]

For Thailand the key to the security of its northern border had been thought to lie with Burmese rebel armies, who served as anti-Communist buffer force between Burma and itself. As John McBeth reported in *Asiaweek*: "For years, successive Thai governments had viewed the activities of minority groups along the rugged northwestern frontier as a buffer force against the southward spread of Communist Chinese influence and, later, a Peking-directed insurgency (BCP) through northeast Burma."[9]

As a result, Thailand always gave minority insurgents the sanctuary they needed. In 1977 Burma's state-run press complained that ethnic Karen rebels caught in Bangkok were given favored treatment as being anti-Communist, while harmless Burmese mine workers in South Thailand were ordered out, and that Shan and other ethnic insurgents enjoyed sanctuary in Thai territory once they had fled across the border pursued by Burmese troops.[10]

Since 1978 Thailand has evidently taken a different attitude toward Burmese tribal insurgents. Early in that year Thai Premier Kriangsak Chamanand declared that the government was determined to evict all minority groups from its territory, at first by lenient means and later by the use of force if the minority groups resisted the eviction. Having laid the groundwork for neighborly cooperation by ordering all armed Burmese rebels to get out of Thai territory, Kriangsak visited Rangoon in May 1978 and on his return to Bangkok he said that he had convinced the Burmese leaders of his government's policy not to provide sanctuaries to Burmese rebels or minority groups taking up arms against the Burmese government.[11]

Three factors may have contributed to the shift of policy toward Burmese tribal insurgents. The first was that Thailand desired better diplomatic relations with Burma, because its connections with the rebels were less important than the threat to its security posed by the Indochina conflict since 1978. The second factor was that Chinese pressure on the BCP to soften its military activities loosened Thai reliance on Burmese tribal rebels to check the BCP's expansion. While visiting in Peking in early 1978 Thai Premier Kriangsak was given assurance that China had no intention of backing the BCP to invade Thailand's northeast area. The third factor was that better trade relations with Burma emerged as an imperative for Thailand's economic betterment.

When Thai Prime Minister Prem Tinsulanonda visited Burma in July

1980, he offered firm assurance that his country "will not give sanctuary to Burma's Karen rebels operating along Thai-Burmese borders by closer control at the frontier."[12] On January 5, 1982, Thai Foreign Minister Siddhi visited Rangoon, where he and Burmese officials reached an agreement to share information and cooperate with possible military operations against insurgents and smugglers along the common border.[13]

In 1985 the Rangoon forces suffered heavy casualties during its thrust into the Karen National Liberation Army (KNLA) enclave at Maw Po Kay. In reply to Burmese protests, Thai authorities insisted that no armed Karens were permitted to operate on Thai soil but blamed the refugee influx on Burmese military operations that Thailand was obligated to accommodate.[14] During Siddhi Savetsila's visit to Burma in February 1986 he said, "We have been trying to convince the Burmese authorities that we do not support the minority groups fighting against the central government in Rangoon. In the past, the pledge might not have been taken seriously enough. Now I am sure that we have demonstrated our sincerity through various means." Burmese Foreign Minister Ye Goung, asked about the outcome of the talks with Siddhi which touched on all the crucial issues, said, "Of course, I am satisfied with the positive trend of our discussions. . . . Things will be followed up."[15]

Thai forces seized military control of some thirty strategic hilltop positions held by Khun Sa's Shan United Army at the end of February 1987, an act to show Rangoon its new policy of fighting against anti-Rangoon ethnic rebel groups active along the two countries' common border. One crucial element lacking from the operation was coordination from the Burmese side. Apparently Burma did not want Thai forces to enter its territory even to do something it highly desired. The visits of Burmese Minister for Defense Thura U Kyaw Htin and Armed Forces Chief of Staff General Saw Maung to Bangkok in mid-1987 and supreme commander of Thai Armed Forces and army chief General Chaivalit Yongchaiyut to Rangoon in April 1988 may be helpful in forging new understanding on matters involving the very active Thai-Burma border.

Drug Trafficking

Burma has remained the largest producer of opium in the Golden Triangle—a 60,000 square-mile wild mountain region that comprises the Burmese, Lao, and Thai frontiers—from which an estimated one-third of the world's supply of illegal narcotics originates. Most of the refineries were situated in Burma, only a few hundred meters from the Thai border, where they could be readily moved out of reach of Burmese authorities if the need arose. Most heroin reached world markets through Thailand. The Shan United Army (SUA) controlled 70 to 80 percent of the trade by 1978. After its hold was broken in early 1982, several other groups, including the BCP, were poised to take over. Ethnic dissidents and the Communists in east and north Burma have come to be increasingly associated with the opium venture in their search for funds and firearms.[16]

Starting with a code named Mohein (Thunderbolt) I in April 1976, the Burmese government has launched hard-hitting military operations every year against opium bank-rolled rebels in an effort to break the back of this drug trade. But the Thai usually chose not to strike against Burmese ethnic rebels conducting the drug traffic because the same rebel forces acted as bulwarks against the Communist presence on its northern border. According to the members from the U.S. House of Representatives Select Committee on Narcotics in 1977, Thailand intercepted only 3 percent of the Burmese opium traffic moving through its territory because tough enforcement would unacceptably weaken the Burmese insurgents.[17]

The year 1978 saw a new spirit of cooperation between Thailand and Burma. During a visit by Thai Prime Minister Kriangsak Chamanand to Rangoon in May, he reached an agreement with Burma to exchange information on narcotics although suppression efforts against the illicit narcotics trade would be carried out separately by the forces of the two countries.[18] In May 1979, a Thai narcotics mission visited Rangoon to discuss drug problems with Burmese senior military and intelligence officers. The Burmese were pleased with their attacks on opium warlord Khun Sa's Shan United Army (SUA), which fled to Thai territory in early 1982. After Siddhi's 1986 visit to Rangoon, the two countries made some concrete proposals to get rid of opium cultivation and narcotics production along the common border. Police Major General Chavalit Yodmani, secretary general of Thailand's Office of the Narcotics Control Board, exchanged telephone numbers with Burma's police director general and they promised to call each other with any tips on the drug problem.[19]

Smuggling

Of the illicit trade routes, the volume of trade moving along the Burmese-Thai boundary has been the biggest. A wide range of good, from Ajinomoto powder, motor car tires, spare parts, radio cassettes, and outboard engines to rubber sandals and textiles, come in from Thailand; jade, rubies, tin, tungsten, rubber, cattle, teak logs, and even antique

Buddha statues are taken to Thailand.[20] The illegal export of commodities from Burma to Thailand avoids Burmese government fixed price policies and duties as well as Thai import duties. The illegal importing of commodities from Thailand to Burma to be sold in the "open" black market is an unfortunate natural by-product of Burma's socialist economic policy. The U.S. embassy in Rangoon once pointed out: "Rigid government controls over all aspects of the economy which ignored or failed to respond to consumer demand created conditions that were ideal for the growth of a black market system."[21]

Insurgent ethnic minorities have played a major role in smuggling. In fact, they rely on this illicit trade for survival. The Burmese Deputy Prime Minister and Minister for Defense General Thura Kyaw Htin stated in his Resistance Day address on March 27, 1982, that these insurgents now "make precarious existence in border regions through vice and black-marketing activities."[22] Among the smugglers, the Karen rebels have enjoyed the lion's share in this border trade, as they are skillful in smuggling. They also extort a tribute from smugglers passing through their territory. In 1982 it was reported that total annual take from the Karen's eight "gates," or frontier toll points, was estimated by rebel sources at anywhere between $6.4 million and $7.7 million.[23]

To Burma, indeed, smuggling creates both a barrier in political unity and a loss in foreign exchange. Smuggling estimatedly amounts to fully two-thirds of Burma's official foreign exchange. In 1974 a U.S. businessman estimated the Thai-Burma illicit trade at $5 million daily,[24] constituting a big leak in the Burmese government's coffers.

Burma has been displeased with Thailand's sympathy for the tribal insurgents and its reluctance to take forceful action to check the smuggling. In 1973 a Burmese-Thai high level committee meeting gave special attention to smuggling and security in the border areas and both sides agreed to a number of practical measures. Both Thailand and Burma agreed to intensify cooperation in suppressing smuggling in the joint statement issued at the end of President Ne Win's visit to Bangkok in July 1977. During the visit by Thai Deputy Prime Minister General Prachab Suntrakoon to Rangoon in March 1982, another agreement was reached to cooperate to combat smugglers along the common border. However, as Albert D. Moscolli observes, it seems that even with the best cooperation of the Thai government, this large-scale illegal trade will not diminish until there are major economic improvements within Burma. Smuggling, especially as conducted by Burmese dissidents in the Thai border area, is likely to remain another major irritant in Burmese-Thai relations.[25]

Illegal Immigration

A major influx of illegal immigrants from Burma has also strained Burma-Thai relations. Most of the immigrants entered the country to work in mines and on plantations at the Pak Tho district and Suan Pluang subdistrict of Ratchaburi and the Thong Phaphoum and Sangkhla Buri districts of Kanchanaburi province. The illegal immigrants were desirable because they would work for lower wages than would Thai laborers. The president of the Bangkok Placement Association, Pichai Sawadsut, who, after having completed a fact-finding tour of labor conditions in the province, said: "Mine operators in Ramong province prefer hiring Burmese who illegally enter the country because they do not have to comply with labor laws regarding the minimum wage and worker welfare benefits as would be the case if Thai were hired."[26]

Prior to 1979, Bangkok had not done anything about these illegal Burmese workers because they believed mine owners' warnings that all mines in Ramong would have to be closed down without the Burmese workers. In 1979 the government declared that stern actions would be taken against illegal immigrants as well as people found guilty of sheltering them. Subsequent measures ordered the Burmese either to leave the country or face three years' jail sentence or a 60,000 baht fine. The employers were also threatened with two years' imprisonment or a 10,000 baht fine if they were found employing illegal Burmese workers.[27] The new policy seemed to reflect Bangkok's concerns that the Communists or other insurgents might infiltrate the Burmese groups, thus damaging Thai-Burmese relations or turning against the Thai government. In spite of these measures, a great number of Burmese illegal immigrants have continually entered Thailand.

Fishing Grounds

Thai fishermen in Burmese territorial waters have also frustrated good Burmese-Thai relations. In a 1963 Thai-Burmese high level committee meeting, Thai authorities agreed that Burma had a sea-fishing industry of its own and that it would not be feasible to let the Thais operate in Burmese grounds.

In 1969 a fisherman on a Thai vessel was short in Burmese waters. In an angry reaction to his incident Thailand announced a naval exercise in the Indian Ocean to protect its fishermen. Soon the issue cooled off when Thailand approached Burma and asked that its fishermen be allowed into Burmese waters after paying a special tax.[28] Either this was a temporary agreement or Thai fishermen did not comply with it, for Thai trawlers were frequently captured by the Burmese authorities. From 1965 to 1976, 273 Thai trawlers had been seized, though for every vessel caught, about twenty escaped. Convicted poachers were usually sentenced to eighteen months' imprisonment plus a fine of $150 to $450 for each person, with another six months' imprisonment in cases of default. Despite such punishment, Thai fishermen went on poaching, because they were tempted by Burmese waters, which they considered contained more fish than the exploited Thai seas.[29]

After Burma declared a 200-mile exclusive economic zone in 1977, Thailand became more concerned about the adverse effect this zone would have on its own fishing industry. During his visit to Rangoon in May 1978, Thai Prime Minister Kaiangsak proposed a joint venture in fishing, but it was not accepted. Instead, Burma agreed in principle to allow Thai trawlers to pass through its "economic zone" waters in order to fish in Bangladesh waters under a joint fishing accord.[30]

In July 1980, the two countries signed an agreement demarking the border of their coastal waters in the Andaman Sea. This would go some way toward ending trespassing by Thai fishermen in Burmese waters. According to Thai officials, however, over 400 Thai nationals were arrested during 1983 and 1984, though an agreement was reached earlier in 1985 to return most of those arrested.[31]

Trade with Thailand

Thailand has not been one of Burma's principal trading partners partly because of the extensive smuggling and also because both export the same major products. According to the International Monetary Fund's statistics, in 1959 the value of Burmese exports to Thailand was at $0.1 million and the value of its imports from Thailand was at $0.4 million. Since 1979, nevertheless, trade between Burma and Thailand has increased remarkably. From that year to 1987 the trade between the two countries totaled $258.45 million, of which sales to Thailand accounted for $176.32 million or averaged $19.6 million per year, and purchases from Thailand accounted for $82.13 million or averaged $9.13 million per year.[32]

INDONESIA

Indonesia was the first of the nations of Southeast Asia with which Burma developed close relations. The Republic of Indonesia was given

de facto recognition by Burma in November 1948 and a representative,
Thakin Tha Kin, was sent to the Indonesian capital to establish relations
with the Indonesian government. Following the Hague Agreement of
December 1949 in which the Dutch extended independence to Indonesia,
Burma recognized the Republic of Indonesia as de jure the sovereign
power of the archipelago on December 27.[33] A five-year treaty of friendship was signed in Rangoon on March 31, 1951, aiming at "closer cooperation and the establishment of peace between the two countries with a
view of strengthening existing ties of friendship and promoting common
benefit."[34] The treaty was the first of its kind signed by Burma with any
foreign country since Burmese independence in January 1948. Prime Minister
U Nu in 1957 described his country's relations with Indonesia as excellent:

With independence the old ties of culture and sentiment, which had temporarily been
severed through Burma and Indonesia having been absorbed in two different empires,
were immediately restored as if by magic. It was as though two long lost brothers who
had forgotten each other's existence had suddenly rediscovered themselves. We lost no
time in making the most of this discovery, and today our relations with Indonesia can
only be described as excellent.[35]

Several factors contributed to the close and cordial relationship between
the two countries in the early years. First, sharing the unpleasant colonial
state experience with Indonesia, Burma supported the Indonesians in their
struggle for independence. Burma was strongly critical of the Netherlands
government when the latter began its second police action against Indonesia in late 1948. U Nu urged Indian Prime Minister Nehru to call a
conference of Asian nations on the Indonesian issue, which was convened
in New Delhi on January 20, 1949. At that meeting, Burma proposed
recognition of the Indonesian government by all Asian nations and called
for Dutch withdrawal and a widened range of sanctions against them. Prior
to the conference Burma had denied the use of its airfields to Dutch planes
and recognized the government of Indonesian Republics.[36] Second, both
Burma and Indonesia pursued an independent and neutral foreign policy,
with the same anticolonialism and anti-imperialism orientation. Third, the
two countries together worked for the solidarity of Asian-African states.
At the Colombo Conference held in Colombo, Ceylon in April 1954, the
participating countries of India, Burma, Ceylon, Pakistan, and Indonesia
resolved to call an Asian-African conference, upon the proposal of Indonesia. The Asian-African Conference was finally convened in Bandung,
Indonesia in April 1955, bringing together twenty-nine countries from
Asia and Africa, including Communist, anti-Communist, and neutral

countries. Fourth, Burma and Indonesia had important trade connections; Indonesia was once the largest customer for Burmese rice. In 1960 its share accounted for 28.9 percent of the total exports of Burmese rice, the dominant product of Burma.[37]

Burmese-Indonesian friendship was cemented by close contacts between the two countries. Indonesian President Sukarno paid his first visit to Rangoon on his way home from a journey to India and Pakistan in 1950. An Indonesian economic mission arrived in Burma on February 21, 1953, increasing economic cooperation between Rangoon and Jakarta. Indonesian Prime Minister Ali Sastroamidjojo visited Rangoon in September 1954. He and his Burmese counterpart U Nu called for close ties between the two states. In November Vice-President Hatta visited Burma, and President Sukarno followed in October 1956. Burma supported Indonesia's claim to West Irian. U Pe Rin, Burmese ambassador to the United Nations, said on February 25, 1957, that West Irian should be consolidated with Indonesia and that the matter should be settled through negotiations during 1957.[38] When President Sukarno visited Burma in January 1958, in the join communique with Sukarno, U Nu reaffirmed Burma's support of Indonesia's claims.[39]

After the military came to power in Burma in March 1962, however, relations between Burma and Indonesia cooled because of Ne Win's self-imposed isolation and Indonesian President Sukarno's new policy in the 1963–65 period of ultranationalist and anti-Western pro-Communist stance. Since Sukarno was replaced by General Suharto in 1967, Burmese-Indonesian ties have remained not close, though the Suharto government has chosen moderation and friendship with all nations regardless of ideological differences. Within the region Indonesian leaders seem to be more concerned about their ASEAN partners and the Indochina states than Burma, which is viewed as a country of political and economic insignificance. Lt. General Ali Murtopo, in a speech on future development in Southeast Asia on January 23, 1976, made no mention of Burma. Statements by other Indonesian leaders in 1977 reflected a similar lack of attention to Burma.[40]

Nevertheless, exchange visits between Burmese and Indonesian officials have continued. Foreign Minister Adam Malik visited Burma in 1967 to sound out General Ne Win about Burmese participation in ASEAN. In June 1973 Ne Win paid an official visit to Jakarta and discussed problems of Southeast Asian security with President Suharto in the wake of the Vietnam cease-fire agreement. During his visit, Ne Win was also interested in Indonesia's oil operation and spent some time getting acquainted with Pertamina, Indonesia's state-owned oil company. The Burmese leader clearly wanted to see if Pertamina's joint venture technique might be emulated by the Myanma Oil Corporation, Burma's state-owned oil company. He had sent his minister of mines, Thaung Tin, to visit Pertamina a month earlier. In 1974 the "service contract" to a consortium of Martaban-Cities Services, Robina Oil Company, and Burma Sun Oil Company, was doubtless born out of the general's study of Indonesian petroleum development.[41] In June Ne Win visited Indonesia again in his new capacity as elected president of Burma.

On December 2, 1976, U Maung Maung Kha, then minister of mines and subsequently prime minister, toured Indonesia and discussed oil production sharing and the training of experts with Piet Haryono, president of Pertamina. On September 24, 1978, a delegation of the House of Representatives of the People's Republic of Indonesia, led by the Deputy Speaker Mohammed Isnaeni, paid a good will visit to Rangoon. At a reception, Isnaeni said, "The tradition of friendship between Burma and Indonesia is well known . . . and the Government and the people of Indonesia will never forget the help rendered by the Government and people of Burma in its struggles for national independence from 1945 to 1949."[42] Burmese Prime Minister Maung Maung Kha, Defense Minister Thura U Kyaw Htin, and Armed Forces Chief of Staff General Swa Maung visited Indonesia in 1987.

Indonesia topped all trading partners in Burma's export trade from 1959 through 1964, except in 1961 when the People's Republic of China purchased Burma's rice fourfold, buying more than Indonesia. The value of exports to Indonesia during this period totaled $210.8 million, or $35.1 million per year. It dropped to $8 million in 1965, reached $48.94 million in 1983, but dropped to less than one million since 1985. Burma's import trade from Indonesia has been insignificant, averaging yearly less than $1 million from 1958 to 1987.[43] Indonesia has reduced its rice imports to the lowest level in over a decade as a result of the "green revolution" in agriculture. And Burma, now self-sufficient in oil, is no longer an Indonesian oil customer, but continues to import small amounts of specialized petroleum products from Indonesia.

MALAYSIA

Burma established diplomatic relations with the Federation of Malaya in 1959. Such relations continued when the Federation of Malaya became the Federation of Malaysia in 1963 and Malaysia in 1965. The two countries share a similar British colonial rule experience and have both pursued the nonaligned policy since Tun Razak assumed Malaysian premiership in 1970. An amicable relationship between Burma and Malaysia has been developed, though, as with other ASEAN states, Burma has no close political ties with Malaysia.

In December 1965 Tun Razak, then Malaysian deputy prime minister, visited Rangoon to promote mutual interests with this neighboring nation after Indonesia had ended the confrontation with Malaysia. As commented on by the *Straits Times* in an editorial, the visit "seemed to show that despite vastly different political systems the opportunities for developing shared interests in commerce and sport and in the economic and cultural fields are rich and varied."[44]

In 1968 chairman of the Burmese Revolutionary Council General Ne Win interrupted his long-time self-imposed isolation and started a tour of some non-Communist countries in Southeast Asia, obviously aiming to develop close relations with these neighbors after the Sino-Burmese rift in mid-1967. He expressed that this visit was an opportunity to learn more about Malaysia and asserted:

The countries of this region ... have a firm determination to safeguard their national independence and to accelerate economic development and social progress with a view to promoting a better standard of living for their peoples. We in Burma believe that this determination of the Southeast Asian nations will prove to be an important factor in determining the future of the group.[45]

On his part, Malaysian Prime Minister Tunku Abdul Rahman said, "We discovered ourselves as close neighbors. We must try to live, think, and work together!" A joint communique issued on April 28 stated they were confident that friendly relations and cooperation could be developed between countries on the basis of mutual respect for each other's independence and sovereignty, the promotion of common good, and non-interference in each other's internal affairs; they agreed that as developing nations, their two countries could derive much benefit by mutual exchanges of experience and ideas in the field of economic development. They therefore decided to intensify efforts to this end, particularly in the technique of development implementation.[46]

Bilateral relations between Burma and Malaysia have largely focused on four matters: exchange of experience in economic development and insurgency suppression; technical and economic cooperation; collaboration in checking drug trafficking; and trade. Both countries are developing countries and have something to learn from each other. During his visit to

Kuala Lumpur in 1968, General Ne Win was briefed by Deputy Prime Minister Tun Rajak on Malaysia's rural and industrial developments, which had been very successful. While Rajak, then Malaysian prime minister, was a state guest of Burma in February 1972, Burma agreed to help Malaysian shipping by sharing the benefit of its experience with the Shipping Conference.

The two countries can also benefit from each other's experience in dealing with insurgency. Malaysia waged successful campaigns against the Malaysian Communist Party during the 1948–60 emergency period and has reduced the rebel party to an ineffective force. Burma, troubled by Communist and various ethnic insurrections almost since the time of independence, has adopted the Malaysian registration card system to control rebel activities with good results. During his visit to Rangoon in November 1982, Malaysian Deputy Prime Minister Musa Hitam offered training facilities at his country's staff college for Burma's police and army. Burma indicated that it would also like to participate in the Malaysian jungle warfare training program.[47] Burmese Defense Minister Thura U Kyaw Htin and Armed Forces Chief of Staff General Saw Maung visited Kuala Lumpur in 1987 to learn more about Malaysian experiences in insurgent suppression.

Under a technical assistance program, Burma's Deputy Minister for Agriculture and Forests Thein Han in December 1976 brought back from Kuala Lumpur palm oil and cocoa seed grains for cultivation. In May 1982 Malaysia supplied Burma with 180,000 palm oil seeds. Later Datuk Musa offered to sell Burma 780,000 rubber seeds to meet the needs of its rubber rehabilitation project. Malaysia has also provided training facilities for Burmese officials in agriculture-based industries, hotel management, and palm oil technology; and Burma sent its doctors and health specialists to Malaysia in 1976 to serve on a contract basis. In November 1982 Datuk Musa received Burma's pledge that a hundred more Burmese medical specialists would be sent to Malaysia.

Burma had agreed in November 1980 to look into a Malaysian proposal to set up joint venture projects on the production of cans as well as the processing of frozen food such as fish and prawns, though the implementation of the projects has not been reported. Malaysian Prime Minister Mahathir Mohammed visited Burma in late February 1988 to reciprocate his Burmese counterpart Maung Maung Kha's visit to Malaysia in the preceding July. Apart from seeking support for Malaysia's bid for a UN Security Council seat, Mahathir intended to maintain the closeness of the ties and explore further avenues for economic and other bilateral cooperation.

Drugs, mainly raw opium, have been smuggled from central Burma to the Andaman Sea or down the coast of Tenasserim division to Malaysia for processing. Malaysia has also been used as a corridor for the export of dangerous drugs to the world markets. The Kuala Lumpur government takes a serious view of the menace and has one of the toughest laws to deal with drug traffickers—a mandatory death sentence for anyone in possession of more than 100 grams of heroin. But the most effective way to deal with the problem is to get full cooperation with the source country. Burma was as concerned as Malaysia with drug trafficking. The Burmese ambassador to Malaysia, Hla Maw, told reporters on July 3, 1975, that his country had already banned the growing of poppies and trading in opium as one measure to check drug trafficking.[48] The drug trade was an important point of the talks held during Datuk Musa's official visit to Rangoon in November 1982. In his talks with Burmese Prime Minister Maung Maung Kha, Musa suggested that Malaysia and Burma police establish a system to exchange information on drug-related development to check the illicit trade.

Burma's trade with Malaysia, insignificant in the early years, has increased considerably since the late 1970s. Burma's exports to Malaysia recorded $0.6 million in 1976, reached $25.93 million in 1983, but dropped to $14.65 million in 1987. Burma's imports from Malaysia amounted to $0.16 million in 1975, rose to $13.68 million in 1977 and $21.39 million in 1981. But in 1987, the purchases were valued at only $5.84 million.[49]

Trade between Burma and Malaysia is recently confined mainly to primary commodities. Burma buys mainly palm oil, palm oil products, and asphalt petroleum from Malaysia, while it sells its smoked rubber, tin concentrates, and teak logs to that country. Rice is not a principal item of Burma's exports to Malaysia as it was before. In 1974 Malaysia bought 100,000 tons of rice from Burma, but it agreed to take only 5,000 tons in 1983 because of improved Malaysian agriculture. In 1980 as much as 92 percent of Malaysian needs were grown domestically. In addition, Malaysians prefer their own rice to Burmese rice, which is more starchy.[50]

SINGAPORE

Burma established diplomatic relations with the Republic of Singapore soon after the latter was separated from the Federation of Malaysia and became an independent state on August 9, 1965. In 1966 Burma elevated its diplomatic mission in Singapore to the embassy level.

Prior to Singapore's independence, Lee Kuan Yew had visited Burma twice as prime minister of the State of Singapore, the Federation of Malaysia. On April 21, 1962, he traveled there to acquaint the Burmese authorities with the facts of his country. Another was in May 1965 when he stopped over at Rangoon for two days on his way home from a socialist conference in Bombay, India. Tok Chin Chye, deputy prime minister of the Republic of Singapore, paid a good will visit to Burma in November 1965, becoming the first high-ranking official of the independent state to arrive in that country.

General Ne Win paid a four-day visit to Singapore in April 1968. It seemed most likely that the mid-1967 troubles in Rangoon caused by Chinese Red Guard diplomacy prompted Ne Win to shift his attitudes toward the outside world and start his tour of Singapore and other countries in the region. A Singapore newspaper in its editorial greeted the Burmese leader with the hope that his visit "holds the promise of strong ties between Burma and its Southeast Asian neighbors all of whom have a stake in protecting their national integrity."[51]

In his speech at a reception, Ne Win said,

The Union of Burma and the Republic of Singapore, being neighbors, have many common interests and it would be to our mutual benefit for our two countries to develop a close relationship and cooperation. . . . We look forward to the kind of Southeast Asia in which every nation would be free to live its own life in its own way. We believe that in such a community of nations, it will be possible for each nation also to live in peace and friendship with its neighbors.

During his stay in Singapore, the general discussed with Lee Kuan Yew matters of security in Southeast Asia after the British military withdrawal from the area. While showing anxiety over the future, he stressed his country's desire to keep out of military alliance.[52] Ne Win visited Singapore again in June 1974, this time in his new capacity as elected president of Burma.

Singapore Trade and Industry Minister Goh Chok Tong led an economic mission to Rangoon in early July 1980. Burma expressed interest in selling more agricultural, timber, and marine products to Singapore. The Burmese also indicated they would be looking to Singapore for equipment and machinery, semi-manufactured goods and some of their raw material requirements to hasten industrial and economic development. Singapore wanted to buy more fish from Burma. Singapore's suggestion that a joint venture in timber processing be set up in Burma did not, however, go over well in Rangoon.

Singapore Deputy Prime Minister Sinnathamby Rajaratnam visited Burma in early August 1980, shortly after Thai Prime Minister Prem Tinsulanond had made a similar journey. Both ASEAN leaders' visits were primarily related to the Cambodian issue. Before leaving for Rangoon, Rajaratnam was certain that as far as the status of Democratic Kampuchea was concerned, Burma would once again be "solidly with us." When Rajaratnam returned from Rangoon several days later, he was somewhat ambiguous about Burma's attitude toward the Kampuchea issue. He said that "Burma will do it in its own style and will let ASEAN take the initiative."[53] Later in October when the UN General Assembly voted for the Kampuchea representation, Burma stayed away from the meeting, taking a different stand from ASEAN.

Lee Kuan Yew visited Burma in January 1986, his first visit in his capacity as prime minister of independent Singapore. Lee's trip was chiefly aimed at renewing contacts with Burmese leaders and promoting trade and economic cooperation. At a banquet Lee said:

After their independence, Burma and Singapore have taken different routes toward their perceived futures. Burma opted for self-reliance, with selected external ties. Singapore had to plug into the world's network of trade and investment flows, which is determined by the free market economics of the industrial nations. We have had very different experiences. However, we still share some common approaches or attitudes to the problems of the contemporary world. So there can be advantage in sharing our experiences.[54]

The Singapore prime minister had talks with Ne Win and other Burmese leaders. In the matter of Singapore participation in Burma's economic development, Singapore hopes to become a transshipment center for Burma and also participate in its public housing, hotel management, tourism, telecommunications, and port development. Other interests are in banking, shipbuilding, and oil exploration.[55] In view of Burma's socialist policies and cautious relations with outsiders, however, the development of economic cooperation is expected to be rather slow, with Burma setting the pace.

Singapore First Deputy Prime Minister Goh Choh Tong visited Burma again in December 1986. He held talks on economic matters with Burmese Deputy Prime Minister and Minister for Planning and Finance Tun Tin. En route home from their visit to Japan in early May 1988, Tun Tin and his delegation stopped over in Singapore where Goh Choh Tong received them.

While Burma's relations with Singapore have been generally amicable, fishing by Singaporeans in Burmese waters caused a sore point. Twelve Singapore trawlers with a total of sixty-seven men and a Singapore fishing research vessel with thirty-one men were reportedly seized by Burmese authorities in the period of 1965–76. In 1978 twenty-three Singapore fishermen in three fishing boats were also arrested and imprisoned by the Burmese for intrusion. According to Ong Chin Guan, secretary of the Singapore Marine Products Workers, the three boats were seized outside Burmese territorial waters.

Singapore is Burma's largest market, taking in 14.8 percent of its total exports in 1984 and overtaking Japan as the major buyer. Singapore is also Burma's third largest supplier after Japan and West Germany, amounting to 9.4 percent of Burma's total imports. In the first nine months of 1985, Singapore exported to Burma goods worth $100 million and imported goods worth $120 million. The balance of trade has been in Burma's favor since 1977.[56]

THE PHILIPPINES

Relations between Burma and the Philippines have been friendly though not close. Far apart in distance, the two countries have paid scant attention to each other. When the Philippines received independence on July 4, 1946, Aung San was among the Asian leaders sending congratulations. In 1949 Burma was one of several nations that Philippine President Quirino consulted about forming an Asian security organization though later Burma showed no interest in joining an association of Asian states. In 1956 Burma established diplomatic relations with the Philippines.

Since the establishment of diplomatic relations mutual visits of Burmese and Philippine high-level officials have been infrequent. Foreign Secretary Salvador Lopez arrived in Rangoon in October 1963. After his talks with General Ne Win and other Burmese leaders, Lopez said he was deeply impressed by the strong national spirit evident in the meeting. A refreshing change, he noted, was the determination of General Ne Win to make Burma stand on its own feet without too much reliance on foreign aid.[57] General Ne Win, accompanied by his wife, paid a good will visit to the Philippines on November 18, 1970. At a banquet given in his honor President Marcos said that "the problems facing both countries transcend distance of geography and even political ideology," and that "it is but proper that both countries exchange information on them" because "problems demand urgent solutions." Ne Win in reply said:

The common problem of the Philippines and Burma is the promotion of the economic and social advancement of their peoples. We in Burma are of the view that this goal will be achieved mainly relying on the effort of our own people and on our own material resources. At the same time, we attach importance to carrying on mutually beneficial relations with other countries in the economic and social fields.[58]

President Marcos and his wife Imelda made a one-day official visit to Burma in May 1976.

While there have not been frequent visits between the officials of Burma and the Philippines, they sometimes make contact through their resident diplomatic personnel and their representatives to the conferences of international organizations located in the Philippines, including the Asian Development Bank.

Burma's imports from the Philippines have been negligible. Burma's exports to the Philippines also have been insignificant except in the period 1963–65. They reached $12.7 million in 1963, $9.1 million in 1964, and $31 million in 1965.[59] The Philippines imported a large amount of Burmese rice in those years due to a severe shortage of this commodity. It purchased 118,000 tons in 1963, 99,000 tons in 1964, and 300,000 tons in 1965.[60]

BURMA AND THE STATES OF INDOCHINA

VIETNAM

Burma's relations with Vietnam are correct and friendly. From the very beginning Burmese leaders, based on their own political aspirations and experiences, apparently sympathized with the struggle of Vietnamese nationalists. They even supported the Viet-Minh in 1946–48 in their national liberation struggle against the French, though they were aware that Ho Chi Minh and the Viet-Minh were Communist in character and received help from the Chinese Communists.[1] However, when the two rival regimes later appeared in Vietnam—the Democratic Republic of Vietnam in the North and the Republic of Vietnam in the South—Burma did not recognize either one, adhering to the position it had taken in 1949 that Burma would not recognize the governments of divided countries.[2] In explanation of Burma's attitudes toward the two Vietnams during his report to Parliament on September 27, 1957, Prime Minister U Nu said:

The Government of each half of Vietnam blames the other for this unhappy state of affairs, and we have done our best to keep out of the controversy. . . . Meanwhile, we have not recognized either of the two Governments in Vietnam as the de jure Government of Vietnam, nor do we propose under present circumstances to recognize both the Governments as de jure Governments since this would imply the existence of two states in Vietnam and help perpetuate the partition.[3]

Consequently, de facto recognition was given to Hanoi and Saigon through exchanges of visits between the leaders of Burma and two Vietnams. Commercial ties and consular relations with both North Vietnam and South Vietnam developed subsequently. After the conquest of South Vietnam by North Vietnam on April 30, 1975, Burma extended de jure recognition to the Democratic Republic of Vietnam and the Provisional Revolutionary Government of South Vietnam on May 28 and 30, 1975, respectively, with the establishment of diplomatic relations at embassy level. On July 2, 1976, the Vietnamese National Assembly named the unified country the Socialist Republic of Vietnam (SRU), and Burma has since maintained formal relations with the SRU.

Burmese Prime Minister U Nu visited Ho Chi Minh, president of the Democratic Republic of Vietnam, at Hanoi in late November 1954 en route to Peking. At a dinner given by Ho, Nu commented on the colonial barriers that had existed between the people of Vietnam and Burma and hoped for future cooperation between the two countries. In a subsequent communique, both leaders agreed on the Five Principles of Peaceful Coexistence previously approved by Nu and Chinese Prime Minister Chou En-lai. Phan Van Dong, then deputy prime minister and foreign minister of North Vietnam, visited Rangoon on his way to Bandung, and a communique issued on April 13, 1955 called for more efforts to promote the Five Principles.[4] Ho Chi Minh paid a good will visit to Rangoon from February 14 to 17, 1958. Ho and Nu exchanged views both on international affairs and on matters of mutual interest to the two countries. A joint statement issued by the two leaders on the occasion of the visit stated:

President Ho Chi Minh and Prime Minister U Nu expressed their deep concern over the continuance of international tension and the consequent danger of the outbreak of a global war in which the employment of all types of destructive armaments, peace could only be maintained on the basis of the five principles of peaceful coexistence. . . .

The President and the Prime Minister expressed their sympathy for all peoples who are struggling to liberate themselves from foreign domination. It is their earnest hope that colonialism wherever it still exists will soon be completely replaced by a new international relationship based on the equality of all nations, mutual benefit and common interest.

The President and the Prime Minister stressed once again their anxiety for the consolidation of peace in Indochina. In this connection they welcomed the implementation of the Geneva Agreement in Cambodia and the recent development toward the political settlement in Laos and emphasized the need for the fulfillment of the Geneva Agreement on Vietnam, with a view to reunifying Vietnam through free general elections as envisaged in the agreement.[5]

In November 1956, U Nu, no longer premier, paid a visit to Saigon at the invitation of President Ngo Dinh Diem. Nu indicated representatives should be exchanged between Burma and the Republic of Vietnam and stressed that the information officer of the Viet-Minh in Rangoon had no diplomatic status, perhaps to remove Saigon's possible misunderstanding about the matter. He called for closer contact through the exchange of students and visits of different groups and also invited the South Vietnamese president to visit his country.[6]

Burma had persistently expressed its desire that the divided Vietnam be reunified by political settlement. This position was manifested by the resolution of the Colombo Conference in April 1954, of which Burma was a participant, that it called for a prompt cease-fire and an irrevocable French commitment to independence for Indochina. In their joint communique at the Bogar Conference in December 1954, Burma and the other four Colombo powers applauded the decision of the Geneva Conference on Indochina for the cessation of hostilities. When Ngo Dinh Diem declared that his government was not bound to hold elections in 1956 to reunify the country by the 1954 Geneva Agreement because South Vietnam was not a signatory, U Nu publicly called on Diem to allow elections.[7]

In the summer of 1965, Burma was reported to have been willing to act as host country in a September 1964 meeting between North Vietnam and the United States. This meeting, proposed by President Ho Chi Minh following the armed conflict between U.S. and North Vietnam forces in the Gulf of Tonkin the previous August, was never held.[8] Ne Win was deeply concerned over the escalation of the Vietnam war after the United States dispatched its combat troops to South Vietnam in February 1965. On February 21, 1966, he sent a letter to Ho to express Burma's sympathy for the Vietnamese people, particularly the people of South Vietnam who had been subjected continuously to untold misery and suffering for the last twenty years, and its hope for the achievement of a truly independent democratic and sovereign Vietnam under the Geneva Agreement.[9]

In a joint communique with President Lyndon Johnson issued at the end of his visit to Washington on September 9, 1966, General Ne Win reiterated Burma's desire for a political settlement of the Vietnam question on the basis of respect for its sovereignty, independence, unity, and territorial integrity.[10]

Following the end of the war, Burma appeared to attach special importance to bilateral relations with the unified Vietnam. In addition to observing a good-neighbor policy, close links with Hanoi may prevent Vietnam's vast store of arms from showing up in the hands of Burmese Communist insurgents. Burma was also interested in better trade relations with the

Communist state. Early in 1976, Burmese Foreign Minister Hla Phone paid a good will visit to Hanoi. In response, Vietnamese Deputy Prime Minister and Foreign Minister Nguyen Day Trinh paid a three-day visit to Burma in April. In July, Hanoi's special envoy and Deputy Foreign Minister Phan Hien visited Rangoon on the last leg of his Southeast Asian trip, during which he had announced his country's willingness to establish friendly relations with non-Communist nations of the region. Phan Hien said that "relations between his country and Burma are developing in a very satisfactory way." He added that recent exchanges of visits between Burmese and Vietnamese foreign ministers were "positive contributions to such friendship and cooperation between the two countries."[11]

In the same month, Burma Trade Minister Hla Aye went to Hanoi and signed a Burma-Vietnam trade agreement, including the sale of Burmese rice to Vietnam on favorable terms. Following that agreement a ten-man Vietnamese trade delegation visited Burma in August to explore possibilities of further developing trade between the two countries. A new ambassador from Vietnam was appointed toward the end of June 1977, and President Ne Win received him with the comment: "Now that favorable conditions have been created for Burma and Vietnam, it is necessary to promote mutual cooperation and assistance in the interest of peace and prosperity in the region."[12]

Before long, nevertheless, Vietnam's aggression against Cambodia (Kampuchea) and confrontation with China have somewhat poisoned the warm relations between Rangoon and Hanoi. After Vietnam invaded Cambodia in early 1979 and installed a pro-Hanoi regime headed by Heng Samrin, Burma declared: "If the overthrow of a country's existing government by forces opposed to it with an outside power's intervention is condoned, elementary rules and accepted norms of international relationships would be greatly impaired."[13] The statement implied blame on Vietnam though without identifying it by name. In 1979 Burma voted for the UN General Assembly resolution calling for the withdrawal of all foreign forces from Cambodia and UN-supervised free elections in Cambodia. At the 1980 UN General Assembly, Burmese Foreign Minister Lay Maung denounced the Vietnamese invasion of Cambodia and the Soviet invasion of Afghanistan and expressed the hope that political settlement could restore the right of self-determination to the Cambodian and Afghan peoples. He said:

The firm and consistent policy of Burma is that it cannot condone the employment of armed intervention by an outside foreign power in the internal affairs of another independent sovereign state to bring about a change in government of the state. . . . Our wish is to see the restoration of unity to the peoples of Kampuchea and Afghanistan and the return of conditions in which they can work out their own destiny free from all external interference and pressures.[14]

The visits of Vietnamese senior officials to Burma in 1980 and 1982 were largely related to the Cambodian question. Prime Minister Pham Van Dong and Foreign Minister Nguyen Co Thach came to Rangoon on April 22, 1980. They met with then Secretary of the Council of State, San Yu, and acting Prime Minister Tun Tin, but not with President Ne Win, who had left the city the day before they arrived. Ne Win's absence was generally interpreted as a sign of coolness toward Vietnam. However, the visit of Dong and Thach might have influenced Burma's position shift on the representation of Democratic Kampuchea in the United Nations. Burma had supported the seating of the Democratic Kampuchea at the 1979 UN General Assembly but was absent from the meeting when the voting for the same issue was taken at the 1980 UN General Assembly. Foreign Minister Nguyen Co Thach made a four-day visit to Burma in late July 1982 as part of a four-nation Southeast Asian tour, apparently with a purpose to sell his new Cambodian plan. Earlier, while meeting in Ho Chi Minh City to discuss how to deal with the new Coalition Government of Democratic Kampuchea (CGDK) headed by Prince Sihanouk, the foreign ministers of three Indochina states—Vietnam, Cambodia, and Laos—had announced a partial withdrawal of Vietnamese troops from Cambodia and called for an international conference to bring peace to all Southeast Asian countries. At a banquet Nguyen Co Thach said, "The problems of the region could not be solved by confrontation. The realities of the past 35 years when Vietnam won wars against the French and the Americans proved that the Indochinese people could not be subjugated." The Burmese reportedly said that Burma insisted on a total Vietnamese troop withdrawal from Cambodia and self-determination for the Khmer people.[15]

There have been no high-level visits between Burma and Vietnam since Nguyen Co Thach's visit in 1982. The intense hostility between China and Vietnam after their hot war in the spring of 1979 has deepened the crisis in the region but has inadvertently benefitted Burma. The Burmese Communist Party was among the only three parties from non-Communist Asian countries publicly invited to attend the fourth Congress of the Vietnam Workers Party (it was renamed Communist Party of Vietnam during the meeting of the Congress) in December 1976. Rangoon has worried about the BCP link-up with Vietnam via Vietnamese-controlled Laos, but the rivalry between Peking and Hanoi reduces such a possibility, as the BCP is still supported by and loyal to Peking. The situation also has strengthened Burma's position in dealing with the two neighboring Communist states, who compete with each other for the support and friendship of the neutral nation.

Burma's exports to Vietnam registered $23.08 million in 1976, the first year after the latter's reunification. But they dropped sharply to $3.55 million in the following year, and no improvement has been shown since. From 1981 through 1987 Vietnamese purchases of Burmese products were worth a total amount of $14.77 million, or an annual average of $2.11 million. Burma's imports from Vietnam have never been appreciable.[16]

CAMBODIA (KAMPUCHEA AFTER 1975)

Burma knew little about Cambodia before the latter was granted independence by the French following the Geneva Conference in July 1954. Burma accorded de jure recognition to the newly sovereign state on August 16, 1954. On January 10, 1955 Burma and Cambodia agreed to establish diplomatic relations, which were maintained with the Lon Nol government after the deposition of Norodom Sihanouk in March 1970. Diplomatic recognition was later transferred to Democratic Kampuchea when Lon Nol's Khmer Republic was overthrown in April 1975.

No important bilateral problems have come up between Burma and Cambodia; therefore, official visits between the two countries have been infrequent. In August 1954, immediately after establishing formal links between the two countries, Burma's home minister visited Cambodia. During the following November Norodom Sihanouk, then king of Cambodia, paid a state visit to Burma. On the occasion of the king's visit, Burmese President Ba U called Cambodia "one of the establishing factors in southeast Asia" and pointed out that the Cambodian people were linked to Burma by common ethnic origin, culture, and religion. He pledged that Burma "shall watch and follow the progress of Cambodia with sympathy, interest and best wishes."[17] After returning home from Burma, where he probably had discussed neutralism with U Nu, King Sihanouk indicated that Cambodia was prepared to adopt a neutral policy. Speaking before a welcoming crowd in Phnom Penh, he said: "In order to safeguard themselves, the large and small nations of Southeast Asia should deploy all of their goodwill in order to create a center of pacific resistance to all pacts or alliances susceptible to providing world conflicts that is to say, a large group of nations should observe neutrality strictly."[18]

On December 16, U Nu arrived at Phnom Penh to meet with his Cambodian counterpart M. Penn Noreth. Prince Norodom Sihanouk, then prime minister of Cambodia, arrived in Rangoon on August 13, 1958, for a two-day visit en route to China. Again he came to Burma on October 7, 1964, and October 16, 1965, in his capacity as Cambodian head of state on his way home after visiting Peking. General Ne Win, then Burmese chief of staff of the defense forces, visited Cambodia in December 1961.

In 1962, Sihanouk proposed an international conference to guarantee Cambodia's neutrality and territorial integrity. In response, General Ne Win reaffirmed Burma's policy of nonalignment and suggested that Cambodia seek the resolution of its difficulties through direct discussion and negotiations. However, he did not close the door on a conference if "all the parties concerned" wished to see one convened. During 1966 and 1967, thanks to the prince's persistence, a growing number of foreign countries declared their respect for Cambodia's territorial integrity. At that point Burma expressed its support of the Cambodian cause.[19]

The Lon Nol government, taking control of Cambodia in 1970, was ousted by Khmer Rouge forces on April 17, 1975. The next day Burma announced that it was "heartened" to learn of the "cessation of bloodshed." Cambodian Deputy Prime Minister Ieng Sary visited Burma from March 10 to 14, 1977, on his tour of Southeast Asia which was aimed at promoting understanding and establishing good relations with the non-Communist countries in the region. Burmese Foreign Minister Hla Phone visited Cambodia in August 1977 and met with the head of state, Khieu Samphan.

President Ne Win arrived in Cambodia on November 26, 1977 and became the first foreign chief of state to visit the Khmer Rouge country. According to Radio Phnom Penh, his visit aimed to strengthen Burma's relations with Cambodia. The radio broadcast stressed the friendly ties between the two countries and their mutual foreign policy of neutrality and nonalignment. However, this visit, which followed the journeys of Ne Win and Cambodian Prime Minister Pol Pot to Peking, might have been stimulated by the P.R.C. to strengthen Cambodia's diplomatic position with Vietnam over border conflicts. It was also viewed as a move to enlist Cambodian support in Ne Win's diplomatic campaign to curb pro-Peking Burmese Communist insurgents, as the Khmer Rouge had close ties with China. During the visit the Burmese president and the Cambodian president emphasized in their speeches nonalignment, national self-reliance, and friendship.[20]

The Democratic Kampuchean government was toppled by the Kampuchean National United Front for National Salvation (KNUFNS) led by Heng Samrin on January 7, 1979, with the support of Vietnamese forces. The Burmese government has denied recognition to the Heng Samrin regime because it came to power through the assistance of an outside nation. Instead, Rangoon maintained nominal diplomatic relations with the Democratic Kampuchean government. In order to seek legitimacy the Heng Samrin regime held general elections in the spring of 1981. Not surprisingly, President Heng Samrin and his colleagues were retained by an overwhelming majority in the elections. But the exercise had little effect on the regime's foreign relations. Burma, like many other countries, ignored this controlled attempt at democracy. On June 22, 1982, thanks to ASEAN's efforts, the Democratic Kampuchean government was reorganized to include Prince Norodom Sihanouk and Son San anti-Vietnamese groups, forming the Coalition Government of Democratic Kampuchea (CGDK) headed by Sihanouk. The reorganized Democratic Kampuchean government aimed to strengthen anti-Vietnamese resistance and improve its international standing. Burma has not expressed its stance toward the CGDK which has been recognized by the P.R.C., North Korea, Malaysia, and some other countries.

LAOS

Burma has maintained good neighborly relations with Laos. When France ended its colonial rule in Laos after the conclusion of the Geneva Conference on Indochina in July 1954, Burma was quick to recognize the kingdom of Laos. In late August 1954, Lao Prime Minister Prince Souvanna Phouma visited Rangoon. On July 12, 1955, the first Lao minister to Burma presented his credentials to the president of the Union, following the establishment of formal diplomatic relations between the two countries. Early in the year Rangoon and Vientiane agreed to resist the KMT soldiers (Chinese irregular forces) seeking refuge in Laos from Burma. Concerned over this neighbor's internal peace, Burma successfully brought Lao Prime Minister Sasorith and Pathet Lao rebel leader Prince Souphanouvong together for talks in Rangoon on October 9, 1955, which resulted in a joint declaration of the two parties to avoid further clashes. In 1961 Rangoon also served as a meeting place for U.S. Ambassador-at-Large Averell Harriman and Lao Prince Souvanna Phouma to discuss Laotian affairs. Burma played a significant role in the Geneva Conference on Laos in 1961–62 by calling for Laos's independence and neutrality. Early in the sessions, Foreign Minister Sao Hkum Hkio made a definite statement on Burmese policy for Laos. He opposed partition for Laos because "it has proved no solution whenever applied." He asserted that any solution for Laos "must be accepted by the Laotian people exercising, through a fully representative government, their full sovereignty."[21]

In 1962 Prince Souvanna Phouma of Laos, then prime minister of the coalition government, stopped at Rangoon on his way home from Paris and had talks with Chairman General Ne Win. The king of Laos, Sri Savang Vatthana, visited Burma in March 1963. The king exchanged opinions with General Ne Win on bilateral relations and the international situation. In a joint communique issued at the end of the king's visit, the two sides agreed to cooperate in political, cultural, and economic fields and reaffirmed their faith in the right of all nations freely to decide internal affairs without outside interference. The two sides also expressed concern over the preservation of world peace and prevention of war through general and complete disarmament.[22]

The amicable relations between Burma and Laos have continued since the Communists took control of Laos in the fall of 1975. The Burmese foreign minister visited Laos in August 1976. In January 1977 Lao President Prince Souphanouvong paid a state visit to Burma. At the state banquet both the host and the guest referred to the closeness of neighborly ties between the two countries. Ne Win said, "We not only place high value on good-neighborliness and promotion of bilateral relations based upon mutual trust and respect, but also wish to make every effort to this end." In reply the Lao president stated, "The rivers and lands of our two countries are physically linked by a common border. As for our two peoples, they have had good neighborly relations since ancient times."[23] In a joint communique both countries agreed: "It would be conducive to the general cause of peace if each country undertook not to interfere in the other's internal affairs, and not to allow its territory to be used by armed forces, indigenous or foreign, as a base for aggression against its neighbors."[24] The communique clearly reflected the two countries' concern over external aggression via each other's territory and internal insurrections through foreign support, as both Burma and Laos had insurgent problems.

President Ne Win paid his first state visit to Laos from October 22 to 24, 1979. The visit was apparently motivated by Laos's increasingly being drawn into the Vietnamese-Soviet orbit since the Vietnamese invasion of Cambodia and Sino-Vietnamese open rivalry in early 1979. The new trends in the immediate neighbor posted a potential threat to Burma's security internally and externally. At the banquet given in his honor by Lao President Prince Souphanouvong, Ne Win said that nations should refrain from activities that might prove to be detrimental to others. "On our parts also," he went on, "we wish to have relations of peace and amity with all nations especially with our neighbors; that wish has continuously guided our endeavors."[25] In the subsequent joint communique, the two countries agreed to make further efforts for a "true and durable peace along their common border" for fostering the common interests of both countries and for promoting peace and stability in the region.[26]

Laos was designated as the representative of the Indochinese bloc during the Indochinese foreign ministers' meeting in Ho Chi Minh City in January 1981. Lao Foreign Minister Phoune Sipraseuth visited Burma in June to seek Rangoon's support for the bloc's position on Cambodia by solving the Cambodian problem through negotiations between the countries of the region. But Burma was still committed to the UN resolution by an international conference. Sipraseuth's talks with the Burmese leaders also touched on the activity of rebels in the northern part of both countries. Laos tried to stress to Burma that both faced a common threat—one from the Peking-supported BCP and the other from Lao ethnic rebels. Deputy Foreign Minister of Laos Souban Salitthilat arrived in Rangoon on March 6, 1988, and discussed bilateral relations with his Burmese counterpart Saw Hlaing.

8

BURMA AND THE
INDIAN SUBCONTINENT

INDIA

Burma's relations with India, its immediate western neighbor, were extremely pleasant and close prior to the military coup in 1962 in spite of Burmese resentment of India's political and economic role in Burma's colonial days. This was especially mentioned by U Nu in his policy address in September 1955:

The governments of India and of Burma have affectionate regard for each other. . . . In Burma's fight for independence, the Burmese leaders and people drew inspiration from Indian leaders and people. . . . Burma has asked for substantial help from India on three different occasions. . . . The reason why we can always approach India for help in our time of need is because there is firm Indo-Burmese friendship.[1]

This excellent relationship between Burma and India may be attributed to political and economic cooperation between the two countries, similar outlook in foreign policy, and the intimate friendship between Burmese Prime Minister U Nu and Indian Prime Minister Jawaharlal Nehru. The Provisional Government of Burma established full diplomatic relations with India on April 15, 1947, immediately after the latter became a dominion. U Nu arrived in New Delhi on December 2, 1947, about one month before Burma's independence, to lay the foundation with the Indian leaders for future talks. On April 12, 1949, when the Burmese government was on the verge of collapse because of the rebellions of Communist parties and ethnic minorities, U Nu went to India to ask Nehru for arms and for help in obtaining funds from the Commonwealth. Indian arms did help to keep the U Nu government in power. In the words of Kyaw Win, who edited the book *U Nu Saturday's Son*, "without the prompt support in arms and ammunition from India, Burma might have suffered the worst fate imaginable. As it turned out, from the middle of 1949, when Mr. Nehru's rifles began arriving, the enemy's threat was first contained, then eliminated."[2] In March 1950, Indian mediation resulted in five Commonwealth countries lending Burma 6 million pounds, of which India contributed one sixth.

Indian Prime Minister Nehru visited Rangoon on June 20, 1950. In a press conference Nehru advised Indians in Burma to act as envoys and work for the land where they live. Burma and India signed a Treaty of Peace and Friendship on July 7, 1951, under which "the two states recognize and respect the independence and right of each other," and "There shall be everlasting peace and unalterable friendship between two states." The two states also agreed in the pact that their representatives would meet occasionally to discuss common matters and to consider ways of mutual cooperation.[3] The treaty came into force on January 31, 1952, by the exchange of instruments of ratification at Rangoon. A Burmese daily, *The Nation*, greeted it as "further strengthening the traditional good will and understanding existing between the two countries."[4]

In 1954, facing economic difficulties, Burma made a deal with India to purchase 900,000 tons of rice from Burma on generous terms. Even more generous to Burma were the terms of settlement in April of the debt Burma owed India arising out of separation with India in 1937. The settlement was linked with an agreement whereby India would purchase 900,000 tons of Burmese rice at £48 a ton, Burma agreed to refund for every ton purchased £13 in reduction of the debt, a total of 44.55 million. The amount of debt remaining would be considered as financial aid to Burma under the Colombo Plan.[5]

On July 14, 1956, Burma and India signed an agreement supplying Burma with Indian textiles. Under the agreement, payment for the textiles would be made in new cotton purchased by Burma from the United States. The Indian textiles to be supplied to Burma would be worth $3,850,000.[6]

The AFPFL leaders, particularly U Nu, relied upon Nehru for inspiration in formulating foreign policy. Moreover, at that time Burma and India faced the same set of international problems in the Cold War and the emergence of the Communist China as a potential force on the other side of a long, and in parts undemarcated, frontier. Hence the two countries took the similar stand of neutrality and nonalignment in foreign policy which had brought them into close cooperation in world affairs. Burma had been consulting India closely on the matter of Kuomintang troops (Chinese irregular forces) inside Burmese territory since early 1951. The CIF problem was also an important topic of discussions between U Nu and Nehru during their tour of the border regions in late March 1953.[7] India vigorously supported the Burmese complaint against the aggression of Kuomintang forces. India along with nine other states jointly submitted a draft resolution that called on the CIF forces once more to submit to disarmament and internment, and urged all states to do what they could to prevent these forces from remaining in Burmese territory. The draft resolution after a slight amendment was adopted by the General Assembly almost unanimously.[8]

U Nu and Nehru attended the first Colombo Conference in April 1954 with the prime ministers of Ceylon, Indonesia, and Pakistan, where the problem of the Indo-Pakistan conflict over Kashmir flared up, and it was only through U Nu's efforts that things were smoothed out.[9] The two prime ministers met again before going to Bogar for the second Colombo Conference in December 1954 to discuss the groundwork for Asian-African Conference at Bandung. At Bogar, U Nu insisted that the P.R.C. be invited to participate in the Bandung Conference. Nu seemed to have treated this as a condition for Burma's participation and his proposal, opposed by Pakistan, Ceylon, and Indonesia, but supported by Nehru, was finally adopted. But the initiative of Burma and India to invite Israel failed, as it would keep the Arab countries away from the conference.[10]

U Nu visited New Delhi on March 25, 1955, to discuss with Nehru the agenda of the forthcoming Bandung Conference and the international situation, especially the U.S.-China conflict. At the Bandung Conference U Nu and Nehru worked closed and preached the Five Principles of Peaceful Coexistence. Subsequently these principles became part of the conference's declaration.[11] U Nu visited India on October 17, 1955 on his way to Afghanistan and the Soviet Union. The object of this visit was doubtless to consult with Nehru about this trip to Moscow where Nehru had visited earlier in June. Nehru stopped in Rangoon for a day on his way home from Japan at a personal invitation from U Nu who had resumed the Burmese premiership in March 1957. U Nu went to India to meet Nehru on December 6, 1957.

U Nu, in his capacity as Burma's prime minister-elect, arrived in Calcutta on March 1, 1960 to meet Nehru and Soviet Premier Khrushchev. The Burmese premier stopped at New Delhi and accompanied Nehru to the nonaligned heads of state conference held at Belgrade on September 1–6, 1961. At the conference U Nu accepted most of Nehru's moderate views over the more extreme views of Tito and Nasser. U Nu traveled to India on January 11, 1962, presumably to mediate the Sino-Indian border dispute. After his return to Rangoon, U Nu expressed his hope that the border dispute between India and China would soon be resolved and good relations restored between the two governments.[12]

Such close consultations between Burma and India seemed likely to have influenced Rangoon's foreign policy. U Nu once stated that Burma was anxious to recognize Communist China but postponed doing so at Nehru's request. According to Nehru, however, U Nu "was not a follower in international meetings in which I participated with him. He had definite ideas of his own and pursued them."[13] In fact, Burma had taken different stands from India's on some international issues. For example, Burma condemned colonialism and communism with vehemence at the First Colombo Conference in April 1954, while India was more concerned with colonialism as a threat to international peace and was hesitant to condemn communism.

Different policies on some issues did not affect the friendship between Burma and India. Nu has attributed the happy Indo-Burmese ties to Nehru's contribution:

The Union of Burma has been privileged to work together with India and to maintain a close contact with her not only in matters of common interest to the two countries, but also in the matter of much wider significance. In this connection I would like to pay my humble tribute to the Prime Minister Jawaharlal Nehru, who has made the greatest contribution to this happy relationship between the two countries.[14]

U Nu and Nehru, both democratic socialists and anticolonial-minded, held each other in high regard. Speaking on the second anniversary of Indian independence U Nu said, "I cannot adequately describe the great personal qualities of Pandit Nehru. He had deservedly earned the respect and admiration of the whole world."[15] On learning that Nu resigned from his prime ministership for the AFPFL reorganization on June 5, 1956, Nehru sent him a letter in which he said "whether you are Prime Minister or not, you will be there as a tower of strength not only to your country, but to others also."[16] Throughout Nu's political career Jawaharlal Nehru was the foreign leader he most frequently met. Whenever he wanted to visit India, U Nu would merely write a letter telling Nehru the date of his arrival and the mode of travel without following the usual diplomatic practice of gaining prior approval. With the exception of his first visit, when he stayed in the Government House, U Nu stayed with Nehru whenever he went to India.[17] On a number of occasions U Nu acted beyond his official relationship with Nehru, as when his government requested Nehru's government to delay its recognition of the P.R.C. so that Burma might be first.[18] U Nu visited New Delhi in October 1951 to consult with Nehru about signing a peace treaty with Japan. After the talks he said at a press conference that Burma had very close relations with India in their foreign policy and that Burma, like India, would have separate agreements with Japan.[19] Nu also asked Nehru for aid in soothing Sino-Burmese relations in 1956 at the time of the Chinese border incursions into Burma. It was through Nehru's efforts that Chinese Prime Minister Chou En-lai invited Nu to visit him in 1956 for a discussion of the frontier troubles between the two countries.

In spite of the affection between Burma and India during the early years of independence, there were still unpleasant moments. Under the Land Nationalization Act of 1948 Indian landlords, whose property in Burma had been nationalized, complained to the Indian government that the Burmese measures were unfair. In June 1950 a delegation from New Delhi conducted talks with the Burmese government; a second Indian delegation came to Burma in December 1953. As a result of these discussions, legislation was introduced into the Union Parliament making compensation for expropriation more equitable. In 1958 interested Indian groups exerted pressure on the Indian government to obtain Burma compensation for Indian landlords quickly. In reply Nehru said that "the only step that we can take is to bring the matter courteously and politely to the notice of the Burmese government." Indian immigrants were also seriously affected by Burma's amendments to the Burma Immigration and Foreigners Registration Act of 1957. On August 25, 1957, responding to a complaint that the Burmese government imposed severe restrictions on stay permits and citizenship rights and was charging exorbitant fees, Nehru said in the Indian Parliament that "it is very difficult for us in an internal matter to protest when there is no discrimination, when it applied to all aliens and foreigners."[20]

After Burma concluded the border pact with China the Indian government was deeply concerned over the map attached by the Sino-Burmese treaty, which showed the frontier separating Burma and China ending where China claimed the Sino-Indian border started. India was also irritated at U Nu's holding up the Sino-Burmese frontier agreement as a model for settling the dispute between the Indians and the Chinese. Nu did make a special trip to New Delhi on November 11, 1960 to explain the situation, but he was unsuccessful in placating Nehru. The Indian prime minister emphasized that his government could not recognize "erroneous depictions of trijunction in the map attached to the Sino-Burmese treaty because these had adverse implications for the territorial integrity of India."[21] In December 1960 the Indian government protested officially to both Burma and China. Rangoon replied that the Burmese did not accept the map as binding and that once India and China settled their dispute, a final adjustment of this part of the boundary line would be made. Later Nehru expressed satisfaction with the official stand of the Burmese government "with whom [the Burmese] we are very friendly, and they do not want to do anything which might injure our interest." He further stated that the Sino-Burmese border agreement was helpful to India, as that agreement respected the MacMahon Line and Himalayan watershed that India favored.[22]

In early 1961 rebel Nagas took refuge in Burma, from which they conducted hostile operations against the Indian government. New Delhi brought the matter to the attention of Rangoon, which then determined to take strong action against the hostile Nagas. The personal friendship of U Nu and Jawaharlal Nehru allowed no disputes to disturb the good relationship between Burma and India.

After the U Nu government was toppled by the military coup on March 2, 1961, India was the first country to recognize Ne Win's government. Since that time relations between Burma and India, however, have not been as warm as previously. This development was influenced by changes in the leadership of both countries, Burma's new nationalization policy, which affected Indian residents' interests, and India's deviation from noninterference and the nonalignment policy. Ne Win and later other Burmese leaders, unlike U Nu, lacked the personal bond with Jawaharlal Nehru and his successors. Consequently, Burma's relations with India have been conducted on a formal footing. On the Sino-Indian border dispute, the military government adopted a strictly neutral attitude and kept silent even after the open hostilities broke out in September 1962. General Ne Win was subsequently invited by the prime minister of Ceylon to attend the Colombo Conference of the six nonaligned nations, which included Cambodia, Ghana, Indonesia, and the United Arab Republic besides Ceylon and Burma, from December 10 to 12, 1962 to discuss the Sino-Indian border question. On arrival at Colombo, Ne Win said that the six countries should together bring China and India back to the conference table without making any attempt to pass judgment in any way on the two parties to the dispute. The conference largely accepted Ne Win's opinions but Ne Win did not participate in the subsequent trafficking between India and China that was carried on by other delegations.[23]

The Burmese Revolutionary government promulgated the Enterprise Nationalization Law in October 1963. Although not directed against any specific foreign group, the law hit the Indian community the hardest, because Indians directly or indirectly controlled 60 percent of the country's commerce at the time. The law put them out of business; even Indians of the middle and poor classes were dislodged from their jobs. Thus relations with India became rather strained. Indian Foreign Secretary Y. D. Gundevia and Minister for External Affairs Sardar Swaran Singh visited Burma in May and September 1964, respectively, to discuss this problem with Burmese officials. An agreement was reached by which Burma made all possible arrangements for repatriation of Indian nationals. After returning to New Delhi, Singh said in the Indian Parliament that he had no doubt that the Burmese government would implement whatever assurances it had given or might give. But the arrangements so far agreed on did not provide much relief to the Indian repatriates. The important question concerning the assets of Indians wanting to return to India still remained to be settled.[24]

Ne Win paid a good will visit to India on February 5, 1965, during which he assured the Indian prime minister, Lal Bahadur Shastri, that the nationalization law was nondiscriminatory, and that resident foreigners who could play a useful role in the new social order in Burma would be able to live and work in Burma as citizens should they desire to do so. The joint communique issued by the two leaders reaffirmed Ne Win's assurance and noted Shastri's satisfaction with it. They also agreed that the problems should continue to be discussed between the two governments with a view to reaching early solution.[25]

Indian Prime Minister Lal Bahadur Shastri arrived in Rangoon on December 20, 1965 for a three-day visit, during which he discussed the issue of Indian residents in Burma with General Ne Win. In a joint communique Shastri and Ne Win reiterated their views that with good will and mutual understanding on both sides solutions would be achieved without much difficulty.[26]

Indian Minister for External Affairs M. C. Chagla visited Rangoon on January 20–22, 1967 in the course of his Southeast Asian tour. While in Rangoon he had also taken up the repatriation question. The Indians leaving Burma were given nothing for their property, forbidden to take even personal articles, and limited to carrying out small sums of currency. During Chagla's visit, Burma agreed to compensate Indians for their nationalized properties in Burma. The problem of compensation was finally settled in December 1973 when Burma announced a compensation schedule. By mid-1968 nearly 158,000 Indians had left Burma.[27]

Indian Prime Minister Indira Gandhi paid a state visit to Burma on March 27–30, 1969. Speaking at a reception accorded to her in Rangoon on March 28 by the All-Burma Indian Congress, Mrs. Gandhi asked the Indian community to face the realities of the situation courageously and find a solution to their problems. She said she realized the difficulties of Indians in Burma, but they had to consider their problems against the realities of the day. They themselves had to answer the question how they could fit into this reality. She told them that they owed their loyalty to the country in which they lived.[28] The visiting prime minister had discussions with Ne Win about their problems. The general promised her that he would sympathetically look into the problem of remaining Indians who, being of poorer classes and noncitizens, were unable to take employment in state-owned organizations. In May the government announced 60,000 foreigners would be granted citizenship. However, Indians were not over-enthusiastic about the announcement because of continuing unfavorable local conditions.[29]

Burma was unhappy at the Indian invasion of Pakistan in 1965, which violated the Five Principles of Peaceful Coexistence. A London periodical commented in an editorial: "India finds herself denuded of friends on this issue. Burma seems to have deserted her; Burma would be glad to see her humbled. . . ."[30] One of the purposes of Indian premier Shastri's visit to Rangoon in December 1965 seemed to seek to win Burma's understanding on the Indo-Pakistan conflicts. At a banquet given in his honor by General Ne Win, Shastri said he was going to Tashkent "with a sincere desire to promote friendly relations with Pakistan in spite of our recent bitter experience. Recently we were involved in conflicts with some of our neighbors which were not of our seeking. Our objective, however, continues to be to strive to do our utmost for peace." In the joint communique Shastri and Ne Win "reaffirmed the devotion of their two countries to the cause of peace and international understanding. They reiterated their faith in the policies and principles of nonalignment and peaceful coexistence," and "their belief in the peaceful settlement of all problems without resort to the use of threat of force." Earlier, Ne Win, who apparently had Indo-Pakistan conflicts in mind, said that India, with her vast human and material resources, had a major role to play in the liberation of colonial countries in Africa and Asia and in the maintenance of peace and security in the world.[31]

The Indians also annoyed Burma by supporting a separatist armed struggle in East Pakistan in 1971. Burma publicly denounced the solution of a country's internal problems by means of the direct help and intervention of a foreign power, a clear criticism of India without identifying it by name. Indian Foreign Minister Sardar Swaran Singh visited Rangoon in the second week of April 1973, the first cabinet-level minister to come to Rangoon since Mrs. Gandhi's 1969 visit. Singh, while in Rangoon, tried to explain the Bangladesh situation to the Burmese leaders. On his return to New Delhi on April 9, Singh told newsmen the Burmese government supported the view that problems of the Indian subcontinent should be resolved by mutual discussions and agreements among the countries concerned. The situation in the subcontinent was well understood in Burma and its attitude had been "one of understanding right from the time when the Bangladesh problem started developing in March 1971."[32]

India has been drawn to the orbit of the Soviet bloc since the Sino-Indian border war in 1962, when the Soviet Union supported India. This led to Rangoon distancing itself from New Delhi for fear of offending Peking. When Indian Minister for External Affairs Atal Bihari Vajpayee visited Burma on August 9, 1977, he stressed India's continued commitment to the nonaligned policy in an effort to regain Burma's friendship and confidence. A statement issued at the end of the visit said Vajpayee had told President Ne Win of India's desire to "strengthen the ties of friendship and cooperation with all nonaligned and other developing countries for a new international order." He pointed out, "Both Burma and India are among the founder-members of the nonalignment movement and believe in its continuing validity for preserving and promoting world peace and international cooperation and for bridging the ever-widening gulf between rich and poor countries." Before leaving for home Vajpayee reiterated that the fundamental Indian foreign policy of cultivating friendship with all countries remained unchanged. "Friendship with the Soviet Union or any other country does not prevent India from maintaining friendly relations with any third countries."[33]

India's "left-shift" policy, nevertheless, became abundantly clear when it sided with the Russia-Vietnam-Cuban group to vote against seating of Democratic Kampuchea in the UN General Assembly and the nonaligned summit conference in 1979. India also extended formal recognition to the Hanoi-installed Heng Samrin regime in Cambodia in 1980. The close of

India's Consulate in Mandalay in 1980 under Rangoon's pressure signaled Burmese disquiet with India's new course. And many saw the return of U Nu from exile in India in 1980 and his public statement supporting Burma's withdrawal from the nonaligned movement as criticism of the Indians.[34]

Burmese Foreign Minister Chit Hlaing arrived in New Delhi on May 9, 1984 on the second leg of his three-nation good will tour, including Nepal, India, and Bangladesh. He had talks with his Indian counterpart, P. V. Narasimha Rao, who invited Burma to join an Indian-sponsored South Asian regional cooperation organization. This organization, comprised of India, Pakistan, Bangladesh, Sri Lanka, Nepal, Bhutan, and Maldives, was scheduled to hold a summit in late 1985 in Dhaka. Hlaing told Rao that Burma had no intention of joining it. Hlaing also met Indian Defense Minister Ramaswamy Venkataraman, who offered Indian assistance to set up a defense industry and provide training facilities for Burmese defense forces, but Burma has not responded to the offer. U Ne Win visited India in December 1984 to meet new Prime Minister Rajiv Gandhi and to promote economic and trade relations. Earlier in the year India had indicated a keen interest in increasing trade with Burma and had also offered to extend credit to Burma.

Indian Minister for External Affairs Khurshid Alam Khan paid a three-day visit to Rangoon in early July 1985 in an attempt to improve ties with Burma. While in Rangoon Khan had talks with Burmese Foreign Minister Chit Hlaing on matters relating to the Indian Ocean as a zone of peace, the Middle East, the arms race, and nuclear nonproliferation. Khan said,

India under the dynamic leadership of our young prime minister was striving not only to attain prosperity for India but also to countries to peace, stability and economic development in the region and the world. We believe that closer cooperation and greater understanding with our immediate neighbors, among whom Burma occupies a prominent place, are essential. . . . India stands ready to share its development experience with Burma and to expand contacts.[35]

India's Prime Minister Rajiv Ghandi paid a two-day visit to Burma in mid-December 1987. Gandhi met Chairman Ne Win and President San Yu to whom he presented a collection of writings by the Burmese hero General Maha Handoola, which had been taken by the British and kept at the Indian museums. Gandhi also had talks with his Burmese counterpart Maung Maung Kha on matters of mutual interest.

Burma shares 875 miles of common border with India. The border demarcations set up by the British had been in complete decay. The question was first taken up by Indian Foreign Minister M. C. Chagla when he visited Rangoon in January 1967. Following subsequent discussions between Indian and Burmese officials, a Boundary Agreement between the two countries was signed on March 10, 1967 and ratified on May 30. The agreement established a Joint Boundary Commission demarking the boundary between the two countries by preparing maps and drafting of a boundary treaty.[36] By early 1976 most of the border between the two countries had been demarcated under the agreement.

On the other hand, the agreement on the delimitation of the two countries' maritime border in the Andaman Sea, the Coco Channel, and the Bay of Bengal was signed by India and Burma during the visit of Indian Minister for External Affairs Shri Narayan Datt Tiwari to Rangoon on December 23–25, 1986. Burmese Foreign Minister Ye Goung exchanged instruments of ratification for the agreement during his visit to New Delhi in mid-September 1987.

India has maintained a modest aid program in Burma during the military rule and the constitutional government since 1974. From 1968 through 1985 India extended $5.319 million to Burma in technical assistance under the Colombo Plan.[37]

In the early years of independence, India was Burma's leading customer and supplier; later Burma-India trade declined. India's purchases from Burma rose to $14 million in 1971 but dropped to $0.13 million in 1975. This situation did not improve until 1981 with $10.16 million in that year, and $12.88 million in 1987. India's exports to Burma had also decreased from $9.2 million in 1972 to $1.9 million in 1973. Between 1981 and 1987, India's sales to Burma totaled $29.15 million, or an average of $4.15 million yearly.[38]

The decline of trade has been a matter of common concern to the two countries. In 1984 an Indian economic delegation headed by Commerce Ministry Secretary Abid Hussain arrived in Rangoon. The delegation held talks with Burmese Trade Minister Khin Maung Gyi, Industry I Minister Tint Swe, Industry II Minister Maung Cho, and Transport and Communications Minister Saw Pru. The Indians offered Burma $10 million in credit to purchase capital goods and expressed India's interest in buying anything that Burma put on the market. The Burmese officials indicated that their country would not turn away Indian goods should their prices be competitive and the quality good.[39] In early February 1988, a Burmese delegation headed by Khin Maung Gyi, minister for trade, visited India to discuss the development of bilateral trade.

PAKISTAN

Relations between Burma and Pakistan have not been altogether cordial for several reasons. First, the cultural bonds are not very close, since Burma is mainly a Buddhist country and Pakistan a Muslim country. Second, Burma's nationalization measures harmed the Pakistan traders and other Pakistanis who had settled in Burma, and third, more tension resulted from Arakanese Muslims who either fled to East Pakistan or turned to Pakistan for protection before the independence of East Pakistan in 1971.

Burmese Prime Minister U Nu flew to Karachi to meet his Pakistani counterpart following his visit to New Delhi to seek assistance on April 12, 1949, when his government was faced with multicolored insurrections. In early February 1950, Pakistan granted a loan of £500,000 to Burma, and in the following March participated with India, Ceylon, Australia, and the United Kingdom in arranging a second but unused loan of £6 million. Pakistan and Burma signed a treaty of peace and friendship in Rangoon on June 25, 1952. The accord envisaged mutual cooperation in matters of common concern to the two countries and, to further this aim, made provision for periodic meetings of Burmese and Pakistani representatives for exchange of views.

Burma and Pakistan had a border problem where the Arakan province touched on East Pakistan. A separate movement of the Arakanese Muslims, the so-called Mujahid Movement, wished to joint Pakistan. The Northern Arakan Muslim League, formed in Akyab in 1946, demanded union with Muslims across the border. The unrest and confusion in Arakan forced 5,000 nonpolitical refugees to flee to East Pakistan by February 1949. In January 1950, after serious communal strife in Burma, another 30,000 Muslims, mostly from Arakan, migrated to Pakistan. On December 19, 1951, Pakistan warned Burma about the influx of Arakan Muslims into East Bengal and asked Burma to repatriate the refugees. The situation eased somewhat when the Mujahid leader Cassim was arrested in East Pakistan in June 1954. During his visit to Rangoon in December 1960, Pakistan's President Ayub Khan was asked by newsmen if the Pakistan government countenanced the activities of the Mujahid leader Cassim; he replied that his government "encouraged Cassim to the extent of having him under home arrest for the last eight years." With regard to the problem of refugees along the Burma-Pakistan border, he said that the complaints were not one-sided. He hoped that with patience on both sides "this very minor problem of refugees" could be resolved.[40] Pakistan's External Affairs Minister Z. A. Bhutto also had discussed the position of Muslims in Arakan with Burmese Foreign Minister Thi Han during his visit to Rangoon in January 1964. The joint communique of the two ministers said:

[Bhutto] expressed his belief that the Burmese government would solve the question of Muslims in Arakan with sympathetic consideration and assured that Pakistan on its part would be glad to extend maximum cooperation in any way possible, consistent with its policy of good neighboring relations. The Burmese Foreign Minister recalled the assurance given in 1961 and said that that question had been largely resolved. It would, however, continue to receive sympathetic consideration.[41]

The Naaf River on the Burma-Pakistan boundary, a winding creek with half-submerged islands and shifting channels, also presented endless possibilities for petty frontier disputes. In December 1952, the two countries agreed to confer on this question after their envoys had completed a joint tour of the border. But no substantial progress could be made for many years, as the issue was linked with other complicated problems connected with the status of people on either side of the border. During his visit to Karachi in October 1959, General Ne Win, prime minister of the Burmese caretaker government, had talks with President Ayub Khan on this question. The two leaders agreed to set up a joint commission to examine the general situation on the Burma-East Pakistan border. General Ne Win paid a good will visit to Pakistan on February 12, 1965, during which the boundary question was a topic of discussion. A communique issued by Ne Win and Pakistan President Ayub Khan on February 19 stated:

The two Heads of State noted with satisfaction the increasing understanding and cooperation between the two countries and the progress made in consolidating friendly relations during the past years. In this connection they especially noted the settlement of the Naaf River boundary and the full understanding and cooperation with which the joint hydrographic survey was being conducted according to schedule.[42]

A Boundary Agreement was finally signed by Ne Win and Khan on May 9, 1966 during the former's visit to Pakistan. Under the agreement, the fluctuating boundary in the Naaf River section of the inherited Burma-Pakistan boundary had been converted into a fixed boundary once and for all by dividing the river along the existing middle line of the main navigable channel.[43]

The nationalization measures adopted by the Burmese government in 1963 affected thousands of Pakistanis and 500 Pakistani shops. By mid-September 1964, 4,845 Pakistanis had left Burma for good. During Ne

Win's visit to Pakistan in February 1965, the matter was brought up for discussions between him and Ayub Khan. In a joint communique the Pakistani president expressed satisfaction that Pakistani nationals would receive due sympathy and consideration from the Government of Burma.[44]

After East Pakistan successfully won independence from Pakistan and became the People's Republic of Bangladesh in 1971, President Bhutto of Pakistan announced that Pakistan would break off diplomatic relations with any countries that recognized Bangladesh. When Burma recognized the new state on January 13, 1972, Pakistan recalled its ambassador from Rangoon. On January 24, however, Bhutto made a statement virtually retracting his earlier announcement which he sensed Pakistan was unable to apply, and diplomatic relations between Burma and Pakistan were returned to normal.[45]

Ne Win visited the Indian subcontinent in April 1974. The visit, made just after India, Pakistan, and Bangladesh agreed to a good-neighbor policy, was the first diplomatic exercise since his election the previous month as Burma's constitutional head of state. During his visit to Pakistan the Burmese president had talks with Pakistani Prime Minister Zulfikar Ali Bhutto on bilateral and international issues. In a joint communique with Bhutto, Ne Win asserted that Burma welcomed any steps toward disengagement and reduction of tensions in the Middle East. He also approved of measures taken to foster lasting peace on the subcontinent and in Indochina.[46]

President Zia-ul Haq of Pakistan paid an official visit to Burma on May 4–6, 1985, becoming the first Pakistani president to visit Burma in twenty-five years and the first such high-level contact between the two countries since Ne Win visited Pakistan in 1974. Speaking at a banquet given in his honor by Burmese President San Yu, President Zia said that friendship and cooperation between Pakistan and Burma were securely founded on sound principles. "Mutual benefit, respect for each other's political independence and territorial integrity, sovereignty and equality and non-interference in internal affairs have been the cornerstone of our bilateral relations." He added, "Relationships between our two countries are wholly free from friction or disagreement." Zia paid tribute to Burmese leader Ne Win for his contribution to deepening mutual understanding between the two countries.[47] The two presidents exchanged views on bilateral relations and the world situation. In a joint communique issued subsequently, they agreed to further develop friendly relations and to expand commerce and expressed grave concern over the increasing ten- dency of some states to resort to the policy of intervention and use of force in the conduct of international relations, pointing out especially the Afghan and Kampuchean problems.[48]

Pakistan had for many years been among Burma's ten principal trading partners. Pakistan's purchases from Burma reached a record level of $25.4 million in 1963, and Pakistan's biggest sales to Burma were $16.1 million in 1964. The trade between the two countries has generally declined since the secession of East Pakistan from Pakistan. Through 1972, the first year after East Pakistan's independence, until 1987, Burma's exports to Pakistan totaled $72.74 million, or an average of $4.55 million per year. Burma's imports from Pakistan during the same period totaled $14.43 million, or an average of $0.9 million per year.[49] Burma-Pakistan trade declined because Pakistan chiefly bought from Burma rice and sold to Burma jute for rice-bagging, but jute has no longer been a major product of Pakistan since East Pakistan's secession from it. Also, Pakistan has greatly reduced its requirements for foreign rice since the mid-1960s as a result of the modernization of agriculture.

BANGLADESH

With Bangladesh Burma maintains good relations. The creation of Bangladesh in December 1971 with India's support was a matter Rangoon most disliked. However, the Burmese government extended official recognition to the fledgling state on January 13, 1972. Burma's recognition was accompanied by the following declaration:

The Government of Burma does not accept as principle, the solution of a country's internal problems by direct help and intervention of a foreign country's armed organization. However, due to the existence of questions requiring immediate communication and action, and also due to a desire to live fraternally as neighbor, the Government of Burma has recognized the State of Bangladesh and its Government.[50]

The declaration was apparently designed to uphold the principle of noninterference and at the same time not to offend India by denouncing it by name.

In early 1972, an official mission from Bangladesh headed by Foreign Secretary S. A. Karim visited Rangoon—the first foreign capital after New Delhi to receive such attention from the newly independent nation. The mission's purpose was to negotiate the purchase of 25,000 tons of rice and the repatriation of Bengalis who had sought refuge in Burma during the "liberation struggle." The mission also reportedly discussed retrieving Bengali diplomats in the Pakistani embassy in Peking who were unable to get out because of close Chinese links with Islamabad.[51] This visit was followed by Foreign Minister Abdus Samad Azad. Kamal Hassain, Bangladesh's new foreign minister, arrived in Burma in late July 1972 on his tour of some Southeast Asian countries. Hassain said the main purpose of his Southeast Asian trip was "to promote and strengthen" relations on a bilateral basis. Undoubtedly Bangladesh was striving to make its presence felt in Southeast Asian countries and to carve out a place for itself in the region.

Ne Win paid a state visit to Bangladesh in April 1974, following his election as president of the Socialist Republic of the Union of Burma the previous month. He had talks with Bangladesh Prime Minister Majibur Rahman about regional and Middle East issues. Majibur took this opportunity to thank Ne Win for providing temporary shelter to thousands of Bengali Muslims fleeing the war between Pakistani troops and Bengali fighters for independence. Majibur, as government head of a Muslim nation, expressed his country's "firm support" for the "just cause of the Arabs" and the "legitimate right of Palestinians." In a joint communique with the host, President Ne Win welcomed "any steps toward disengagement and reduction of tension in the Middle East," and gave his "firm support" for keeping the Indian Ocean free from superpower rivalry.[52] In Bangladesh the visiting president also met the minister for industry, commerce and foreign trade for discussions of expanding Burma-Bangladesh trade as envisaged in the bilateral trade agreement signed in 1973.

President Ziaur Rahman of Bangladesh paid a state visit to Rangoon on July 20–28, 1977. In a joint communique President Ziaur outlined the foreign policy of Bangladesh which sought the promotion of peace in the South Asian region. He also mentioned the successful measures taken by his government for forging a balanced relationship with all countries. The communique said that President Ne Win stressed the importance of strengthening good neighborly relations for promoting a lasting peace in the region.[53]

Burma's relations with Bangladesh became strained in the first part of 1978 when some 200,000 Burmese Muslims in the northeastern areas of Rakhine State (formerly Arakan State) fled the country and crossed the border into Bangladesh after Burmese officials entered the areas to check up on illegal immigrants. President Ziaur Rahman accused Burma on May 7 of "inhuman eviction of Moslems" who alleged that murder, rape, and arson had been committed by Burmese troops, and he demanded the repatriation of these people to Burma. The president's accusations were officially denied in Burma on May 10, when it was reaffirmed that those who had fled across the border were, in Burma's view, Bangladesh nationals who had been illegal immigrants in Burma.[54]

Fears arose that a major religious clash might ensue involving some of the Islamic nations of the Middle East, but the tension eased when an agreement was finally reached between the governments of Bangladesh and Burma during June and July 1978, with intensive diplomatic activity by Bernard Zagarin, the chief representative of the UN High Commissioner for Refugees, and by the ambassador of Saudi Arabia to Bangladesh. Under the agreement Burma would repatriate the refugees in various stages. Up to the end of 1979 about 187,000 refugees had been repatriated.[55]

President Ne Win arrived in Dhaka for a three-day visit in May 1979. Earlier in July 1978 the refugee repatriation agreement also covered demarking the land boundary between Burma and Bangladesh. During his visit Ne Win signed a border agreement. On that occasion the Burmese president reiterated the Five Principles of Peaceful Coexistence as the basis for Burma's policy on relations with its neighbors.[56] A joint communique issued by presidents Ne Win and Ziaur Rahman stated: "Burma and Bangladesh firmly believe that their common border will always remain a border of peace."[57]

Ne Win paid a third visit to Bangladesh in 1980. In Dhaka on August 24, Burma and Bangladesh signed the ground rules for border arrangements and cooperation aimed at preventing border incidents of the kind that happened in 1978. In February 1982, Bangladesh President Abdus Sattar visited Rangoon to conclude agreement on the demarcation of the Naaf River boundary, among other things. In reference to border disputes, Burma's President San Yu said: "We have been able to approach our problems in a conciliatory spirit and to resolve them on the basis of sympathetic consideration of each other's difficulties." Sattar and San Yu also agreed to cooperate in economic, trade, cultural, and technical fields.[58]

Lieutenant General H. M. Ershad, Bangladesh's martial law administrator and president of the Council of Ministers, paid a good will visit to Burma in March 1983. The subsequent joint communique issued by Ershad and Burma's Prime Minister Maung Maung Kha underscored the traditional good-neighborly relations between the two countries. On the international situation, both sides reiterated full support for the 1971 UN Resolution on the Declaration of the Indian Ocean as a Zone of Peace and reaffirmed their commitment to establishing a New International Economic Order based on justice and equality.[59]

Burma's Foreign Minister Chit Hlaing made a tour of Nepal, India, and Bangladesh in early May 1984. At Dhaka, Chit Hlaing's talks with Bangladesh Foreign Minister A. R. S. Doha were concerned mainly with the question of a maritime boundary between the two countries. Burmese and Bangladesh officials later met in Rangoon to sign strip maps of the border from the mouth of the Naaf River to the junction of the borders of Burma, Bangladesh, and India.

U San Yu, president of Burma, visited Bangladesh on November 27–30, 1986. The Burmese president held talks with the president of Bangladesh, Hussain Muhammad Ershad, on bilateral, regional, and international matters of common interest. In a joint communique the two presidents agreed to further strengthen the bonds of friendship between the two countries and to explore the possibilities for further expanding the area of cooperation in various fields. They reaffirmed their two governments' firm commitment to the cause of peace and progress in the region and the world and emphasized the need for all states to strictly observe the principles of sovereign equality, territorial integrity, noninterference in the internal affairs of other states, and peaceful settlement of disputes.[60]

Bangladesh President Hussain Muhammad Ershad paid a three-day visit to Burma in late April 1988. During this talks with Burmese President San Yu the Burmese side agreed to release Bangladeshi fishermen detained in Burma soon. Both sides explored the possibility of setting up joint venture industries in Bangladesh and Burma. Bangladesh and Burma also agreed to take necessary measures for delineating the marine boundary between the two countries in a spirit of accommodation and cooperation.

Burma's trade with Bangladesh has been significant but has fluctuated a great deal. The two-way trade in 1972, the first year of commencing trade relations between the two countries, was worth $12.2 million, but in 1973 it dropped sharply to $2.6 million. It reached $35.77 million in 1979 but only $3.99 million in 1983. Burma's exports to Bangladesh up to 1986 averaged $5.1 million yearly.[61]

SRI LANKA (CEYLON BEFORE 1972) AND NEPAL

Burma and Sri Lanka agreed to exchange legations on June 6, 1949. They were later raised to embassies. The two countries were drawn together increasingly in subsequent years because of their Theravada Buddhism common heritage as well as their commercial ties. This bond was especially apparent when Sri Lanka agreed to jointly sponsor the Sixth World Buddhist Council at Rangoon between May 1954 and May 1956.

The membership of the two countries in the Colombo Plan and in the Colombo Powers, which met in April and December in 1954, as well as in the six-nation conference of 1962 at Colombo that mediated the Sino-Indian border conflict, all helped to maintain friendly but not over-active relations.[62]

As a member of the British Commonwealth Sri Lanka participated with India, Australia, Pakistan, and the United Kingdom in arranging an unused loan of £6 million to Burma in March 1950. In September 1953, Sri Lanka agreed to a four-year rice trade agreement calling for the purchase of from 200,000 to 400,000 tons of rice annually at annual prices ranging from £50 to £44 per ton in each succeeding year. This agreement provided some compensation for Burma's poor rice exports at that time. Burma and Sri Lanka exchanged trade missions frequently during the early years.

General Ne Win, then chairman of the Revolutionary Council, paid a good will visit to Sri Lanka on February 10–16, 1966. At a banquet given in his honor by Governor-General W. Gopallawa, Ne Win said:

The relationship between the Union of Burma and Ceylon rooted in their age-old contact has been one of friendship, cooperation, mutual understanding and respect. We in Burma desire to continue and further develop this relationship because we believe that in the context of the present international situation it not only promotes the interests of our two peoples but also serves the cause of world peace and international understanding.[63]

In a joint communique issued by Ne Win and Sri Lanka's Prime Minister Senanayake, the two leaders noted with satisfaction that the relations between Burma and Ceylon had been marked by mutual goodwill and understanding and expressed their determination to promote the development of these relations. They also reaffirmed their faith in the policies of nonalignment and of peaceful coexistence among nations irrespective of their social systems.[64]

Sri Lanka provided a small amount of technical assistance to Burma under the Colombo Plan totaling $12,300 from 1952 to 1986, including nineteen Burmese to be financed for training in Sri Lanka.[65] Sri Lanka was once a major purchaser of Burma's products, principally rice. Among Burma's customers, Sri Lanka ranked third from 1958 through 1960, following Indonesia and India, averaging $25.5 million per year. However, Sri Lankan purchases from Burma fell sharply to $1.85 million in 1975, returned to $28.97 million in 1983, and registered only $2.69 million in 1987. Burma's imports from Sri Lanka, principally tea and electric appliances, have been inappreciable.[66]

Nepal has for a long time had a consulate in Rangoon to look after the sizable Gurkha population in Burma, a number of whom are members of Burma's armed forces. The Nepal prime minister, B. P. Koirala, paid a visit to Burma on March 7–9, 1960. During his stay at Rangoon the visiting prime minister exchanged views with his Burmese counterpart General Ne Win on the international situation as well as on matters of direct interest to Burma and Nepal. In a joint communique issued on the conclusion of the visit, the two leaders announced their decision to establish diplomatic relations between Burma and Nepal at the embassy level in order to promote friendly relations. The communique also expressed their satisfaction with a strong similarity between the foreign policies of the two countries and their welcome of the efforts now being made by the great powers for the reduction of tension in the world and for the settlement of outstanding world problems by peaceful means.[67]

General Ne Win paid a state visit to Nepal from November 30 to December 3, 1966. In a subsequent joint communique, the chairman and King Mahendra Bir Bikram Shan Deva noted with satisfaction that the relationship between Burma and Nepal had been fundamentally one of friendship and good will toward each other, and that it was the common objectives of the two governments to develop their national economies and promote social progress by methods suiting the traditions of their respective peoples. The chairman expressed particular appreciation of the loyal services rendered by the Nepalese nationals in Burma, and the king expressed his appreciation for the sympathy and good will shown by the chairman toward them. They reaffirmed the adherence of their countries to the policies of nonalignment and peaceful coexistence among nations regardless of differences in the social systems and also strongly opposed any form of colonialism.[68]

Nepalese Foreign Minister Gehendra Bahadur Rajbhandary arrived in Rangoon on October 26, 1969. He called on Chairman Ne Win and met with acting Foreign Minister Hla Han. Prior to departure, the visiting foreign minister said that he had cordial talks with Burmese officials on promoting friendly relations and extending educational and cultural contact between the two countries. In answer to questions raised by the media, he said that there were about 80,000 Nepalese nationals in Burma, many of whom had taken up Burmese citizenship.[69]

King Mahendra and the queen paid a state visit to Burma from April 5 to 9, 1970. Chairman Ne Win and the king held talks on the question of further strengthening the friendly relations and cooperation between the two countries. In March 1980, King Birendra Bir Bikram Shah Deva and the queen visited Burma. The royal couple, accompanied by Burmese

Prime Minister Maung Maung Kha, visited the Shwedagon Pagoda and presented a Buddhist relic that is being enshrined at the pagoda. Burmese Foreign Minister Chit Hlaing visited Nepal in May 1984 in his tour of the Asian subcontinent. He had an audience with the king as well as discussion with his Nepalese counterpart. Under the Colombo Plan, Burma awarded fellowship to one Nepalese in 1970 for training in agriculture and scholarships to three Nepalese in 1975 to study medicine in Burma.[70]

BURMA AND OTHER COUNTRIES IN ASIA AND THE PACIFIC

JAPAN

Burma's relations with Japan, primarily in the areas of economic cooperation and foreign trade, have been very close. Despite resentment of the harsh policy of Japanese occupation during World War II, principal Burmese national leaders were trained and aided by the Japanese in the early forties. This, coupled with reparations funds, trade agreements, and economic assistance that contributed to Burma's economic reconstruction and development, helped maintain a special relationship between the two countries.

The inauguration of diplomatic relations with Japan, however, was delayed by the U Nu government's refusal in 1951 to attend the Japanese Peace Conference at San Francisco. Burma believed the multination Japanese peace treaty would allow Japan to evade reparation payment. As U Nu put it: "We felt that it did not sufficiently take into account our reparations claims against Japan . . . our best interest would be served by our entering into bilateral negotiations with the new Japan both as regards reparations and a peace treaty."[1]

Postwar Japan was eager to gain an entry into Southeast Asia and to eliminate the ill will caused by the war. The successive Japanese governments had set an Asian policy to normalize political relations and establish a new base for economic ties. As a result, Burma and occupied Japan signed a trade agreement on August 4, 1951. The state of war between the two countries officially ended on August 30, 1952; the 1951 trade agreement was extended by an exchange of letters in 1952 and superseded by a four-year trade agreement on December 8, 1953, which included a stipulation that Japan would encourage private concerns to give technical assistance to Burma.[2] Finally, a reparations and economic cooperation agreement, together with a treaty of peace, was signed in Rangoon on November 5, 1954. Japan agreed to pay 7.2 billion yen, or $200 million, for reparations in goods and services, and 1.8 billion yen or $50 million for joint venture investments in Burma over a ten-year period. The peace treaty provided for "firm and perpetual peace and amity" between the two countries and agreed to negotiate treaties or agreements at the earliest practicable date to place trade, maritime, aviation, and other commercial relations between the two countries on a stable and friendly basis. It included a clause allowing Burma to claim just or equitable treatment whenever a final reparations settlement with the other Southeast Asian countries was attained.[3]

The Philippines received $550 million in goods and services in 1956, as well as $250 million in private loans and investments, and the Indonesian claims were concluded in 1958 for $223 million in reparations goods and services, plus $400 million in private loans and investments. In April 1959, when the figure of South Vietnam reparations was announced, Burma applied for reparations revision and asked another $150 million to be added to the pact. Japan refused to increase its reparation payment on the ground that it might set off a chain reaction among the other signatories, but instead offered $50 million to Burma as a gift. Burma resented what it regarded as "shabby treatment." Japan's failure to satisfy Burma's additional requests for reparations and unfavorable trade balances provoked Burma to terminate further reparations discussions and boycott Japanese goods in December 1959.[4] Negotiations for reparations were soon reopened, but it was not until March 1963 that a new agreement of economic and technical cooperation was signed. The delay was due partly to the transition in the Burmese government and partly because Japan was a tough bargainer. Under the agreement Burma was to receive an additional $140 million in goods and services over a twelve-year period from 1965 as well as commercial loans totaling $30 million. Burma agreed to make no further reparation claims.[5]

After the first reparation settlement in 1954, normal diplomatic relations between Burma and Japan were established and the leaders of the two countries began to exchange visits. Burmese Prime Minister U Nu stopped in Tokyo on July 19, 1955, on his way home from visiting the United States. At a luncheon in his honor, U Nu heard Japanese Prime Minister Ickiro Hatoyama praise him for his statesmanship and diplomatic wisdom. Hatoyama referred especially to Japan-Burma reparations negotiations, which made Burma the first country to settle this issue and open diplomatic relations with Japan. He added: "We warmly approve of this friendly gesture, which augurs well for the future relations of our two countries and which reveals a high statesmanship on the part of the Prime Minister of Burma." Nu and Hatoyama discussed relations between Japan and Burma and pledged continuing efforts to further friendship and cooperation between the two countries.[6] Japanese Prime Minister Nobusuke Kishi visited Burma on his tour of Asian countries in 1957. While in Burma Kishi stressed Japan's peaceful purposes and its intent to cooperate fully with Burma.

Japanese Prime Minister Hayato Ikeda paid a visit to Rangoon on November 23–26, 1961. At a news conference Ikeda parried questions on the further reparations talk between Burma and Japan that was in progress and explained that he had come to Burma on a good will visit and not to participate in the reparation negotiations. Replying to a question, he said that it was for Burma to determine what sort of economic cooperation it needed from Japan. He added: "We on our part will do what we can to meet Burma's requirements to the fullest extent." Ikeda had talks with Burmese Prime Minster U Nu on topics including particularly economic cooperation between the two countries. A joint communique issued on November 26 said in part:

The Prime Ministers expressed satisfaction that the current reparations program, under the 1954 Agreement between the two countries concerning reparations and economic cooperation, is making smooth progress and contributing to the economic development of the Union of Burma. As to the review of the Agreement, it was agreed that negotiations for an increase in the amount of reparations would be continued between the two countries.

Prime Minister Ikeda assured Prime Minister U Nu that Japan would be prepared to strengthen her economic and technical assistance to Burma within her capacity in future.[7]

General Ne Win visited Japan for eight days on his way home from Washington in September 1966, during which he conferred with Japanese Prime Minister Eisaku Sato and had an audience with Emperor Hirohito. His trip to Japan was primarily economic in purpose, and Sato expressed Japan's readiness to help improve Burmese agriculture. On major international issues, the two leaders found themselves in agreement. In a communique issued on the occasion of the visit Ne Win and Sato agreed that the 1963 agreement between the two countries on economic and technical cooperation "is being satisfactorily implemented and has contributed toward the economic development in Burma" and reaffirmed the support of their respective governments for "the purposes and principles of the United Nations as well as the inalienable right of every nation to choose its own political, economic and social systems and its own way of life free from any outside interference or pressure." They expressed their deep concern over the situation in Vietnam and hoped a just solution would be found to secure a lasting peace in that country.[8]

Eisake Sato visited Rangoon On September 20–22, 1967. Sato said upon his arrival that the relations between Japan and Burma were so close that there was no particular problem requiring immediate solution and emphasized that the main purpose of his current tour was to find out how to stabilize Asia. Sato and General Ne Win exchanged views on Vietnam and China, and the two leaders agreed to work for peace in Vietnam from their own respective positions. Sato, talking to journalists, expressed the hope that Burma would make best use of its neutral position to help solve the Vietnam problem. There would not be any change in their respective policies toward China—Burma remained pro-Peking and Japan, anti-Peking. The joint communique said:

The Chairman and the Prime Minister reviewed the development in Southeast Asia and discussed its future. They reaffirmed the importance for countries of the world to maintain peaceful and friendly relationships on the basis of equality, of mutual support to each other's position and of non-interference in each other's domestic affairs. They considered that while the primary responsibility for raising the levels of living in developing countries rested with the governments and peoples concerned, international cooperation toward this could be of much help.[9]

In late April 1970 General Ne Win arrived in Tokyo and conferred with Prime Minister Eisaku Sato. The two leaders agreed to cooperate in trade and technology. General Ne Win visited Tokyo again in April 1973. In November 1974, Japanese Prime Minister Kakuei Tanaka came to Rangoon. In a speech during his visit, he described Burma-Japan friendship as "one of the closest in the world."[10]

In August 1977, Japanese Prime Minister Takeo Fukuda came to Rangoon after his consultations in Kuala Lumpur with leaders of the five members of ASEAN following the ASEAN summit meeting. In a joint communique issued at the conclusion of the talks between Fukuda and his Burmese counterpart Maung Maung Kha, the two leaders asserted that all Asian nations should work together to build a prosperous and peaceful

Asia. The Japanese prime minister also reportedly briefed Burmese President Ne Win on his conversations in Kuala Lumpur with the leaders of the ASEAN nations.[11] Fukuda tried to promote mutual understanding and cooperation between Burma and the ASEAN states for a peaceful Asia that would benefit Japan's economic growth.

In late 1979 president of the Japanese Overseas Economic Cooperation Fund Kaneo Ishikara arrived in Rangoon to discuss Burmese projects aided by Japanese government loans and assistance. As a gesture of good will to Japan, Burma named six serving officers of the Japanese Imperial Army southern branch, which led the Burmese operation together with the Burma Independence Army in 1942 of which Ne Win was an officer, in the 1981 independence "honor list" and conferred on them the "Banner of General Aung San," the highest award for distinguished services for Burma.[12]

President San Yu paid his first state visit to Japan on July 1–11, 1984. During his stay there he met Emperor Hirohito and held discussions with Prime Minister Yasuhiro Nakasone. At a state banquet give in his honor, San Yu conveyed to Hirohito Burma's appreciation of Japan's long-standing and valuable assistance in helping to raise the living standard of Burma's people. Earlier, the emperor noted that the friendly ties between Burma and Japan were strengthening in economic, technical, cultural, and other fields in recent years. At a reception the following day Nakasone lauded Burma for strictly adhering to the principle of nonaligned neutrality and for endeavoring to develop its foreign relations on the basis of international good faith.[13]

In early May 1988, a Burmese delegation headed by Tun Tin, deputy prime minister and minister for planning and finance, visited Japan. During the stay in Tokyo, the deputy prime minister and his delegation had meetings with Japanese Prime Minister Noboru Takeshita, Deputy Prime Minister and Minister of Finance Miyazawa as well as other Japanese cabinet members to discuss matters of economic cooperation between the two countries.

Japan is Burma's foremost foreign aid donor. The annual Japanese reparations as they became effective in 1955 represented one-quarter to one-third of Burma's public capital for the next ten years. They amounted to a major share of total foreign aid to Burma, averaging 84.7 percent yearly between 1960 and 1964. Through additional reparations and later Japanese grants and loans in Burma, Japan has retained its dominant position in Burma's foreign aid throughout the years. The Japanese aid to Burma, including reparations payments, during 1960–86, excluding 1968 for which the figures are not available, totaled $1,659.91 million out of which $617.41 million were in grants and $1,042.5 million were in loans.[14]

Japan has long been Burma's foremost goods supplier. Japanese domination of Burma's import trade results from the great amount of its financial flows to Burma. At first reparations were paid in Japanese goods and services rather than in cash. As well, Burma has used a good bit of Japanese grants and loans to buy Japanese products. Of Burma's exports Japan shares only a small fraction. Between 1960 and 1987 Burma's imports from Japan totaled $7,878.52 million, or an average of $281.376 million yearly, and Burma's exports to Japan totaled $673.76 million, or an average of $24.063 million yearly.[15]

AFGHANISTAN AND MONGOLIA

Naim Khan of Afghanistan stopped in Rangoon to accompany Burmese Prime Minister U Nu on the way to and back from Bandung Conference in 1955. U Nu paid a brief visit to Afghanistan in October 1955. Burma and Afghanistan signed a Treaty of Friendship in London on November 8, 1956, providing for the establishment of perpetual peace and friendship as well as diplomatic and consular relations between the two countries. King Mohammed Zohir Shan and Queen Homaire of Afghanistan stopped at the Mingaladon Airport on April 18, 1969, on their way home from Japan, and were entertained by Foreign Minister Thi Han at the airport. Burma continues to maintain diplomatic relations with the Kremlin-backed Kabul regime despite its unpopularity in Afghanistan.

Burma and Mongolia agreed to enter into diplomatic relations on October 4, 1956, and the two countries exchanged legations the following year. In early 1962, their respective legations were raised to embassy level. On April 11, 1969, a Mongolian good will mission headed by First Deputy Foreign Minister Bayaryn Jargalsaikhan arrived in Rangoon via Cambodia for a four-day visit and met with Burmese Foreign Minister Thi Han.

AUSTRALIA AND NEW ZEALAND

Burma has established direct diplomatic relations with Australia since their legations were first set up in 1952. On April 18, 1956, the Australian and Burmese governments announced their agreement on raising their respective legations in Rangoon and Canberra to the status of embassy. An Australian trade mission visited Burma in November 1954. Through frequent visits to Rangoon, the Australian Foreign Minister Richard

Cassey developed a good acquaintanceship with Burmese leaders and senior officials. Friendly relations between Burma and Australia were strengthened when a thirteen-member Australian parliamentary delegation led by Postmaster-General C. W. Davidson visited Rangoon on June 27, 1963 to study economic and social development programs in Burma. On arrival at Mingaladon Airport, Davidson announced that over the next two or three years his country would provide Burma with 100 buses to help the government modernize the Rangoon city transport service.

In June 1967, National Planning Secretary Kyan Uyun visited Australia to study the facilities available for the development of the cooperative partnership between the two countries. Deputy Prime Minister Douglas Anthony of Australia paid a visit to Rangoon in 1982. Australian Foreign Minister Bill Bayden, who had visited Burma in 1978, returned in November 1983 with a three-member team on a three-nation tour and discussed matters of mutual interest with his Burmese counterpart, Chit Hlaing.

Australia was Burma's third largest contributor of technical assistance from 1952 to 1986 under the Colombo Plan. It contributed a total of $5,438,900, including 1,401 scholarships and fellowships for Burmese to study and train in Australia and 265 Australian experts to help implement Burma's various development programs. Burma awarded two fellowships to the Australians, one in 1974 for training in education and the other in 1976 for studying humanities in Burma.[16]

Burma has maintained a considerable import trade with Australia that amounted to $175.95 million from 1958 to 1987, or an average of $5.87 million per year. Burma's export trade with Australia, on the other hand, has been inappreciable.[17]

Burma's relations with New Zealand are largely confined to economic cooperation and commercial activities. New Zealand extended to Burma $786,400 in technical assistance from 1952 to 1986 under the Colombo Plan, including 159 scholarships and fellowships for Burmese to study and train in New Zealand and sixteen New Zealand experts to help Burma's development programs.[18] The two countries have maintained limited trade relations. Burma's exports to New Zealand have been inappreciable except in 1979 when they registered $3.31 million. Burma's imports from that country were below half a million dollars in most of the past years.[19]

SOUTH KOREA AND NORTH KOREA

Relations between Burma and the two Koreas are not similar. On December 8, 1949, in the United Nations Political and Security Committee

Burma voted in favor of a U.S.-Australian-(Nationalist) Chinese-sponsored resolution "to regard the Seoul (Southern) Government as the only legal government of Korea." The Burmese delegation asserted, however, that Burma would not recognize either government in Korea since it did not want to contribute to the division of a country. Burma later voted for the establishment of a UN Commission for Korea to work toward unification.[20] In July 1950, following the North Korean attack on South Korea, Burma endorsed the UN Security Council's action in declaring North Korea an aggressor and sending troops to fight North Korea in the name of the United Nations. In the subsequent votes regarding the Korean war at the UN General Assembly, the Burma delegates insisted that Burma stood for a peaceful settlement that could only be achieved by bringing all parties together for peace talks.[21] Despite lack of official recognition of both the Republic of Korea (ROK) and the Democratic People's Republic of Korea (DPRK), Burma subsequently developed contacts with them on economic and cultural matters. U Nu had this to say:

So far as Korea is concerned, the unfortunate division of the country poses for us the same problem as divided Vietnam does. Consequently we do not recognize the Government of either North or South Korea, as the de jure Government of Korea, but this has not prevented us from having economic and cultural contacts with them.[22]

In mid-May 1975 Burma finally established diplomatic relations with the two Koreas and raised their links from consulate to embassy level. Such a move was probably influenced by the Communist victory in South Vietnam in the previous month, after which Burma was ready to extend diplomatic recognition to the Democratic Republic of Vietnam and the Provisional Government of South Vietnam. But Burma broke off diplomatic relations with North Korea in November 1983 after an official investigation found North Koreans responsible for the October bombing of the Rangoon mausoleum.

Contacts between Burma and the Republic of Korea started in the early 1960s. A seven-member South Korean cultural good will mission arrived in Rangoon in September 1962 for a four-day visit. A South Korean trade mission headed by Chul Seung Lee, assistant trade minister, visited Burma on January 11, 1964. As a result of the mission's visit, the first trade agreement was reached between the two countries. In October 1982, Burmese Foreign Minister Chit Hlaing visited South Korea, apparently to counterbalance his visit to North Korea three months before. A good will delegation headed by Yi Young Sup, a member of the Advisory Council on State Affairs of the Republic of Korea, visited Burma for four days during the last week of May 1983.

South Korean President Chun Doo Hwan paid a state visit to Burma in October 1983 in the first leg of a six-nation tour of Asia, which was designed to improve Chun's legitimacy at home and strengthen his relationship with the countries in the region. The visiting president was scheduled to officiate at a wreath-laying ceremony at the Aung Sang Martyr's Mausoleum in Rangoon at 10:30 A.M., October 9. A few minutes before he reached the site, a remote-controlled bomb concealed in the roof of the mausoleum exploded and killed seventeen of Chun's entourage, including four cabinet ministers, and four Burmese. Chun was clearly the principal target of the assassins, and practice notes played on a Burmese soldier's bugle appeared the inadvertent signal that set off the bomb and saved his life. The South Korean president cut short his tour and returned home immediately, but before he left Rangoon the distressed president was met at the Government Guest House by Burmese leader Ne Win, who offered his condolences. President San Yu, who saw him off at the airport, gave an assurance that "those responsible for this odious and cowardly act will not go unpunished." Nevertheless, Seoul was quick to blame Pyongyang for the blast and asked Rangoon to back a move to bring the affair to the United Nations General Assembly. But Rangoon maintained its policy of unwavering neutralism and refused to cooperate with the South Koreans. It organized its own investigation.[23]

A South Korean delegation headed by Foreign Minister Won Kyun Lee arrived in Rangoon on July 23, 1984 for a three-day visit, the first high level visit to Burma since the North Korean attempt on the life of President Chun. The delegation held talks with Prime Minister Maung Maung Kha and other Burmese officials. Kim Yong Chu, special envoy of the South Korean president, paid a good will visit to Burma in late June 1988.

Burma has good economic ties with the Republic of Korea, which is currently building a $75 million commercial dam near Mandalay, the largest construction project ever undertaken in Burma. Rangoon's exports to Seoul were negligible in the 1960s and 1970s, generally much less than $1 million per year. But the sales have increased in recent years, reaching $23.79 million in 1981 but only $5.39 million in 1987. Imports from Seoul were also insignificant in the 1960s. Purchases have increased since the mid-1970s. They were $24.6 million in 1982, and $15.57 million in 1987.[24]

Burma's relations with North Korea were once closer than those with South Korea. Mutual visits of Rangoon and Pyongyang officials took place more frequently. A North Korean trade and friendship delegation, headed by Vice Premier and Minister of Foreign Trade Lee Jo Yun, paid a visit to Rangoon on May 6–16, 1961. The delegation held talks with Burmese officials resulting in an understanding to promote reciprocal trade and exchange consular representatives "without involving diplomatic recognition." A joint communique issued at the conclusion of the talks noted an understanding between the two countries on trade items and an agreement to exchange various cultural groups at a favorable time to develop cultural relations between the two countries.[25]

North Korean Prime Minister Kim Il Sung made a brief stopover at the Rangoon Airport on April 10, 1965, on his way to Indonesia. Burma and North Korea signed an agreement for exchange of news between the two countries on July 23. In 1974 North Korea received the leaders of the BSPP and some Burmese ministers and sent dignitaries to Burma. A special envoy from North Korea paid a friendly visit to Rangoon in 1975 following Burmese diplomatic recognition. In February 1976, North Korean Deputy Prime Minister and Foreign Minister Ho Dam came to Burma and held talks with Burmese officials on bilateral and international affairs. President Ne Win paid his first state visit to North Korea in September 1977, which resulted in the development of warm relations between the governments and the ruling parties of the two countries. The joint communique issued by Ne Win and Kim Il Sung, president of the DPRK, specifically stated that they "exchanged views on further expanding and developing the friendly and cooperative relations between the Workers Party of Korea and the Burma Socialist Programme Party, between the Democratic People's Republic of Korea and the Socialist Republic of the Union of Burma, and on international matters of common interest."[26] As such, North Korea became the first Communist state to establish fraternal party links with the BSPP. Burmese Prime Minister Maung Maung Kha paid a good will visit to North Korea on July 13, 1979, after visiting the P.R.C. He met with President Kim Il Sung, his North Korean counterpart Li Jon Ok, and Deputy Prime Minister and Foreign Minister Ho Dam.

A delegation of the Burma Socialist Programme Party led by Secretary Htwe Han arrived in Pyongyang in October 1980 at the invitation of the Democratic People's Republic of Korea. The delegation attended the Sixth Congress of the ruling Workers Party and the concurrent celebrations of the thirty-fifth anniversary of the founding of the DPRK. In July 1982, Burma Foreign Minister Chit Hlaing visited North Korea, followed by a forty-member Burman cultural troupe in August for a performance tour of that state. In late August 1983, a delegation from the Supreme People's Assembly of the DPRK, led by Youg Hyong Sop, chairman of its standing committee, paid an eight-day good will visit to Burma.

The friendly ties between Burma and the DPRK became a casualty of the terrible blast at the Rangoon Martyr's Mausoleum on October 9, 1983, as the latter attempted to kill the visiting president of the Republic of Korea, Chun Doo Hwan. Two Korean assassins were captured within three days, and a third Korean assassin was killed in an escape bid. After nearly one month of painstaking investigations, the Burmese government finally announced on November 4 that "the statements of the two captured Koreans, the articles seized and other facts obtained from the investigation have firmly established that the explosion was the work of saboteurs sent by North Korea." Meanwhile Rangoon took the drastic step of not only severing diplomatic relations with the DPRK but also derecognizing it, the first time for Burma to do so with another country. All twelve North Korean diplomats assigned to Burma were given forty-eight hours to leave. Ne Win was reported to have been personally appalled by North Korean President Kim Il Sung allowing the attack to be made on Burmese soil, and the government actions were taken upon his personal decision.[27]

In early September 1985, Toyko's *Tongil Ilbo* reported that North Korea asked other Communist countries to help it resume diplomatic relations with Burma. North Korea asked the Soviet Union, China, East Germany, Poland, and Yugoslavia to convey to Rangoon its willingness to pay a considerable amount in indemnity and provide millions of dollars in economic aid as a way of apologizing for the Rangoon incident. The source said North Korea also had expressed its intention to dispatch a mission to Rangoon headed by a top-ranking official to express its apologies.[28] But no subsequent news on this matter has been reported.

Despite the severance of diplomatic relations between Burma and North Korea, their trade relations have continued. Prior to 1977, Burma's exports to North Korea were negligible. Since 1978 they have shown considerable increase and registered a total of $41.29 million up to 1986, or an average of $4.59 million per year. Before 1980, Burma's imports from that country were also negligible. Since 1981, however, they have grown significantly and totaled $84.3 million up to 1986, or an average of $14.05 million per year.[29] As to other economic ties, the North Koreans had only a small tin-smelting project near Rangoon which they withdrew from in late 1983, after having failed at a number of hydropower projects.

RELATIONS WITH THE UNITED STATES AND OTHER WESTERN COUNTRIES

THE UNITED STATES

Burma's relations with the United States have been friendly but low key. Soon after the Second World War, the U.S. Consulate General at Rangoon was reopened. When Burma was a provisional government within the British Commonwealth, the United States raised its consulate general to embassy level. U.S. Secretary of State Marshall also sent good wishes to Thakin Mya, chairman of the Constituent Assembly on June 10, 1947 and said, "Burma's peaceful and steady progress in rehabilitation is being watched with sympathetic interest. Freedom loving people throughout the world hope that you will lay the foundation for a stable and peaceful nation." In reply Mya assured Marshall that "free Burma will regard it as its special duty and privilege to maintain most cordial and friendly relations with your country and to make all possible contributions to the peace and happiness of the world."[1] On the occasion of Burma's independence on January 4, 1948, U.S. President Truman also sent a message of greetings to Burma's President Sao Shwe Thaike, which welcomed Burma into the brotherhood of free and democratic nations and assured Burma of U.S. firm friendship and good will.[2]

After independence, however, some unpleasant events occurred between Burma and the United States. The leaders of the rebellious Karen

National Defense Organization were for the most part Baptist Christians, and the rebellion began in three mission centers. The Burmese government blamed the U.S. missionaries and dubbed the uprising the "Baptist Rebellion." A U.S. medical missionary, Gordon Seagrave, was charged with aiding the rebels by the Rangoon authorities and sentenced in January 1951 to six years' imprisonment that was later quashed after appeal.

In the early 1950s the Burmese government also suspected U.S. involvement in the activities of the KMT forces (Chinese irregular forces) in Burma. When Burmese forces attacked a headquarters of the KMT forces located at the northern border of Thailand, they found the opposing KMT forces had recent U.S.-made arms, presumably delivered to them by U.S. planes and pilots from Taiwan via Thailand. In March 1953, the press reported that "three white men," presumed to be Americans, had been killed in battle at Loikaw, capital of the Kayah state, while aiding the KMT forces. In 1961 an anti-U.S. riot in Rangoon erupted after Burma shot down a KMT plane and discovered new U.S. military equipment in captured KMT strongholds. The progovernment press made the following comment: "The sooner the KMT are taken out of Burmese territory by the Formosa (Taiwan) Government to whose designs the American Government is privy, the better it will be for Burmese-American friendship."[3]

The United States was well aware of the effect the KMT question had produced on U.S.-Burmese ties. During his visit to Rangoon in November 1953, U.S. Vice President Nixon stated that "the presence of Chinese Nationalist troops in Burma is a major point of irritation in U.S. relations with Burma."[4] After a debate on this question at the UN General Assembly in spring 1953, the United States was included in a four-nation committee along with Burma, Thailand, and Nationalist China to work for the voluntary repatriation of KMT troops from Burma.

The Burmese were also displeased with the U.S. policy of disposing its surplus rice to needy countries that Burma counted on for its rice market. The *New Times* of Burma, a progovernment newspaper, declared in an editorial that "A broad hint was also implied in press reports that the United States Government may be behind an insidious plan to cut off rice markets from Burma so as to force the Burmese to come to terms, economic as well as political, which will once again envelope Burma in the American sphere of influence."[5] During his visit to Burma in 1955, United States Secretary of State John Foster Dulles was asked about this question and he said that "every country was free to protect itself by tariff restrictions and that at any rate the U.S. did not give food to countries that did not want food. . . . The basic principle for the U.S. in these matters," he went on, "as long as there were people who were hungry surplus food should not be allowed to rot, or to be thrown into the sea."[6] Though Dulles justified U.S. policy, the Burmese nonetheless protested U.S. dumping of its surplus rice when rice prices and normal market outlets for Burma declined sharply in the wake of the Korean War.

The United States was unhappy about Burma's "xenophobic" policy after the coup in March 1962. The Fullbright, Asia, and Ford Foundation programs were terminated and the United States Information Agency in Rangoon was closed. Western missionaries were expelled and foreign tourists and scholars excluded from the country. U.S. diplomats in Rangoon, as well as other diplomats, were subject to travel restrictions as well. But there was no protest from the U.S. government. The U.S. ambassador to Burma, Henry A. Byroade, said, "My country is committed to belief in a world of diversity where each nation can evolve its own political and economic forms."[7] A *New York Times* editorial considered the Burmese move more nationalistic than politically anti-Western:

The motivation for the new military Government's move, in so far as it can be ascertained, appears partly to be a xenophobic, totalitarian desire to end the relations between Burmese and Western individuals and agencies, not entirely subject to Government channels and supervision. This trend seems more nationalistic than politically anti-Western.[8]

In spite of these unhappy events normal relations between the two countries continued. U.S. Vice President Richard Nixon paid a visit to Burma on November 24, 1953. U.S. Secretary of State John Foster Dulles traveled to Rangoon after the close of the Manila Pact Powers' Council meeting in Bangkok in February 1955, the first time a U.S. secretary of state had ever visited the Buddhist country. Asked by the Burmese press if he had come here to woo U Nu, Dulles replied that the purpose of his visit was neither to woo nor to be wooed.[9] It was obvious, however, that he wanted Burma to join SEATO or at least to court Rangoon's friendship, which the United States needed during the Cold War.

U Nu made his first state visit to the United States in the summer of 1955, wherein he attempted to mediate the conflicts between the United States and the People's Republic of China, as he did during his visit to Peking at the end of 1954. It was Nu's opinion that the hostility between the two giant nations would lead to a world war with a disastrous consequence of global destruction.[10]

During his stay in the United States the Burmese prime minister met with President Eisenhower and Secretary of State Dulles, addressed a joint session of Congress, and appeared before the United Nations in New York and the National Press Club in Washington. Through his talks publicly and privately, U Nu made a plea for rapprochement between Washington and Peking. In addition, he asked the United States to help Burma sell its rice stocks for cash or credit. The Burmese leader also gave the United States $5,000 to help the children of the U.S. armed forces who were killed or incapacitated in the Burmese campaign in the Second World War. A joint communique summed up U Nu's visit as follows:

The President and the Prime Minister discussed many matters of common concerns and exchanged views on current international problems. . . . They had a frank discussion of the complex economic problem arising from the existence of substantial surplus of exportable rice both in Burma and in the United States. The problem of imprisoned American fliers in Communist China was reviewed. . . . Our two peoples . . . share fundamental goals: a peaceful world and a democratic way of life. The two leaders reaffirmed their dedication to peace and friendly relations among the nations based on international justice and morality, and joined in supporting the United Nations Charter as the surest and most practical avenue in the search for peace and justice. The two leaders also deplored the conditions which force the peoples of the world to divert their energies and talents from single-minded effort to improve and expand cultural and economic opportunities by which men can raise the levels of their existence.[11]

The communique made no mention of the China problem. According to William C. Johnstone, however, the Burmese credited U Nu's efforts when the United States and the P.R.C. agreed to open talks in Geneva,[12] less than a week after U Nu's American visit.

General Ne Win, chairman of the Revolutionary Council, visited Washington in September 1966, presumably to counterbalance his trips the previous year to Peking and Moscow. The general's visit changed the cold and suspicious attitude Burma had adopted toward the United States since he took power in March 1962. In his statement on arrival at Washington on September 8, Ne Win said:

My visit is essentially a visit of friendship and goodwill. The Union of Burma and the United States have no problems between them to settle. . . . I know that through personal contacts and discussions with them I shall have a deeper understanding of the position of the American leaders on important international problems.[13]

During the visit Chairman Ne Win and President Johnson discussed the further development of U.S.-Burmese ties and exchanged views on international questions of common interest. A joint communique issued on September 9 stated the United States' policy to help the people of the Republic of Vietnam to defend their freedom and to reconstruct their war-torn society as well as Burma's desire for a political settlement of the Vietnam question on the basis of respect for her sovereign independence, unity, and territorial integrity. The two leaders reaffirmed their earnest desire for an early and peaceful settlement in Vietnam. They also reaffirmed their belief that mutual respect, non-interference, and equality among all states are the basic principles underlying the creation of a stable, peaceful international order.[14] Burma had disagreed with the U.S. policy toward Vietnam but did not denounce it publicly. Undoubtedly, the general's visit afforded an opportunity for both sides to make a gesture of friendship without attempting to modify policies.

Prior to Ne Win's visit, an official delegation from Burma's Information Ministry had made an extensive forty-day tour of the United States in June and July 1966. U.S. astronauts Charles Conrad, Jr., Richard Gordon, Jr., and Alan Bean and their wives visited Rangoon on March 16–18, 1970, under the Burmese-U.S. cultural exchange program. A small Union of Burma flag taken to the moon along with the flags of other nations on the *Apollo 12* space vehicle and brought back to earth was presented by Conrad to Brigadier Thaung Dan, minister for culture and information.

Thanks to Sino-Soviet hostility and Sino-U.S. rapprochement, Burma has been more flexible with the United States since the early 1970s. This and the need to improve its lagging socialist economy have led to a modest increase in Burmese-U.S. cooperation throughout the years. In June 1974 the two countries signed an agreement with the United States providing civilian helicopters to help suppress illicit narcotics production and trafficking. Eighteen helicopters were subsequently delivered. As a result, Burma's opium harvest dropped from 450 tons in 1975 to 390 tons in 1976. And the average number of opium plantations destroyed by the Burmese troops increased from 300 acres in 1974 to 8,050 acres in 1975–76. U.S. President Gerald Ford praised Burma's "active role" in suppressing international drug trafficking when he accepted the credentials of Burma's new ambassador to the United States in 1975.[15]

A four-man congressional delegation led by Lester L. Wolff, chairman of the U.S. House of Representatives international relations subcommittee on Asian and Pacific affairs, made a visit to Rangoon, when Burma proclaimed an antidrug week from January 2 to 10, 1979, during which antidrug exhibitions and mass rallies denouncing drug abuse were held. Wolff and his party were also taken to Laikow, Lashio, and Mony Hsat in Shan state to witness the destruction of poppy fields. Later, Wolff, in a press conference held in Bangkok, Thailand, praised the Burmese government's action, describing its efforts as being sincere.[16]

In August 1975, U.S. Senate Majority Leader Mike Mansfield arrived in Rangoon for a fact-finding visit. Under the Burma-U.S. Educational Exchange Program, Maung Maung Kha of the Rangoon Arts and Science University visited the United States to study the university correspondence degree system in July. Burmese Deputy Education Minister Myint Aung traveled to Hawaii to study the university educational system in August, and four academics took a trip to the United States to study the community college system in May 1977.

In November 1981 Burma received a U.S. naval delegation headed by the chief of the United States naval operations in the Pacific, Admiral Robert Long, the first visit by such an important military delegation in over thirty years. John Holdridge, then U.S. assistant secretary of state for Asian and Pacific affairs, also visited Rangoon. Former U.S. President Richard Nixon paid a private visit to Burma on September 15, 1985. In January 1986 a U.S. congressional delegation, headed by Charles B. Rangel, chairman of the U.S. House of Representatives select committee on narcotics abuse and control, visited Rangoon, followed by U.S. assistant secretary of state for international narcotics matters, Dominick L. DiCardo.

The bilateral relations between Burma and the United States has been particularly characterized by economic cooperation. On December 22, 1947, just before Burma's independence, the United States and Burma established the United States Educational Foundation in Burma with a joint Burma-U.S. board with funds derived from the sale of surplus property in Burma. This was followed by an air-transport agreement and several other minor agreements. After the Communist rebellions started, however, the United States transferred eight to ten patrol boats, and some lend-lease ammunition to Rangoon but avoided any significant measures to aid the Burmese government. In September 1948, the U.S. government turned down a Burmese request for military assistance, suggesting that Burma turn to Britain and to U.S. commercial channels for help.[17] Obviously, Burma was then not considered a major concern of the United States.

The United States took a new approach to the countries in Southeast Asia following the Communist victory in China in October 1949. Ambassador-at-Large Philip C. Jessup was assigned to a tour of Asia in December 1949, and in February 1950 the Griffin Economic Cooperation Administration mission was also assigned to a similar tour. Both the Jessup and Griffin missions included visits to Burma. The result of these and later Jessup's second visit, coupled with the outbreak of the Korean war which prompted a strong U.S. anti-Communist policy in Asia, led to an economic cooperation agreement on September 13, 1950. The purpose of the agreement was "to assist Burma to achieve those sound economic conditions and stable international economic relationships so necessary for the maintenance of individual liberty, free institutions, and independence." It provided for $8 million for the year ending June 30, 1951.[18]

On March 17, 1953, Burma notified the United States to terminate the U.S. aid program as of the end of the coming June, but said "the action is not intended in any way to cast a reflection on existing programs nor on the activities of E.C.A. personnel in Burma." Certain projects already started were allowed to continue and a number of American technicians were even employed by the Burmese government. The note expressed appreciation and gratitude for materials and services received by the Burmese government under the ECA.[19] U.S. assistance to Burma under the program for fiscal year 1951 to 1953 totaled $31.4 million appropriated and approximately $21.2 million expended.[20]

The Burmese decision to abrogate the aid program was influenced by a variety of factors. First, it was the unnerving presence in the northeast of Burma of the KMT forces allegedly aided by the United States. As U Nu later stated publicly, "The cessation of American assistance in 1953." was related to the "aggression [of] the Chinese Kuomintang group which owes its very existence to American support."[21] Second, Burmese leaders were dissatisfied with the administration of the program. The U.S. Technical Cooperation Administration (TCA), lacking previous contact with the program in Burma, determined its content and allotted funds for it for fiscal year 1953. The TCA, again without consulting Rangoon, cut the proposed budget to half of that in the previous years. And the programs of social capital investment prepared by U Nu were rejected by the TCA. Third, Burma objected to the transfer of its direction from the Technical Cooperation Administration to the Mutual Security Administration in October 1952. In Burma's view, this suggested the service of Cold War needs and undermined its neutralist stance. Fourth, the increase in price of rice and other primary export products during the Korean war resulted in a rapid growth in Burma's foreign-exchange earnings. A lack of U.S. aid would not substantially harm economic development of their country.[22]

Feeling a pinch of a recession in 1954, Burmese Prime Minister U Nu urged the United States to offer indirect economic aid by buying rice for allocation to needy Southeast Asian nations and promised that Burma would use the money to hire U.S. technicians and buy U.S. machinery for a stepped-up economic program. He stated that Burma would accept U.S.

aid but not as a free gift. The United States, however, would not negotiate an aid agreement based on rice purchases.[23]

Economic cooperation between Burma and the United States was resumed in February 1956 under a Public Law 480 agreement delivering to Burma $21.7 million surplus agricultural products with payment in local currency. About 80 percent of the funds, equivalent to more than $17 million, was to remain in Burma for the purpose of promoting economic development, and the balance was to be used for U.S. local expenditures in Burma. In the view of Professor Frank N. Trager, this agreement renewed the government-to-government aid relationship and benefited both parties. The United States was able to reduce its agricultural surplus; Burma was able to conserve foreign exchange in implementing its development programs.[24] In June 1958, a military sales agreement was signed between the two countries in which the United States agreed to sell, for local currency, equipment and material that Burma needed in suppressing internal and external insurgencies.[25] Burma requested no new aid from the United States under the strict socialist policy after the military coup in March 1962. A few aid projects previously initiated, however, continued.

In June 1966, Burma and the United States agreed to liquidate Burma's obligations under P.L. 480 agreements. Under the terms of the agreement, the United States returned kyats 82.3 million; 57.6 million was given for school and hospital construction, while the remaining 24.7 million was to be a loan repayable in dollars over a thirty-year period at 3 percent interest.[26] Following Rangoon's breach with Peking in mid-1967, the United States supplied substantial quantities of arms and equipment to the Burmese forces under a new deal that replaced the newly expired ten-year arms agreement between the two countries. This military aid program ended in June 1971 when the Burmese government rejected a United States offer for renewal at a time when Sino-Burmese relations were normalized, making obsolete the very reason for the 1967 agreement. U.S. military assistance to Burma totaled about $88 million from its beginning in 1958 through its termination in 1971.[27]

In 1980 Burma and the United States resumed direct economic cooperation, and U.S. military aid to Burma also resumed in 1981. The reestablished economic aid program concentrated on health care and agricultural production. On August 28, Burma and the United States signed a two-year $5 million aid package to improve Burma's primary health care projects by providing training and basic medical equipment for half of Burma's 284 townships. To help Burma buy fertilizer and equipment for maize and oilseed production a $30 million grant was extended in October 1981. U.S.

aid totaled $14.5 million in 1985 and $12.2 million in 1988. It seems unlikely to develop a major bilateral aid program in the foreseeable future such as the United States had in Burma in the 1950s because of Burma's socialist economy and America's own scaled-down foreign aid programs.

The volume of Burma's trade with the United States was very small during the first three decades. Trade between the two countries has increased since 1978, both in export and in import, but not steadily. Burma's sales to the United States rose to $3.55 million in 1978 from $0.94 million in 1977. Between 1981 and 1987, the sales totaled $82.36 million or an average of $11.77 million per year. Burma's purchases from the United States rose to $33.22 million in 1978 from $17.79 million the year before, and totaled $158.18 million from 1981 to 1987, or an average of $22.6 million per year.[28] Burma's liberalized socialist policy and the improvement in relations between the two countries allowed the trade expansion between Burma and the United States.

THE UNITED KINGDOM

Burma's relations with the United Kingdom, its former colonial master, have been cordial. Under a treaty known as the Nu-Attlee Treaty, signed by Britain and the provisional government of Burma on October 17, 1947, the parties stated the desire "to define their future relations as the Governments of independent states on the terms of complete freedom, equality and independence and to consolidate and perpetuate the cordial friendship and good understanding which subsist between them." Great Britain recognized the Republic of the Union of Burma "as a fully independent sovereign State" and the parties agreed to exchange diplomatic representatives.[29] As a fully independent state Burma was free to join or not to join the British Commonwealth. Earlier, the Burmese had decided not to join. According to William C. Johnstone, this decision was influenced by many factors. Among these were Britain's immediate postwar policies, which caused considerable ill will among many political segments of the AFPFL, and an emotional desire to sever all ties with the former colonial ruler. The most important fact was that the Communists and their supporters were violently opposed to retaining any ties with Britain. The need for political unity within the AFPFL and with other political parties overrode other considerations.[30] When Burma withdrew from the sterling area on October 18, 1966, it severed the last of formal ties it had inherited from British rule.

In early years relations between Burma and the United Kingdom were

somewhat tarnished by two incidents. One was related to the Karen
rebellion. The Karens joined the multicolored insurrections against the
government in January 1949. Many British who had served in Burma
became alarmed at the possibility of warfare between Burmese and the
Karen minority, who were traditionally loyal to London and considered
anti-Communist. The Commonwealth representatives met in New Delhi
in late February 1949 and proposed that the Burmese resolve their differences with the Karens with the aid of Commonwealth mediation. The
proposal was sharply rebuffed by Prime Minister U Nu as unwarranted
interference in Burma's internal affairs.[31] Furthermore, a few British
nationals were found by the Burmese government to be supporting the
Karen revolt. British agents were charged as being behind the operations
though the British government denied it.[32] The other incident concerned
the nationalization of British property. After independence the Burmese
government nationalized the Irrawaddy Flotilla Company and certain
other British interests on June 1, 1948. Disputes arose between the Burmese and British governments over the compensation to be paid to the
nationalized firms. Under Ne Win's socialist policy, all foreign agencies
were either nationalized or purchased, which affected British interests in
Burma.

Burma and the United Kingdom signed a defense agreement on August 29, 1947, which was incorporated in the Nu-Attlee Treaty of October 17. Under the agreement, the United Kingdom, at Burma's request,
would send to Burma a service mission of military, naval, and air force
personnel to help train and strengthen Burmese armed forces. The duration
of the agreement was three years in the first instance and thereafter subject
to a twelve months notice on either side. On January 5, 1953, Burma
notified Britain to terminate this defense agreement. In Frank N. Trager's
opinion, Britain and Burma never agreed upon the quantity and types of
arms to be supplied, which eventually led to the abrogation of this pact.[33]
However, Burma had no urgent need for foreign military assistance as the
domestic insurrections had lessened and its neutralist foreign policy
seemed to be working. In retrospect, the United Kingdom had made
significant contributions to the development of Burmese armed forces, and
the British arms proved vital to preserving the integrity of the new Burmese
state against the insurgency. This was publicly acknowledged by U Nu in
1949:

Frankly speaking, we have been now able to equip our fighting forces with the necessary
arms through the good offices of the British Labor Government which has very kindly
met our requirements in spite of their own urgent defense problem. For this friendly act,

I wish to place on record the Union Government's heart-felt gratitude to the British Labor Government.[34]

There have been frequent visits between Burmese and British officials. Burma's Foreign Minister U. E. Maung and Commander of the Armed Forces General Ne Win went to Britain in 1949 to discuss economic and military assistance with the British authorities. In 1950 Premier U Nu visited London. Clement Attlee, former British prime minister, was a distinguished participant at the Asian Socialist Conference of January-February 1953 at Rangoon. In 1955, U Nu stopped in London for a week on his way to the United States. He had talks with Sir Anthony Eden and other British leaders on Taiwan, Bandung, and other international issues. British Under-Secretary for Foreign Affairs Peter Thomas visited Rangoon on March 25, 1963. Lord Louis Mountbatten and Deputy Foreign Secretary Lord Carrington came to Burma in early 1964 to discuss problems arising out of Burma's socialist policy. Chairman of the Burmese Revolutionary Council General Ne Win, accompanied by his wife, paid a visit to England in November the same year. They had an audience with the queen and were guests of honor at a luncheon given by Prime Minister Harold Wilson. As a gesture of Britain's good will and friendship, the British government returned to Burma a collection of Burmese art, known as the "Mandalay Regalia," which had been in Britain since 1886. Ne Win visited London in 1968 and reviewed the general situation in Asia with Prime Minister Harold Wilson.

President Ne Win made many subsequent trips to England, some of which were for medical treatment. In 1979, the president planned a trip to London to attend Earl Mountbatten's funeral, but Ne Win had to fly back to Rangoon because of his health after a stopover in Singapore. In his condolence message to Queen Elizabeth, Ne Win said: "The death of Earl Mountbatten means an irreparable loss to Burma of a good friend and unfailing well-wisher, and to me of a personal friend and a constant support."[35]

Great Britain has given Burma economic aid either on a bilateral basis or through a multilateral arrangement. On October 12, 1948, it agreed that Burma might draw on central reserve up to £2 million to meet its essential need for hard currency. Upon Burma's request for economic help, the Commonwealth countries agreed in March 1950 to loan Burma £6 million, of which Britain provided £3,750,000. Because of a U.S. grant and the great profit Burma earned from the sale of rice abroad in 1950, however, the loan was never used. Three months before, a short-term loan of £500,000 from London helped Burma finance rice purchases and ease its financial problems. On November 3, 1955, the British government agreed to reduce Burma's obligations to Britain from £26 million under the 1947 agreement to £7.3 million so that Burma might be able to apply all available funds to reconstruction and development.[36]

The United Kingdom was Burma's second largest contributor, next to Japan, among the members of countries in aid for technical cooperation from 1952 to 1986 under the Colombo Plan. It had extended a total of $6,522,200, including 1,632 scholarships and fellowships to be awarded to the Burmese for studying and training in England and 209 British experts in helping Burma's various development programs. In addition, a total of $59 million had been extended for capital assistance (official development assistance) for the same period.[37]

The United Kingdom is a major trading partner of Burma. Burma's commerce was integrated with that of Britain and India in the colonial period, and this triangle has remained the basis of trade into the 1950s. However, British traders later encountered difficulties in view of the withdrawal of agencies for British goods held by British nationals on October 1, 1961, and deregistration of British importers along with all other foreign importers from October 1, 1962, which debarred them from doing import business. In 1957 the United Kingdom was still Burma's leading supplier and the fourth customer, following India, Ceylon, and Japan.[38] Britain received from Burma in trade $231 million from 1961 to 1970 and $245.5 million from 1971 to 1980, remaining the second supplier to Burma during the two periods, also following Japan. On the other hand, Britain provided to Burma in trade an annual average of $15.59 million from 1961 to 1970 and an annual average of $10.46 million from 1971 to 1980. Since 1981 West Germany has overtaken Britain as Burma's leading supplier in Europe. In 1987 British sales to Burma were valued at $44.78 million, and British purchases from Burma were valued at $5.72 million.[39]

THE FEDERAL REPUBLIC OF GERMANY

Burma formally ended the state of war with Germany on July 9, 1952. From the beginning Burma had high regard for the Federal Republic of Germany (F.R.G.) for its industrial achievements and recognized it as a source of assistance. Formal diplomatic relations with the F.R.G. were established in 1956, disregarding the Burmese principle of not recognizing a divided country. Relations between Burma and the F.R.G. have since been friendly and close, particularly in the field of economic cooperation.

A Burmese trade mission headed by Finance Minister Bo Khin Maung

Gale and Trade Development Minister U Tin visited Bonn in early July 1956, resulting in the first trade agreement with West Germany. A West German loan mission led by the director of the West German Banking Corporation for Reconstruction, F. R. Kesseler, and the assistant director, R. Hopfen, came to Rangoon on June 20, 1963, to discuss a loan with the Burmese authorities.

Burma's Foreign Minister Thi Han, accompanied by Industry Secretary Colonel Maung Maung Kha, visited West Germany on June 16–25, 1965. They were received by President Heinrich Luebke and discussed Burma's economic development problems with Chancellor Ludwig Erhard. Ralf Lahr, the West German state secretary for economic affairs, paid a three-day visit to Burma in May 1967, and discussed West German aid to Burma with General Ne Win. Chancellor G. Kiesinger of the F.R.G. and his wife arrived in Rangoon on a state visit on November 22, 1967. Ne Win visited Bonn in October 1968. A German vocational education study mission headed by Herr Ballerstedt of the Economic Cooperation Ministry arrived in Rangoon at the end of 1970 to hold talks on educational aid programs.

In January 1972, the West German Minister for Economic Cooperation Frau Marie Schlei led an eleven-member delegation to Rangoon resulting in several aid agreements between the two countries. In March 1984 a West German delegation headed by Minister for Economic Cooperation Juergen Warnke visited Burma and had talks on matters relating to economic cooperation with a Burmese delegation headed by Deputy Prime Minister and Minister for Planning and Finance Tun Tin. Both sides also reviewed the German-aided projects and discussed future cooperation.

In July 1984, Ne Win, Chairman of the BSPP, accompanied by a number of high officials including Deputy Prime Minister and Minister for Defense and Chief of Staff General Kyaw Htin, visited West Germany. President of the F.R.G., Richard von Weizsacker, accompanied by his wife and entourage, paid a state visit to Burma on February 5, 1986. The economic orientation of West Germany's relations with Burma was emphasized by the fact that the only government minister accompanying the president was Juergen Warnke, the economic cooperation minister. Ne Win visited West Germany in 1987, as did President and BSPP Vice-Chairman San Yu.

The close economic cooperation between Burma and West Germany is reflected by West German aid to Burma's economic development. Between 1969 and 1986 Bonn extended to Rangoon $419.7 million, of which $77.4 million were in grants and $342.3 million were in loans. This aid accounts for 17.8 percent of the total contributions to Burma from the Development Assistant Committee (DAC) countries during that period, second only to Japan.[40]

West Germany has been a major supplier of commodities to Burma but not its important customer. Burma's imports from Bonn averaged $10.93 million per year during the 1960–70 period and averaged $23.38 million per year during the following decade. The purchases have increased in recent years, totaling $540.22 million from 1981 to 1987, or an average of $77.17 million per year. On the other hand, Burma's exports to Bonn averaged $5.8 million yearly during the 1960–70 period and averaged $8.37 million yearly during the following decade. The sales reached $16.55 million in 1981, but dropped to $6.97 million in 1987.[41] Burma has always had adverse trade balances with the F.R.G. The imbalance is due partly to foreign aid from the F.R.G. and partly to Burma's needs for Bonn's products for development projects.

OTHER WESTERN COUNTRIES

Burma has maintained good relations with other Western countries. After the state of war with Austria was formally ended on July 9, 1952, Burma established diplomatic relations with that country and later with Belgium, Denmark, Finland, France, Italy, the Netherlands, Norway, Sweden, and Switzerland. After 1957 diplomatic links were extended to Turkey, Canada, and Spain.

Burma's relations with France have been harmonious but not free of unpleasant incidents. In July 1955 Burma criticized France's delay of self-government to Morocco and Tunisia. In the meeting of the Colombo Powers held in New Delhi in November 1956, Burma and three other Colombo Powers—Ceylon, India, and Indonesia—condemned France for using force to suppress the Algerian struggle for freedom. Burma also described the Anglo-French-Israeli military action against Egypt in 1956 as aggression and called for an immediate withdrawal of all foreign troops from Egypt in accordance with the UN resolution.

U Ne Win paid his first visit to France in 1949 when he was commander of Burmese armed forces, and he visited France again on July 26, 1984, at the invitation of long-term business acquaintance Jean Ribaud. French authorities took the unusual step of according Ne Win head-of-state status for which he did not strictly qualify as BSPP chairman. The Burmese leader was to have remained in France for two weeks on this trip and had been scheduled to meet with President Mitterrand, but after staying barely two days he suddenly cut short his visit and canceled the scheduled meetings. Diplomatic sources suggested that he flew into a temper when he discovered Ribaud had been delayed in New York on business and would not be there to meet him.[42]

France has provided economic assistance to Burma and is a member of the Burma Aid Group formed in 1976. Between 1976 and 1986 France has extended to Burma a total of $41.8 million in official development assistance, of which $2 million was a grant and $39.8 was a loan.[43] Low-interest bearing loans were given on a case-by-case basis. French Transport Minister Charles Fiterman visited Burma on May 26–30, 1984, and talked with Burmese officials on economic cooperation between the two countries, especially in the railway transport sector. For a similar purpose French Transport Minister Jacques Douffiagues visited Rangoon in early February 1988.

France is Burma's fourth largest trading partner among European countries, following West Germany, Britain, and the Netherlands. From 1958 to 1987 Burma's exports to France totaled $56.11 million, or an average of $1.87 million per year. Burma's imports from France during the same period totaled $264.55 million, or an average of $8.82 million per year.[44]

Canada extended to Burma a total of $2,199,200 in technical assistance from 1952 to 1986, becoming the fifth largest contributor to Burma under the Colombo Plan, next to Japan, the United Kingdom, Australia, and India. This technical assistance included scholarships for 67 Burmese students and 230 Burmese trainees in Canada, 9 Burmese students and trainees in other countries, and 54 Canadian experts to help Burmese development programs. In addition, Canada extended to Burma $36 million in official development assistance during the same period, of which $28.4 million was a grant and $7.6 million was a loan.[45]

Burma's exports to Canada have been always inappreciable except in 1986, when they registered $1.12 million. Its imports from that country had also been negligible up to 1969, rose to $3.45 million in 1970 and reached $15.65 million in 1980, but dropped to $2.23 million in 1981.[46] No improvements have been shown in recent years. The Burmese embassy in Canada had been closed for many years as an economy measure. But it was reopened in 1986, reflecting the importance in relations between the two countries.

There have occasionally been mutual visits between Burmese officials and officials of other small European countries. Most significant were Burmese Prime Minister U Nu's good will visit to Sweden, Denmark, and

Finland in November 1955; the visits to Burma of Danish Prime Minister H. C. Hansen in March 1957, Danish Foreign Minister Per Haekkerup in early 1964 and Danish Foreign Minister Uffe Ellemann-Jensen in January 1988; Chairman of the Burmese Revolutionary Council General Ne Win's visit to Austria and Switzerland in July 1962; Burmese Deputy Minister for Transport and Communications Ko Gyi's visit to Norway in June 1979 to observe the work of building vessels for Burma Five Star Shipping Corporation; Burmese Deputy Trade Minister Khin Maung Gyi's delegation tour to European countries in July 1979 to find new markets for Burmese rice; Finland Minister for Foreign Affairs and Foreign Trade Esko Rekola's visit to Burma in April 1980; Italian Deputy Foreign Minister Bruno Corti's visit to Burma in early June 1985; and Norwegian Minister of Health and Social Affairs Tove Strand Gerhardsen's visit to Burma in December 1987.

These European countries provide small aid to Burma. Burma received from Denmark grants of $1.5 million and loans of $43.6 million during the 1976–86 period; from Finland grants of $6.1 million and loans of $9.4 million during the 1973–86 period; from Italy grants of $7.7 million and loans of $4.2 million during the 1979–86 period; from the Netherlands grants of $19.4 million and loans of $8.2 million during the 1975–86 period; from Norway grants of $13 million between 1978 and 1986; from Sweden grants of $0.69 million in 1965 and 1967 and $0.5 million in 1981; and from Switzerland grants of $0.1 million in 1974 and $3.2 million between 1979 and 1986.[47]

The Netherlands is one of Burma's principal trading partners. Burma's exports to the Netherlands totaled $167.04 million from 1958 to 1987, or an average of $5.57 million per year. Burma's imports from the Netherlands totaled $277.04 million during the same period, or an average of $9.22 million per year.[48] Burma also has maintained limited trade relations with other small European countries.

11

RELATIONS WITH THE SOVIET UNION
AND EASTERN EUROPEAN COUNTRIES

THE SOVIET UNION

Relations between Burma and the Soviet Union have been correct and polite. The newly independent Burmese government was soon recognized by the Soviet Union and the two governments had agreed to exchange ambassadors in February 1948. But it was not until February 17, 1951, that Burma sent its first ambassador to the Soviet Union and received the first Soviet ambassador on May 21. The Soviets originally viewed Burma as a British puppet, though they did not oppose Burma's admission to the United Nations. Moscow had been cool toward Rangoon and did nothing to develop relations of any kind with the Burmese before 1954. However, with the advent of Khrushchevist amiability and flexibility following the death of Stalin in 1953, Burma's need to dispose of its surplus rice, its estrangement from the United States over the vexing problem of Chinese Nationalist forces in northern Burma, and the groundwork for good relations between Burma and the Soviet's ally P.R.C. laid down by Chinese Prime Minister Chou En-lai, a new era in Burmese-Soviet relations ensued.[1]

In September 1954, a Burmese delegation led by the minister of agriculture and forestry visited the Soviet Union and the following

December another Burmese delegation led by a cabinet official arrived in Moscow to negotiate the sale of rice. Earlier in April and again in November, China had signed two barter trade agreements with Burma. An unusual clause in the November protocol called for a separate account to be maintained by both parties for 20 percent of the purchases which would be paid in goods from the U.S.S.R. and Eastern European countries.[2] On July 1, 1955, Burma and the Soviet Union concluded a three-year trade agreement. The Soviets agreed to purchase 150,000 to 200,000 tons of Burmese rice within one year. In return, they would supply Soviet machinery, industrial goods, and technical services. The pact was extended to five years on April 1, 1956, providing that the Soviet Union would take 400,000 tons of Burmese rice each year for five years, if Burma desired, in exchange for Soviet goods and services. Later Burma encountered difficulties with this arrangement that were attributable in part to the inexperience of the Burmese government and in part to the hazards of trading with the Soviet bloc. Delays in deliveries, evidence of over-pricing and poor quality, and the purchase of goods not actually needed had all dampened Burmese enthusiasm for barter deals.[3] The *New York Times* had this report:

It is difficult for Burma to find qualified representatives to go on trade missions. Persons of unusual qualification are required to understand the complex of goods required by Burma's economic development program. Furthermore, there is the difficult language barrier. For the Burmese, the pricing is very important. The goods offered by the Soviet Union in barter do not have to be priced competitively. There is no competition. If the Burmese do not want to pay the Soviet price, they have no choice but to move along to the next item.[4]

Prime Minister U Nu paid his first state visit to the Soviet Union from October 20 to November 31, 1955. During his stay, U Nu had discussions with Soviet Prime Minister Nikolai A. Bulganin and other leaders of the soviet government and called upon President Voroshilov. At a banquet given in his honor, U Nu praised the Soviet Union for saving Burma from a severe crisis by purchasing rice, and reiterated his support for the coexistence of countries with differing political and social systems. A joint communique issued by Bulganin and Nu contained the following parts, reflecting Nu's endorsement of many of the stated aims of Soviet foreign policy:

1. The Soviet and Burmese Prime Minister "unanimously condemn the policy of creating blocs, and agree that a policy of nonparticipation in blocs guarantees security for the peoples and plays a positive part in establishing world peace."

2. The Soviet Union and Burma would have their mutual relations on the "Five

Principles" agreed upon by Bulganin and Nehru during the latter's visit to Moscow, viz.—non-aggression; noninterference in internal affairs, peaceful coexistence; cooperation based on equality and mutual economic benefit; and respect for each other's sovereignty and territorial integrity.

3. Both premiers welcomed the recent ease of international tension as expressed in such developments as the ending of the Korean and Indo-Chinese Wars, the normalization of Soviet-Yugoslav relations, the success of the Bandung Conference of Afro-Asian countries, Nehru's visit to the Soviet Union, and the "summit" conference in Geneva.

4. Both countries were agreed that special attention should be paid to the "problems of Asia and the Far East," including Formosa, and that the Chinese People's Republic should be seated in the U.N.

5. The two prime ministers called for the unconditional prohibition of nuclear and thermonuclear weapons, substantial reductions in conventional armaments, and "effective control" of disarmament.[5]

Soviet Prime Minister Nicholai A. Bulganin and Nikita S. Khrushchev, Soviet Communist Party First Secretary, visited Burma on December 1–7 the same year in connection with their trip to India and Afghanistan. The Soviet leaders used the occasion to criticize the policy of the West in Asia and the world and to play the role of friends of the Burmese people. A joint statement issued by Bulganin and Nu on December 6 clearly paralleled their previous Moscow communique.[6] On December 7, 1955, details of the Soviet-Burmese economic agreement were announced in Rangoon, under which the Soviet government would provide the Burmese government with materials and services for agricultural development and industrial plants, and Burma would supply "an appropriate quantity of rice and other products of Burmese origin" to the Soviet Union.

Anastas Mikoyan, the Soviet First Deputy Premier, visited Burma from March 30 to April 2, 1956, during a tour of Asian countries. The Soviet government subsequently offered to construct and equip in Rangoon a hospital, a theater, a cultural and sports center, and premises for industrial and agricultural exhibitions, as a gift from the Soviet people. In reciprocation, Burma offered an appropriate quantity of rice to the Soviet people.[7] In January 1958 the Soviet Union agreed to lend Burma between 4 and 7 million rubles at 2.5 percent interest for twelve years to build two dams, and to supply teams of experts for related agricultural projects,[8] which were completed in 1967.

In 1959 two Soviet embassy officials in Rangoon defected. One was taken back to the Soviet Union, and the other, Alex Urevitch Kaznacheev, was allowed to go to the United States. The tape-recorded statement Kaznacheev made at the U.S. embassy and released to the press subsequently gave, among other things, a rather full account of Soviet espionage and intelligence activities in Burma. But the Burmese government confined itself to increasing its vigilance against subversion and espionage and brought no complaints against the Soviet government.[9]

Nikita S. Khrushchev, then Soviet prime minister, visited Burma on February 16–18, 1960, on his way to Indonesia. A communique issued at the end of Khrushchev's visit stated that it had been agreed upon to develop a program for cultural and scientific exchange in 1960. It also referred to Soviet support of Burma's neutralist policy and Burma's support for Khrushchev's disarmament proposals, and it called for the suppression of nuclear tests.

When the military toppled the U Nu government in March 1962, the Soviet Union was slow in recognizing the new government. A leading Soviet expert on Burma at the time asserted that, although Ne Win's policies were supported by all progressive organizations, his government did not recognize the special role of the working class and the decisive significance of Marxism-Leninism as a theoretical weapon in the Burmese effort to introduce scientific socialism.[10] After some time of hesitation, however, the Soviet government proceeded with its diplomatic, economic, and cultural activities in Burma, mainly for fear of Burma's domination by Peking's influence.

In July 1962, Soviet First Deputy Premier Anastas Mikoyan made a brief stopover in Rangoon and had discussions with Brigadier Aung Gyi, a key figure in the Revolutionary Council. They agreed to set up a fertilizer plant with Soviet aid. An economic cooperation agreement was signed in August under which the Soviet Union agreed to provide Burma a long-term loan of 3.5 million rubles (Kyats 30.4 million) to build a dam and to introduce the Russian language into Burma's schools and colleges.[11] Soviet Defense Minister Marshal Radion Yakovlevich Malinovski visited Burma in April 1963. In his address at a dinner given in his honor by General Ne Win, Malinovski pictured his country as a Burmese ally in the struggle for peace and anticolonialism:

The Burmese people, building a new life, will meet the comprehension and support from the Soviet Union. . . . The Soviet Union as the consistent fighter for peace and friendships between the peoples comes out in the united front with Burma and the other states which recently embarked on the road of independent development in the struggle for the preservation of peace, liquidation of the remnants of colonialization on the globe.[12]

General Ne Win paid a state visit to the Soviet Union in mid-September 1965, presumably to counterbalance his trip to the People's Republic of

China the previous summer. He had an exchange of views with Soviet leaders, including Soviet Communist Party First Secretary Leonid Brezhnev, Prime Minister Alexei Kosygin, and Chairman of the Presidium of the Supreme Soviet of the U.S.S.R. Anastas Mikoyan. A joint communique, issued at the conclusion of the talks, said that Burmese-Soviet relations were developing successfully on the basis of peaceful coexistence. The communique also denounced imperialism and colonialism and said that the Vietnam problem should be settled under the 1954 Geneva Agreement. It stressed the importance of Afro-Asian cooperation and stated that the second Bandung Conference in Algiers should strengthen it. Both sides considered important and unshakable the right of all peoples to choose and develop freely the political, economic, and social systems which in the best ways met their aspirations and strivings.[13]

Anastas Mikoyan came to Rangoon in later September 1965. The forthcoming second Bandung Conference in Algiers and the Vietnam situation were again major topics the visiting Soviet president brought up for discussion with General Ne Win in an effort to win Burma over to the Soviet side on these two issues. The Soviet Union had worked hard to defeat Peking's efforts to exclude itself from the Afro-Asian conference and severely denounced U.S. interference in Vietnam after the United States sent combat troops into South Vietnam early in the year. As generally expected, Burma, adhering to its neutralist stance, neither endorsed Soviet participation in the scheduled Algiers conference nor criticized U.S. action in Vietnam.[14]

Contacts between Burma and the U.S.S.R. increased following Peking's Red Guard diplomacy in mid-1967. The ensuing Sino-Burmese rift afforded the Soviet Union an excellent opportunity to increase the influence in this Buddhist nation. The Soviet leadership was quick to criticize Mao Tse-tung's group of its provocation of Burma and stepped up efforts to develop close diplomatic and economic ties with Burma. On July 7, 1967, a Moscow radio commentary in Burmese on anti-Chinese riots in Burma spoke of the conspiracy of a Peking directive to Chinese in Burma to steer Burma toward China and to encourage Peking's supporters infiltrating Burmese society. When Peking leaders realized the failure of their plan they decided to attack Burma and call for the overthrow of the Burmese government.[15] Immediately after the Sino-Burmese rift, Soviet Premier Kosygin reportedly sent Ne Win a message pledging full support and sympathy for Burma in its troubles with China and offered the Burmese military aid and increased economic support.[16] Soviet party leader Leonid Brezhnev, in his report to the Soviet Communist Party's Twenty-fourth Congress in 1971, praised Burma for being on the non-capitalist road of development along with Syria, Algeria, and the United Arab Republic.

Soviet diplomatic activities reached the height by Nikolai Podgorny's visit to Burma on October 3, 1971. During his stay, the Soviet president held talks with General Ne Win on Burmese-Soviet economic relations and the situation in South and Southeast Asia. At receptions, Ne Win expressed appreciation for the technical and economic assistance Burma received from the Soviet Union. In his reply, Podgorny expressed sympathy for Burma's struggle for

complete elimination of the colonial past for further strengthening of the political and economic independence of Burma. . . . Experience of international relations during recent times shows that young developing countries constantly come up against attempts of imperialism and international reactionism to avenge defeat they suffered and to prevent the peoples who won their freedom from following the path of independence and progress chosen by them. There are attempts to create such obstacles for Soviet-Burmese relations.[17]

Clearly, his remarks implied criticism of the West and China.

Nevertheless, historical ties, geographical proximity, cultural similarity, and fear of Peking's support to internal insurgency give China clear advantages over the Soviet Union in Burma. Burma welcomed the Soviet friendship gesture but kept the Soviet aid program and Soviet military assistance at a low level on neutralist grounds. For the same reasons Burma expressed no enthusiasm toward the Soviet proposal of an "Asian Collective Security System" that Soviet President Podgorny had discussed with Ne Win while visiting Rangoon in 1971. As Professor Robert C. Horn points out, "Despite obvious Soviet efforts and interests, the policy of neutralism and efforts at cooperation with China have proven insurmountable obstacles thus far to the establishment of real Soviet influence in Burma."[18]

Burma's displeasure over the Soviet alliance with Vietnam and its aggressive policy toward the Third World has affected Burma's relations with the Soviet Union and its domestic policy. The year 1977 saw a sweeping purge of the Burma Socialist Programme Party that removed all politburo members suspected of pro-Moscow leanings. Burma withdrew from the nonaligned movement in September 1979 because of its apparent alignment with the Soviet Union. Mutual visits between Burma and Soviet leaders have been infrequent in recent years.

In nonbilateral issues between Burma and the Soviet Union, Burmese response has been very careful not to offend the Soviet Union unless the reaction would seriously compromise its neutralist stance or other fundamental principles of its foreign policy. When the Soviet Union invaded Hungary to suppress that country's revolt in 1956, Burmese leaders strongly condemned the Soviet action. After Soviet troops marched into Afghanistan in December 1979 to rescue the wobbly Marxist regime, Burma sent a token team of three to the Moscow Olympics in 1980 as a gesture of protest against the Soviet action. Foreign Minister Lay Maung also made implicit criticism of Soviet action to expand its sphere of interest in his statement before the UN General Assembly on September 29, 1980.[19] The Soviet destruction of a South Korean airliner on September 1, 1983, provoked most nations to voice horror and accusations. Nonetheless, Burma kept silent, anxious to avoid displeasing Moscow.

Burma and the U.S.S.R. have not been major trading nations. For many years prior to 1960 Burma made 2 percent of total sales to the U.S.S.R. and brought 1 percent of its requirements from that country. During the ten-year period from 1971 to 1980 Burma's exports to the U.S.S.R. averaged $2.04 million yearly and Burma's imports from that country averaged $2.65 million yearly. The trade between the two countries has shown considerable increase in recent years. From 1981 to 1987 goods going to the U.S.S.R. totaled $113.55 million or $16.22 million per year and goods coming from that country totaled $104.6 million or averaged $14.94 million per year.[20]

EASTERN EUROPEAN NATIONS

Burma established correct ties with the socialist countries in Eastern Europe during the early years of independence. After the military coup in 1962, relations with these states seemed to become closer. The 1974 Burmese Constitution drafted by the Revolutionary Council is largely modeled on Eastern European fundamental laws in terms of the organizational character of the government, its recognition of the sole legitimacy of a single political force, and its stress on theoretical social justice. Fear of growing Soviet influence in Southeast Asia since the later 1970s, however, has had some negative impacts on Burma's relations with Soviet satellite countries in Eastern Europe. In 1977 all East European diplomatic missions in Rangoon were placed under heavy surveillance and all aid from these countries was seriously curtailed.[21]

Yugoslavia

Yugoslavia was the first state in Eastern Europe to establish diplomatic relations with Burma. The first Yugoslav ambassador presented his credentials in February 1951. Thanks to a personal friendship between Premier U Nu and President Tito, the common conviction of nonalignment, and military assistance to Burma from Yugoslavia, a special affinity between the two countries quickly developed. U Nu said, "Both Yugoslavia and Burma share the belief that a socialist state was the best means of raising general prosperity, and this fact, plus common belief in peaceful co-existence, had drawn Yugoslavia and Burma close together."[22]

U Kyaw Nyein, Burmese cabinet minister, party leader, and leading socialist theoretician, spent a month in Yugoslavia in 1952 in partial preparation for the Asian Socialist Conference held in Rangoon in 1952–53. At the Asian Socialist Conference Burma invited the Communist party of Yugoslavia to attend. Yugoslavia signed the first barter agreement with Burma on June 19, 1953 when the latter faced problems of poor exports. This agreement became the model used for later agreements with the U.S.S.R. and countries of the Communist bloc. In October 1955, the Yugoslav envoy to Burma turned over to the defense minister the equipment necessary for one brigade in the Burmese army as part of the barter agreement.

President Josip Broz Tito of Yugoslavia paid a state visit to burma on January 6–17, 1955, the first head of a European state to do so. Tito received an exceptionally warm welcome. At the reception, U Nu said, "Both countries since their independence had been on the friendliest relations, and Marshal Tito's visit would further strengthen these relations and promote international cooperation." U Nu stressed that both countries had a "common goal—namely to build a socialist state." The visiting president stated in an interview that the principles of coexistence advocated by him and the Indian prime minister in their joint statement were applicable to all countries. Coexistence became a new form of solving international disputes without the use of armed forces. It was the only way out of the vicious circle of an armament race. There was no reason by coexistence could not be applied to the relations between the United States and the Soviet Union.[23]

On the occasion of his visit, President Tito attempted to gain support wherever he could for his own middle course in foreign policy and there was talk that he was attempting to promote a "neutralist" third force. The Burmese leaders, however, were pleased to find that Tito apparently understood their basic aims of building a socialist state, and that he seemed to be a firm supporter of their policy of active neutralism. In a joint communique issued at the conclusion of his visit, Tito and U Nu affirmed that neither passive neutralism nor an alignment with either of the power blocs would aid the cause of peace. Only active neutralism could achieve peace.[24]

In June 1955 U Nu paid a return visit to Yugoslavia and received a spectacular welcome as "Our Friend." Both U Nu and Tito laid great emphasis upon active coexistence. In a subsequent joint communique the two leaders stated:

It was noted . . . that the policy of active co-existence is gaining increasing support as the only sure way to achieve permanent peace and develop international cooperation. The two Governments reaffirm their determination to continue their efforts toward the fullest possible application of the policy of co-existence and agreement in the first place through the United Nations; and to work for the establishment of peaceful relations among nations on a basis of equality.

Special significance was attached to the development and extension of economic cooperation between the two countries, as an exceptionally important element in the consolidation of friendship and cooperation between them.[25]

President Tito paid a second visit to Burma on January 8–10, 1959, and had talks with Burmese Prime Minister General Ne Win. A communique issued by the Burmese Foreign Office on the visit said that "those talks had fully confirmed the common views which have already been expressed on several occasions in past contacts between the statesmen of the two countries, both as regards the development of Yugoslav-Burmese friendship, the further advancement of mutual relations and the strengthening of peace and international cooperation."[26]

Yugoslav President Peter Stambolic paid a four-day state visit to Burma in February 1983, a month ahead of the nonaligned summit conference in New Delhi. With Burma's withdrawal in September 1979 from the nonaligned movement in mind, Stambolic said at a reception, "Nonalignment has been and remains the only option for general stability, equal security and peace and progress for all." Burmese President San Yu, however, said in his welcoming address that certain members had deliberately tried to exploit the movement to gain their own grand designs, and there was no change in Burma's attitude toward the movement.[27] The joint communique issued on the occasion of Stambolic's visit reaffirmed the long-standing friendship and good will between the two nations and noted a desire to develop further cooperation in the sphere of science, technology, education, and information. It stressed the need to respect the principles of the Charter of the United Nations, the importance of launching a global negotiation on economic cooperation and development, and the urgent need for genuine disarmament. Both sides also denounced all forms of imperialism, hegemony, and domination as impermissible.[28] On return to

Belgrade, President Stambolic, referring to talks with President San Yu, said that although Burma was no longer a member of the nonaligned movement, "in its foreign policy it consistently addresses to precisely those principles which constitute the basis of the policy of nonalignment."[29]

The volume of trade between Burma and Yugoslavia has been very small. Burma brought only 1 percent of its needs from Yugoslavia and solid to it about the same in the 1950s. Since 1960 Burma's sales to and purchases from that country have shown no change in proportion to its total foreign trade. In value the largest selling was $7.64 million in 1980 and the smallest selling was $0.18 million in 1974, while the largest buying was $26.6 million in 1987 and the smallest buying was $0.65 million in 1985.[30]

German Democratic Republic

Burma declared the termination of the state of war with Germany on July 9, 1950; Burma and the German Democratic Republic (G.D.R.) established consular relations in October 1960 and full diplomatic relations in the following year. But prior to the establishment of official ties the two states had made contacts with each other. On February 27, 1955, Burma and the G.D.R. signed the first trade agreement of three year's duration, calling for 50,000 tons of rice to be shipped to the G.D.R. within one year.

The 1960s saw frequent visits between government officials and cultural groups of the two countries. But since 1970 such mutual visits have seldom occurred. The situation may in part reflect a change in Burma's relations with East Germany as a result of its closer ties with West Germany.

The G.D.R. provided a small amount of aid to Burma. In 1964 it advanced a credit equivalent to $14 million for health, educational, and sports projects. In 1966 it extended another credit of the same amount to be used by 1970 for the purchase of industrial plants and equipment from the G.D.R. But as part of checking growing Soviet influence in Burma in the late 1970s, East Germany, a satellite state of the Soviet Union, was compelled to phase out its aid projects.

Czechoslovakia

Burma and Czechoslovakia signed a trade agreement of three years' duration on February 14, 1955. On July 25, Burma and Czechoslovakia agreed to establish full diplomatic relations, and the consulate general in the Burma capital would be raised to legation status effective January 1, 1956. Czech President Antonin Novotny paid a visit to Burma on January 27–30, 1963. In a joint communique issued at the end of the visit, Chairman Ne Win and President Novotny expressed their conviction that all international issues could be settled through negotiation. Reference was also made in the communique to the need for further economic and trade cooperation between the two countries. It further stated that Czechoslovakia agreed on Burma's request to supply machinery and equipment, and to send a group of specialists to cooperate with their Burmese counterparts in considering concrete measures for the intensification of mutual cooperation.[31]

General Ne Win paid a four-day state visit to Czechoslovakia in June 1966. Though a study was done on Czechoslovakia's planned economy, industrial and labor set-up, little political significance was attached to the visit. The Burma-Czech joint communique issued on the occasion of the general's visit noted the similarity of views on international issues—world peace, disarmament, prevention of the spread of thermonuclear weapons, and peaceful coexistence. The Czech government agreed to help develop the Burmese economy by delivering plants and engineering equipment.[32]

Czechoslovak Prime Minister Lubomir Strougal paid an official visit to Burma from February 23 to February 26, 1984. At a reception, Burma Prime Minister Maung Maung Kha said that

the limited conflicts in some regions and the spiralling arms race have created tensions in international relations. We regret to observe the parallel emergence of recession in the world economy. These adverse factors constitute a threat to world peace and security and tend to hinder the national efforts of developing countries.

In reply Strougal called for an end to the "new gunboat policy and colonial practice of aggression and intervention,"[33] by which he probably referred to Western powers. In a joint press statement issued at the end of the visit the two prime ministers expressed their satisfaction at the successful development in Burma-Czech relations, discussed the prospects for future cooperation, and reiterated their common desire to sustain relations on the basis of mutual respect and understanding.[34]

Burma has implemented a number of Czech-aided projects under the economic cooperation program between the two countries. A tractor plant started June 16, 1966, was to produce spare parts for Zeta tractors, engines, gear boxes, hydraulic parts, trailers and parts, and molds for waterpumps run with Zeta engines. Other projects included a tire and rubber factory in

Thaton, a diesel injection pump and nozzle project at Malun, a sugarmill project in Zeyawaddy in lower central Burma, extension of the beer brewery in Mandalay, and a leather factory also in Mandalay.[35]

Romania

Burma and Romania established diplomatic relations on March 15, 1956. On February 17 in the previous year, Burma signed a three-year trade agreement with Romania patterned on previous trade pacts between Burma and other Eastern European countries. Under the agreement, Romania would buy annually 20,000 tons of Burmese rice and supply its equivalent in value of consumer goods and machinery. It also established a trade mission to Rangoon. The agreement was extended annually for many years since 1959.

President of Romania Gheorghe Gheorghiu-Dej visited Rangoon on October 20, 1962 and held talks with General Ne Win. In a joint statement issued on October 22, the two leaders expressed their determination to increase their efforts toward settling all international issues through negotiation in helping ensure lasting world peace. They considered a total nuclear test ban to be a necessary first step toward general disarmament and appealed to all nations possessing nuclear capability to enter into such a nuclear test ban agreement. They deplored the continued existence of colonialism and affirmed every nation's right to self-determination. The president and the chairman also reviewed the existing trade relations between the nations and agreed that trade relations should safeguard the interests of the developing nations.[36] Following the Romanian president's visit, a technical cooperation agreement provided for oil and natural gas surveys and development of oil, mining, and chemical industries in Burma.

General Ne Win paid a return visit to Romania on June 24–27, 1966. Talks between the visiting Burmese leader and President Stoica centered on the economic field, particularly the petroleum industry. Six Romanian experts had been working at Burma's People's Oil Industry since the industry was nationalized on January 1, 1963. Ne Win devoted much time to observing the latest techniques in Romania's oil centers, which produced roughly 11.6 million tons a year, making Romania the largest producer of petroleum in Europe at that time. In a joint communique issued at the end of the visit, the two sides agreed to cooperate further with each other and expressed their interest in maintaining peace.[37]

Romanian Prime Minister Constantin Dascalescu visited Burma in May 1985 as part of the general tour of southeast Asia. Dascalescu indicated his country's interest in increasing economic cooperation in oil exploration, chemical industries, transportation, energy, building materials, and agriculture. Burmese Prime Minister Maung Maung Kha paid an official visit to Bucharest in July 1986 and had talks with his Romanian counterpart Constantin Dascalescu on matters of mutual concern to their countries. President San Yu visited Romania in 1987.

Hungary

Burma and the Hungarian People's Republic agreed to establish diplomatic relations on March 5, 1956. The two countries had signed the first trade agreement of one year's duration on February 21, 1955, providing for shipment to Hungary of 20,000 long tons of Burmese rice. Trade between Burma and Hungary has been negligible. In 1972 Burmese Trade Minister Maung Lwin was sent to Budapest to discuss the possibility of increasing the trade between the two countries without results. General Ne Win later paid a state visit to Hungary. He reciprocated Hungarian Premier Jeno Fock's brief visit to Rangoon in February 1971, but principally, he studied the economic reforms that Hungary had implemented since 1968: decentralization, the shouldering of greater responsibilities by plant managers, and incentives.[38] Ne Win wanted to find ways of using such techniques with the peculiarly Burmese socialist environment.

Burmese President San Yu visited Hungary from September 5 to September 9, 1983, his first trip aboard as the chief of state. He said in Budapest: "We seek to build good relations with all countries, irrespective of their economic, social and political systems and we expect other countries to observe these principles in their relations with us."[39] The visiting president held talks with his Hungarian counterpart on bilateral, regional, and international issues of mutual interest.

Poland, Bulgaria, and Albania

Burma has also established diplomatic relations with Poland, Bulgaria, and Albania but made less contacts than with other Eastern European countries. Burma and Poland signed the first trade agreement in Rangoon on November 1, 1955, under which Burma agreed to deliver rice and other agricultural products, minerals, ores, timber, and rubber, in return for Polish supplies of consumer goods, machinery, ships, and other capital equipment. On November 11, 1955, Burmese Prime Minister U Nu arrived in Poland on his good will trip. During his visit it was announced that the Polish and Burmese governments had agreed to exchange diplomatic missions headed by Minister Plenipotentiary. Polish Prime Minister Jozef Cyrankiewicz paid a return visit to Burma from March 18 to March 21, 1957.

Burma and Bulgaria signed a one-year trade agreement for exchange of 20,000 tons of Burmese rice for Bulgarian machinery and other goods on June 26, 1956. Another pact was signed on April 27, 1967, to develop economic and trade relations between the two countries. Bulgarian Deputy Foreign Minister Marinlotov paid a good will visit to Burma on August 8, 1979. Burma's Prime Minister Maung Maung Kha visited Bulgaria in late June 1988. Albanian Prime Minister Mehmet Shehu and members of a delegation stopped over in Rangoon on May 12, 1966, on their way back from the People's Republic of China.

RELATIONS WITH THE MIDDLE EAST, AFRICA, AND LATIN AMERICA

ISRAEL

Burma's relations with Israel, once very close, are now proper and correct. At the very beginning Burma appeared content to subscribe to the general Arab-Asian line of thought and inaction regarding the State of Israel. Although it voted with the Arab-Asian group against Israel's admission to the United Nations in May 1949, Burma recognized the Israel government on December 7, 1949. It was not until July 13, 1952, however, that the Burmese government announced the exchange of diplomatic missions between Burma and Israel and the appointment of the first Israeli minister to Burma.[1] Rangoon's view of Israel took a significant turn after the visit in December 1952 of a top-level Burmese delegation headed by U Kyaw Nyein, the Socialist party leader. The delegation, en route home from a study tour of several European countries, stopped over in Israel at the invitation of the Israeli government. The Burmese visitors were highly impressed by what they saw in Israel.[2] The participation of an Israeli delegation, led by former foreign minister Moshe Sharett, in the First Asian Socialist Conference at Rangoon marked the beginning of Burmese-Israeli friendship. Moshe Sharett in his speech nominating U Ba Swe for the chairmanship of the conference paid high praise to Burma by saying: "I believe, comrades, that all of us know that this has not been merely a trip to a conference but also a voyage to Burma, a country which has a special place in the hearts of all of us, a country which has gone through a heroic struggle, and a country in the independence of which we all rejoice."[3] Before long special affinity between Burma and Israel developed because the Burmese were pleased to receive aid and technical advice from Israel, a new and small state, without fear of political strings attached and "imperialist influence." They also admired the Israeli political system and national goal which provided them with a model for building a modern country on the basis of socialism and democracy. Israel, on its part, in the arid desert of Arab hatred, sought close friends in the international community.

Burma's intimate relations with Israel were manifested by its support of Israel on several occasions. At the Bogor Conference held in December 1954 to prepare for the Asian-African Conference, Burmese Prime Minister U Nu insisted on inviting Israel. He had even threatened not to attend a conference from which Israel would be excluded. But since Israel's participation would provoke all Arab states to boycott the conference, thereby denying Africa adequate representation, U Nu finally withdrew his proposal.[4] At the Bandung Conference held in April 1955, U Nu opposed the Arab countries to gain the conference's support in their quarrel with Israel.[5] During his trip to the Middle East after the Bandung Conference, U Nu planned to visit both Egypt and Israel. When Egypt asked him not to visit Israel, he carried out his trip to Israel and cancelled the one to Egypt.[6]

U Nu arrived in Israel in late May 1955 for a nine-day good will visit, the first to be paid to Israel by the prime minister of a foreign country. The visiting prime minister traveled extensively throughout Israel and took great interest in the Israeli kibbutz system of self-defended frontier settlements. Four villages modeled in this system were later built in the Shan state west of the Salween River about 125 miles from the Chinese border. A joint communique issued by U Nu and his Israeli counterpart Sharett declared that the two countries were willing to pool their efforts for their mutual economic, social, and cultural advancement, and dedicated "to the principles of the U.N. Charter and the ideals of peace, progress, democratic freedom and social justice."[7]

Burma and Israel signed a three-year trade agreement in December 1955 on a barter basis with Burmese rice for Israel's goods. On March 5, 1956, an economic cooperation agreement was signed which included, among other things, provisions for setting up a rubber tire factory, a ceramic and glassware factory, a paint and varnish plant, and a $30-million agricultural development in Shan state.

Israeli Prime Minister Moshe Sharett arrived in Rangoon on September 21, 1956, for a seven-day visit. In August 1957 the Burmese Defense Services Institute sponsored a joint construction and housing venture with an Israeli company Solel Bone, which would bring in engineers, technicians, machinery, and equipment. Subsequently many other joint-venture enterprises between the two countries developed. On January 2, 1958, Israeli Chief of Staff of the Defense Forces Major-General Moshe Dayan and Director-General of the Defense Ministry Shimon Peres visited Burma.

General Ne Win, prime minister of the caretaker government, paid an official visit to Israel on June 8–15, 1959. During the visit the general toured immigrant settlements in rural areas and visited industrial and research establishments and military installations. At the close of his visit, he said: "Impressions which I gained during my visit are deep and will surely be lasting, and I shall be able in future to appreciate more fully all questions relating to our two countries. . . . It is my firm belief that the bonds of friendship and cooperation between our two countries will grow from strength to strength."[8]

Israeli Prime Minister David Ben-Gurion visited Burma on December 5–21, 1961, principally to explore the possibilities of establishing relations with the People's Republic of China and of lessening tension with the United Arab Republic (of which Egypt was a part), with both of whom Burma was friendly. During his visit, the Rangoon University Council conferred him an honorary LL.D. degree. In a joint communique issued on December 21, Burmese Prime Minister U Nu and Ben-Gurion noted with great pleasure the development of friendly relations between their two governments and peoples, and affirmed their hope that these relations would continue to grow. The prime minister of Israel, as a token of his faith in the great potentialities of Burma's agriculture, offered a team of Israeli technicians to help the development work of the dry zone for a period of two years. The prime Minister of Burma gratefully accepted this offer.[9]

Israeli Foreign Minister Golda Meir visited Burma on February 4, 1962. Israel agreed to prepare an architectural design for a new mausoleum to house the tombs of the late General Aung San and his martyred colleagues. The Namsam Resettlement Project would be expanded with Israel's help. Since the 1960s mutual visits between high-ranking Burma and Israeli officials have been infrequent.

In spite of its close relations with Israel in the early years, the Burmese unanimously deplored Israel's incursion into the Sinai Peninsula in 1956. The Rangoon government, adhering to the principle of settling disputes by negotiations without force, voted to condemn the Israeli action at the UN General Assembly as an act of aggression. In explanation of Burma's position on this incident, Prime Minister U Nu said:

Despite our friendship for Israel, we were compelled to join in the condemnation of this invasion as an act of aggression. We recognize that Israel could plead extenuating factors for the attack. The Arabs make no secret of their hostility toward her, and the large scale shipments of arms to Egypt during 1956 must have been a source of considerable concern to Israel. But we cannot subscribe to the doctrine of "preventive war." We do not think it can ever be morally justified. Besides, today the world lives on the edge of a volcano. Any disturbance may cause that volcano to erupt. In our view, no nation has the right to take such a risk. We were therefore gratified when Israel bowed to the authority of the United Nations and withdrew from Egyptian soil.[10]

EGYPT

Burma and Egypt established diplomatic relations on August 12, 1953, and their respective legations in Rangoon and Cairo were raised to the status of embassies on October 1, 1957. Earlier in January 1953, the Socialist party of Egypt had sent representatives to Rangoon to take part in the Asian Socialist Conference. President Gamal Nasser of Egypt met U Nu in Rangoon before and after the Bandung Conference in April 1955 and accompanied U Nu to and from Bandung. The two developed a personal friendship that promoted good relations between Burma and Egypt, and later with the United Arab Republic (U.A.R.). A zealous pacifist, U Nu once fancied himself a mediator of the Arab-Israeli conflict, but President Nasser reportedly expressed his displeasure at Burma's Israeli ties.[11]

The Israeli invasion of Egypt in 1956 drew Burma to Egypt's side in denouncing the Israeli action. However, Burma did not agree with Egypt that the Suez Canal should be kept closed. Prime Minister U Ba Swe stated that as an international waterway the Suez Canal should be kept open to all nations.[12]

Prime Minister Ne Win arrived in Cairo in September 1959, and he visited Cairo again in December 1961, probably to mediate Arab-Israeli relations at the suggestion of Israeli Prime Minister Ben-Gurion following Ben-Gurion's visit to Burma. But no discussion of this matter with Nasser was mentioned publicly. During his visit, Ne Win showed particular interest in Nasser's new socialist policy, which he thought might be able to provide the basis of some ties between the two countries.

OTHER COUNTRIES IN AFRICA, THE MIDDLE EAST, AND LATIN AMERICA

Burma developed commercial ties with the Union of South Africa in its early years. Burma imported from South Africa goods worth $4.6 million in 1962—mainly agricultural products, manufactured goods, metals, and minerals. To South Africa Burma exported wood, oils, fibers, and other products worth $1 million in 1962. Early in November 1962, Burma voted at the UN General Assembly for sanctions against South Africa because of its apartheid system, and from November 15 it banned trade with that country. Hence the trade between the two countries dropped sharply in 1963—supplies to South Africa were $0.7 million and purchases from South Africa were $0.5 million. Since 1964 Burma-South Africa trade has become almost nonexistent.[13]

The 1960s saw the emerging of many independent countries in Africa which were former French, British, and Belgian colonies. Burma extended "a warm welcome to all these new nations as they enter the community of nations and has given official recognition to all those which have already declared their independence."[14] However, normal contacts between Burma and these newly independent countries as well as other countries in Africa, the Middle East, and Latin America have been sporadic and meager. Apart from Egypt and Israel which have exchanged ambassadors with Burma as noted above, Algeria, Argentina, Brazil, Chile, Cuba, Iran, Iraq, Mauritius, Morocco, Nigeria, and Syria have embassies in Rangoon, but find no Burmese embassy in their countries. Burma also has no diplomatic mission in any other countries in Africa, the Middle East, and Latin America.[15] This lack of diplomatic missions evidently results from the shortage of trained diplomatic personnel, insufficient funds, and the minor commercial business carried out between Burma and those countries.

The meetings of the UN General Assembly and its specialized organizations as well as specific regional and international conferences have provided opportunities for Burma to contact these Third World countries. The Afro-Asian group in the United Nations to which Burma belonged was one arena for diplomatic interplay among its members in the 1950s. The nonaligned summit conference, which consisted of participants from ninety-four nations until Burma's withdrawal in 1979, brought Burma into contact with almost all Third World countries.

Official visits between Burma and these countries in Africa, the Middle East, and Latin America have been few in number. Shaikh Sabah Al-Ahmed Al-Sabah, minister of foreign affairs of Kuwait, paid a good will visit to Burma in May 1964. President Farik Ibrahim Abboud of the Sudan stopped over at the Rangoon Airport on May 16, 1964, en route to the People's Republic of China. the president of Mali made a brief stopover in Rangoon on November 10, 1964, on his way home from Indonesia. Ali Lakdari, personal envoy of Algerian President S. Guellal and Algerian ambassador to India, arrived in Rangoon on June 7, 1965. Burma's Deputy Minister for Trade Khin Maung Gyi and members of his delegation toured countries in Africa in July 1979 to find new markets for Burmese rice. Flevio B. Pardo, vice-chairman of the council of ministers and special envoy of the president of Cuba visited Burma in August 1979, apparently related to the forthcoming nonaligned summit conference in Havana in September.

Burma's trade with countries in Africa, the Middle East, and Latin America has been limited or nonexistent, with a few exceptions. Mauritius has been a steady customer of Burmese rice. In recent years Niger, Senegal, Iran, Kuwait, United Arab Emirates, and Saudi Arabia have become Burma's customers, and Morocco and Egypt have become Burma's suppliers. Irregular trade relations exist between Burma and Cote d'Ivoire, Venezuela, and Brazil. Burma's exports to Cote d'Ivoire registered $21.01 million in 1979 and $8.6 million in 1980; to Venezuela, $14.18 million in 1979 only; to Brazil, $14.26 million in 1979, $23.43 million in 1980, and $18.25 million in 1981.[16]

13

RELATIONS WITH INTERNATIONAL AND REGIONAL ORGANIZATIONS

THE UNITED NATIONS AND ITS SPECIALIZED AGENCIES

Burma is a member of the United Nations and a member of all but two of its specialized agencies: International Fund for Agricultural Development (IFAD) and World Intellectual Property Organization (WIPO). On February 27, 1948, less than two months after attaining independence, Burma applied for membership in the United Nations and became its fifty-eighth member on April 19 following the unanimous approval in sequence by the Security Council and the General Assembly. The Burmese derive a feeling of pride and prestige from participating as an equal member with large nations in the world organization. But Burma's foremost objective in joining the United Nations was to protect itself against aggression. In the words of Prime Minister U Nu, "When we joined the United Nations organization . . . what was foremost in our minds was the expectation of U.N. assistance when our country should be subjected to aggression by a stronger power."[1]

Burma supported UN military action against North Korea in June 1950. U Nu considered this as a noble precedent for the world organization to protect small member nations like Burma. He said: "As soon as aggression started in South Korea, the United Nations went to its assistance. This has set up a noble precedent. Henceforth, if aggression occurs elsewhere, there too the United Nations must step in. . . . This is the great hope, the hope for small member nations like us."[2]

Nevertheless, Burma was somewhat disillusioned with the United Nations' response to its complaint against the Kuomintang troops in March 1953. The resolution adopted by the General Assembly deplored and condemned the presence of foreign forces in Burma which must be disarmed and either agree to internment or leave forthwith, without referring to Nationalist China as the aggressor, as Burma had requested, but the Burmese delegation voted for the resolution.[3] Later at the Bandung Conference in 1955 U Nu expressed disappointment with this UN action when he said:

We found the United Nations, which acted with speed and energy in Korea, unwilling even to bring in a verdict of "aggression" against the Kuomintang regime. It seemed to us that the United Nations had more than one yard-stick for measuring aggression. In our view aggression is aggression regardless of the source from which it comes.[4]

Despite disappointment with the United Nations, Burma still has faith in it as an instrument for the promotion of world peace and progress. During his visit to the United States, U Nu said:

The Charter of the United Nations is in effect one great mutual security pact. Despite its failure to come up to our expectations, our faith in the United Nations remains undiminished. . . . A divided world stands in greater need of a common forum to discuss differences than a world united. . . . Our task therefore is to strengthen it, and to make it the effective organization which had been planned by its founders.[5]

Burma has been a faithful member of the United Nations throughout the years. As a developing nation, it also has profound interests in UN development programs in economic development, health, education, and social advancement. The United Nations Children's Fund (UNICEF), the World Health Organization (WHO), and the Technical Assistance Board (TAB) set up offices in Rangoon in the early 1950s at the invitation of the government of Burma. Since then many more UN specialized agencies have been created, and cooperation between these agencies and Burma has grown tremendously. Technical assistance extended by the UN specialized agencies to Burma is in the form of advisory services, feasibility studies, equipment, and fellowships, and is done through three offices. The United Nations Development Program (UNDP) is in charge of its own undertakings as well as that of other specialized agencies except UNICEF and WHO, which maintain their own representation, but the UNDP has been assigned the role of coordinating all UN technical assistance to Burma.[6]

Table 13.1
United Nations System Technical Assistance (in US dollars) 1973–87

	1973	1974	1975	1976	1977	1978	1979	1980	1981	1982	1983	1984	1985	1986	1987	Total
UNDP	2,503,880	3,069,000	5,967,165	3,908,124	4,794,600	4,575,774	7,091,680	9,169,698	10,169,725	11,065,213	8,799,716	7,772,178	12,667,896	12,189,193	10,646,000	114,416,842
UNICEF	1,117,000	1,129,400	1,362,300	2,635,000	6,058,520	8,780,520	4,042,700	6,646,000	3,813,700	4,912,900	6,737,800	12,934,100	10,072,500	8,033,200	5,879,000	84,154,640
WHO	493,109	515,400	513,000	629,700	881,500	889,100	996,900	1,292,600	2,714,100	2,950,613	2,128,180	3,451,704	4,366,891	4,127,021	1,995,000	28,044,818
ESCAP													122,932	41,291	24,000	188,723
FAO				119,702		347,000	347,000	282,000	729,000	51,000	2,545,940		6,500	946,024		5,374,166
IAEA					66,800	96,905	39,782	137,800	114,658	161,227	186,828	152,885	190,869	113,807	93,000	1,384,561
ILO													101,100	3,321	12,000	116,421
UNESCO			1,000,000	52,150		72,850	28,410	38,410	26,000	48,850			56,260			1,327,930
UNFDAL				657,100	1,333,000	2,910,000	2,529,700	495,000	786,340	1,579,250	1,208,750	832,600	661,300	2,207,167	2,503,000	17,703,207
UNFPA			431,091		47,000	195,640	2,600	49,196	80,450	49,701	225,878	143,033	44,687	69,482	125,000	1,463,763
UNIDO				10,800		11,818				15,019	5,327	21,177	37,408	30,500		132,049
WFP			1,735,700				3,273,500									5,009,700
WHO					35,600	47,200	98,500	122,100	28,430		24,841	42,600	57,200	33,000	27,000	516,471
UNHCR						400,000	2,700,000	730,252	1,085,000	865,000	250,000					6,030,252
UNIDRO												15,000				15,000
TOTAL	4,113,989	4,713,800	11,009,259	8,012,576	13,217,020	18,326,807	21,150,772	18,990,056	19,577,403	21,698,773	22,213,260	25,365,279	28,385,543	27,794,006	21,304,000	265,872,543

Source: Compiled by the author from the Annual Reports of the United Nations Development Corporation on the Socialist Republic of the Union of Burma from 1973 to 1987.

The expenditure of technical assistance to Burma from the United Nations system had jumped to $21.3 million in 1987 from $37,000 a year in the early 1950s, with a total of $265,872,543 between 1973 and 1987. An organizational breakdown of such assistance is shown in Table 13.1.

In addition, Burma has received capital assistance from the World Bank. Burma became a member of the International Bank for Reconstruction and Development (IBRD) in 1952 and of the International Development Association (IDA) in 1962. Between 1956 and 1961 the IBRD made three loans to Burma totaling $33.1 million, all for transportation projects. No lending was requested between 1962 and 1973 because of the military government's strict socialist policy. Burma resumed borrowing from the World Bank in 1973 after its economic situation worsened. Since then, all World Bank assistance to Burma has been from the IDA, which does not charge interest but only a service charge of 3/4 to 1 percent to cover administrative costs. IDA credits are repayable in fifty years including a grace period of ten years. As of the end of 1987 the IBRD/IDA had extended to Burma forty-one loans totaling $1,036.05 million.[7]

THE NONALIGNED MOVEMENT

The nonaligned conference was first held in Belgrade in September 1961 with twenty-five countries in attendance. The participants had to pursue a foreign policy of national independence based on peaceful coexistence, support of national liberation movements, and avoidance of multilateral or bilateral military alliances with the great powers—the criteria for participation as agreed on at the Cairo preparatory meeting held the previous June.[8] Since then the number of nonaligned countries has increased and there were 101 represented at the eighth nonaligned summit in Harare, Zimbabwe in September 1986, including almost all the countries of the Third World.

The First Nonaligned Conference dealt with the same basic themes as the Bandung Conference before it, but while Bandung's emphasis had been on decolonization and economic development, the Belgrade meeting's first priority was world peace. At that early stage nonalignment did not take on any East-West factionalism; the United States and the Soviet Union were equally held to blame for international tensions, and pleas for peace were made of both without prejudice. Once the issue of colonization and international economics came to the fore in 1973 following the transition of the Cold War to detente, the nonaligned movement took on a decidedly anti-Western hue, because the developed capitalist countries held colonial possessions and dominated the international economic system to which the Third World belonged. Subsequently, the movement became a pro-Soviet group, the "alignment of the nonaligned" in Henry Kissinger's words, under the domination of the radicals led by Cuba. For the radicals the Soviet-bloc socialist countries, by the very nature of their system and their politics, were natural allies of the nonaligned. The Sino-Soviet rivalry and the split of the developing countries into oil-exporting and oil-importing groups have also intensified the internal tensions and conflicts within the movement.[9]

Although a founding member, Burma placed relatively low priority on its role in the nonaligned movement. This was reflected by the fact that except for the first and fifth summits, in which Prime Ministers U Nu and Sein Win participated, all other summits had not been attended by the Burmese head of state or government. Burma had expressed concern over the movement's involvement in bloc politics. On October 16, 1964, a state-run newspaper's editorial had this comment:

The nonaligned nations do not and should not constitute any bloc. Nor is nonalignment merely the striking of an attitude between the different power blocs. Nonalignment preserves independence of thought and action. It is characterized by the qualities of detachment, good sense and goodwill. That is why nonalignment does not believe it is its duty to condemn this or that nation in any conflict or controversy. Its entire effort is dedicated to the search for peaceful solutions acceptable to all parties to a conflict. It is prepared to search till all peaceful means have been exhausted.[10]

At Belgrade in July 1969 the Burmese delegate to a Consultative Conference of Nonaligned Countries officially argued against the formation of a Third World bloc. He said, "the launching of a process of intensified activity of nonaligned countries would sooner or later bring the nonaligned countries as a group into a confrontation with power blocs and organizations [and] . . . the policy of nonalignment would be jeopardized."[11]

At the Sixth Nonaligned Summit Conference in Havana on September 6, 1979, when the question of Cambodian representation was deliberated, Cuba, the host country, manipulated the meeting by leaving the Cambodian seat vacant. The following day, Burmese Foreign Minister Myint Maung proposed that the nonaligned movement dissolve itself and make a fresh start with only those countries genuinely subscribing to the philosophy of nonalignment. Otherwise Burma would withdraw from the movement. Myint Maung said:

The delegation of Burma has come to Havana in the hope that the principle which inspired the founding members of the Nonaligned Movement can be preserved and given new life here. The trends of discussions we have seen so far have, however, deeply disappointed us. . . . The principles of the Movement are not recognizable any more; they are not merely dim, they are dying. . . . And it is not enough for the Movement to just exist in name . . . there are those . . . who deliberately exploit the Movement to gain their own grand designs. We cannot allow ourselves to be so exploited. The delegation of Burma therefore puts this motion . . . before the Summit: that we do resolve to begin anew, dissolving the Movement as it stands torn and divided today; that we do appoint a committee of members to draft a Charter, defining with clarity the inviolable principles to which the Movement should be dedicated, the qualifications and code of conduct for membership and the consequences of its violation, the functions and powers of the principal organs of the movement and the procedures. When the draft charter is done, let us consider and adopt it, admit qualified members and start again, purified and renewed. . . . Should the Summit reach no decision and let things drift, the delegation will withdraw from the Conference and Burma will end her participation in the Movement.[12]

The conference took no action and at the thirty-fourth regular session of the UN General Assembly held on September 28, 1979, Burmese Foreign Minister Myint Maung officially declared his government's decision to quit the nonaligned movement. He added his government did not plan to organize a new movement in the cause of nonalignment. If, however, "like minds" should move one day toward a community of nations sharing similar views and values, willing to dedicate themselves to clear principles of nonalignment, Burma might become a member of that community.[13]

The foreign ministers of the nonaligned countries met in New York on October 4–6, 1979 to discuss a proposed common policy statement for presentation to the UN General Assembly, agreed that the Coordinating Committee of the Nonaligned Movement should ask the government of Burma to rescind its decision. However, General San Yu, then the secretary of the Burmese State Council, reaffirmed the Burmese position toward the nonaligned movement in his speech to the Burmese People's Assembly in Rangoon on October 8, 1979.[14]

Several factors may be attributed to Burma's dramatic decision to withdraw from the nonaligned movement at the Havana Summit. First, the movement, since it was no longer truly nonaligned, would exacerbate bloc antagonisms and endanger world peace. Pe Kin, a distinguished Burmese diplomat, had this to say: "As a founder-member, Burma had no wish to see a movement so ideologically launched to become an instrument that favored any particular bloc, and an instrument that would bring tension once more into this world."[15] Second, the movement, as it stood then, would compromise Burma's own neutralist policy in foreign affairs. An editorial in *The Guardian* made this point clear when it stated, "Burma does not favor the systems of blocs as such and does not wish to place itself in a position where politically speaking it is just lined up with a particular group or bound to it in regard to its future activities in the field of foreign affairs."[16] Third, Burma's decision may have signaled an implicit protest against the Soviet influence on the movement. Burma had already felt uneasy at the growing power of the Soviet Union and its Southeast Asian surrogate, Vietnam, in Indochina, following the new Indochina conflicts in 1978. Fourth, Fidel Castro, the Cuban leader, strongly accused "the ruling clique in Peking" as the new ally of U.S. imperialism in his opening address at the Summit. Burma's open challenges of Cuban actions at the summit were undoubtedly intended to give moral support for China. Not surprisingly, in the wake of the summit, Chinese Foreign Minister Huang Hua was sent to Rangoon to express the deep appreciation of his government and people for Burma's just stand in upholding justice and resolutely safeguarding the principles of the non-aligned movement.[17]

SEATO

There are three considerations for Burma to join any regional organization: the fundamental principles of foreign policy, China's attitude toward the organization concerned, and the internal situation. In other words, to join a regional organization Burma must not violate its neutralist foreign policy, must not antagonize China, and must benefit domestic policy. Consequently, Burmese participation in regional organizations is very limited. Since the end of World War II, the following groupings have come into existence in Asia: the Colombo Plan, the Southeast Asian Treaty Organization (SEATO), the Association of Southeast Asia (ASA), MAPHILINDO, the Asian and Pacific Council (ASPAC), the Asian Development Bank (ADB), and the Association of Southeast Asian Nations (ASEAN). Burma has not associated with any of them except the Colombo Plan and ADB.

Starting with the discussion between U.S. Secretary of State John Foster Dulles and British Prime Minister Anthony Eden for united action against Communist expansion in Southeast Asia in London on April 13, 1954, SEATO was founded under the Manila pact by the United States, the Philippines, France, Pakistan, Australia, the United Kingdom, Thailand, and New Zealand in Manila on September 8, 1954. Its aim was to provide for "collective defense action to resist armed attack . . . and to counter subversion directed from without against the territorial integrity and sovereignty of any of its members." The Manila pact signatories also designated Laos, Cambodia, and South Vietnam as countries against which an armed attack would be considered as endangering their own security.

But as the years went on, the Cold War with China gave way to detente, and SEATO began to look less and less practical to changing circumstances in Southeast Asia. In 1973, the alliance's military aspect was played down. With Communist forces winning in Indochina in 1975, Thailand and the Philippines accommodated their policies to the new regimes in Indochina as well as to China and proposed that SEATO be scrapped altogether. The United States, Britain, Australia, and New Zealand agreed to this suggestion. The two other members—Pakistan and France—had already left SEATO. France stopped taking part in the organization's military activities in 1967 and stopped providing funds in 1974, and Pakistan pulled out in 1973 after secession of its Eastern section and the creation of Bangladesh. SEATO was finally dissolved on June 30, 1977.[18]

Throughout the negotiations of setting up the regional defense organization, the British government was in favor of associating India, Pakistan, Burma, Ceylon, and Indonesia—known as the Colombo Powers—with any proposed guarantee or defense treaty relating to Southeast Asia. From the point of view of the United States, bringing the five Asian Colombo Powers prominently into the situation would be regarded as important and welcome.[19] British Undersecretary for Foreign Affairs Arthur Dodds-Parker went to Rangoon in August 1954. He was followed later by U.S. Secretary of State John Foster Dulles. They did not succeed in getting Burma to join SEATO. SEATO proved to be too much of a pro-Western and anti-Communist, particularly anti-China, military alliance to attract Burma. Burmese Prime Minister U Nu asserted: "We will not be a party to the proposed SEATO. We must not be caught under the clash of swords."[20] On September 13, 1954, five days after the formation of SEATO, he reaffirmed: "In foreign relations, we refuse to align ourselves with any power bloc and at the same time we are friendly with both."[21] During his visit to the United States in the summer of 1955, U Nu again spoke of Burmese alliance with a great power military bloc (meaning SEATO) as incompatible with its existence as an independent state. He said:

In the present circumstances of Burma her membership in any alliance with a great power military bloc is incompatible with her continued existence as an independent state. . . . Burma has no choice but to pursue her policy of neutrality if she wishes to preserve her independence, and that to us is more important than anything else. It is part of her defense, and an important part, against subversion.[22]

Moreover, SEATO had been bitterly denounced by China. In his address to the National People's Congress, Chinese Prime Minister Chou En-lai said that "the purpose of the United States [in forming SEATO] is to destroy the Geneva Conference agreements . . .to split Asia, show its hostility to the People's Republic of China . . . and create new tensions."[23] Hence, Burma could not take the risk of offending Peking by joining SEATO. In addition, Burma's preoccupation with stabilizing and improving its own internal conditions at that time did not permit it to join SEATO. In practice, nevertheless, Burmese potential association with SEATO was effectively undermined by Chou En-lai's "successful diplomatic coup" in visiting Rangoon for talks with U Nu in June 1954. The Five Principles of Peaceful Coexistence proposed by Chou and agreed to by Nu in their joint statement gave Burma a strong assurance of peaceful and friendly relations with China, thus mitigating Burma's need to join a military alliance. Though Burma refused to join SEATO, many Burmese were secretly glad to have such a defense organization that might well serve to protect Burma's independence. The *New York Times* had this to report:

The other day a Burmese said in private, "Sure we say we are opposed to the mutual defense organization in Southeast Asia. We say it because we don't want to antagonize China. It is easy to take a strong stand when you are small if you've got an ocean or buffer country between you and a large nation. We act the way we do as a matter of self-preservation. . . . Many of us are secretly glad there's a defense organization even though we are not part of it. It is almost like having one's cake and eating it too."[24]

ASA

ASA (Association of Southeast Asia) was created by the Philippines, the Federation of Malaya, and Thailand—the three non-Communist countries with active Communist-supported insurgent movements in Southeast Asia—under the Bangkok Declaration of July 31, 1961. This was the first regional grouping inspired and organized by Asians, and it was an outgrowth of the South East Asia Friendship and Economic Treaty (SEAFET) initiated by Prime Minister of the Federation of Malaya Tunku Abdul Rahman during his visit to Manila in early January 1959.[25] According to Tunku, the countries of Southeast Asia were so small that unless they could work together for the good of the whole, there was no possibility of them ever becoming economically strong. And he was convinced that poverty would facilitate the expansion of communism. The aims of ASA, as set out in the Bangkok Declaration, were to establish effective machinery for friendly consultations, collaboration, and mutual assistance in the economic, social, cultural, scientific, and administrative fields; provide for exchanges of facilities and information in these fields; promote regional studies; provide machinery for cooperation in resource use, trade promotion, industry, and transport; study problems of commodity trade; and generally, consult and cooperate with one another so as to achieve the aims and purposes of the association as well as to contribute more effectively to the work of existing international organizations and agencies.[26]

During the first two years, ASA gained momentum. In 1963 the Philippines renewed its century-old claim to Sabad in response to the formation of the new Federation of Malaysia. The claim caused severance of relations between the two countries, which resulted in the suspension of ASA's activities. With Filipino-Malaysian rapprochement following the inauguration of new Philippine President Ferdinand Marcos in December 1965, ASA was reactivated in March 1966. Soon after the formation of ASEAN (Association of Southeast Asian Nations) in August 1966, spokesmen for the Philippines, Malaysia, and Thailand announced that most ongoing ASA programs would be incorporated into ASEAN in order to prevent duplication of activities and secure optimum use of available resources.[27] It hence implicated a virtual merger of ASA with ASEAN.

ASA was an economic and cultural cooperation organization and was not highly ideological. In the words of Tunku Abdul Rahman:

This organization is in no way intended to be an anti-Western bloc or anti-Eastern bloc, or, for that matter, a political bloc of any kind. It is not connected in any way with the various organizations which are in existence today; it is purely a Southeast Asian economic and cultural cooperation organization and has no backing whatsoever for any foreign source.[28]

As such, the founding member countries of ASA hoped to leave the door open to new members. But throughout ASA's life, it never succeeded in enticing a fourth member. As for Burma, the decidedly pro-Western connection of the three member countries and China's hostile attitudes toward ASA[29] were undoubtedly its major reasons for not joining it. Burma had made its position clear even before ASA was formally set up. Earlier in October 1959, Tunku Abdul Rahman sent letters to the leaders of all non-Communist Southeast Asian states, soliciting their comments on his proposed group and suggesting that they meet to discuss it. In reply Rangoon found it "inadvisable" to participate "at this stage." Nevertheless,

Thai officials continued to hope almost to the actual forming of ASA that Burma might join, for the purpose of broadening the organization's political orientation to include a neutral.[30]

MAPHILINDO

MAPHILINDO was formed by Malaya, the Philippines, and Indonesia under the Manila Declaration on August 15, 1963. It was named after the initial letters of the member countries and an outgrowth of MAPHI. Earlier in July 1962 when the idea of a Malaysia Federation had taken firm root and its implementation by London seemed assured, Philippine President Macapagal announced his proposal of a "Greater Malay Confederation" comprised of the Philippines, Malaya, Singapore, Sarawak, Brunei, and Sabah, a grouping of MAPHI as a means to forestall Sabah's inclusion in Malaysia. At that time the Philippines was pressing the historical claim of the Sulu sultanate to this portion of North Borneo. Coincidentally, after Indonesia's success in acquiring West Irian, Jakarta began its own campaign against the formation of Malaysia, which was considered a malicious British scheme to encircle Indonesia. President Macapagal welcomed Indonesian cooperation in opposing the formation of Malaysia. It also afforded the Philippines opportunities to improve its relations with Indonesia, its powerful neighbor, and forge for itself an "Asian identity," which it badly needed because of its reputation as only a follower of the United States. Accordingly, Macapagal was determined to extend his MAPHI proposal to include Indonesia. Indonesia was pleased to obtain extra help in its opposition endeavor. During that period, furthermore, President Sukarno of Indonesia was also particularly interested in grouping like-minded states (ASA, the then exiting Asian organization, was suspected as a subregional counterpart of SEATO) and expanding Indonesian influence among Southeast Asian countries to eliminate Western military presence in the region, including the withdrawal of U.S. installations at Clark Field and Subic Bay in the Philippines. Malaya also wanted close relations with these two neighbors in order to settle any differences with them and to keep its future federation from becoming isolated in the archipelago.[31] The Philippine president's initiative, after months of complex tripartite negotiations, led to a summit meeting in Manila of Malaya, the Philippines, and Indonesia from July 30 to August 5, 1963, in which three agreements—the Manila Declaration, the Manila Accord, and the Joint Statement—were finally reached and signed by the leaders of the three countries.[32]

The three leaders agreed to use a UN survey team to determine how the peoples of Sabah and Sarawak felt about the Malaysia Federation. Finally in accordance with the Bandung Declaration, the agreement required the participants to abstain from making any collective defense arrangements that would serve the particular interests of any of the big powers. The three countries took initial steps toward the establishment of MAPHILINDO by holding frequent and regular consultations at all levels with the objectives to strengthen fraternal relations and cooperation among their peoples in the economic, social, and cultural fields and to maintain the stability and security of the area, free from subversion in any form.[33]

MAPHILINDO soon began to die down when Indonesia and the Philippines disputed the UN survey's results that the Borneo peoples wished to join Malaysia, on the pretext that the procedures agreed upon in Manila were not followed properly. Indonesia renewed its confrontation against Malaysia, and the Philippines insisted on its claim to Sabah within the framework of the principle of self-determination. Consequently, MAPHILINDO was in a state of suspension. At the initiative of the Philippine president, the leaders of the three countries met again in Tokyo in June. But the summit conference failed to break the deadlock in the Malaysian dispute.

MAPHILINDO was further weakened by the formation of a new Indonesian government under General Suharto, which adopted a new policy toward Malaysia. The Philippines viewed the suspension of MAPHILINDO as a demise. In January 1966, the Malaysia prime minister formally turned its back on MAPHILINDO as an undesirable racial concept.[34] For their national interest all three states soon indicated a preference for broad regional political and economic cooperation.[35]

MAPHILINDO never consisted of more than the three charter members. During the earlier days of the talks between the presidents of the Philippines and Indonesia in Manila in January 1964, it was agreed that MAPHILINDO could be extended to include other Southeast Asian countries, perhaps Thailand, Burma, Laos, and Cambodia. But the joint communique merely said in the end that it was "essential to strengthen MAPHILINDO as a living reality in the firm belief that within its framework constructive and equitable solutions can be found for many of the serious problems of the region," including the Malaysian dispute. Burma definitely had nothing to do with MAPHILINDO. In view of the three countries' involvement in serious politics among themselves during the organization's short life, it seemed most likely that Burma was neither asked nor pressed to join it.

ASPAC

The Asian and Pacific Council (ASPAC) was established by nine countries on June 16, 1966, at the meeting of their foreign ministers held in Seoul. The nine charter members were Australia, the Republic of China (Taiwan), Japan, South Korea, Malaysia, the Philippines, New Zealand, Thailand, and South Vietnam. The organization grew out of a proposal by Lee Tong Won, the South Korean foreign minister, in September 1964, and a preparatory meeting at the ambassadorial level was held in Bangkok in March 1965.[36] Several unofficial reasons led to ASPAC's creation: (1) fear that a weak and largely destitute non-Communist but pro-Western Asia would have to come to terms with the future modes of regional—that is, collective—security; (2) apprehension that the Communist states, on the other hand, were moving into positions where they could increasingly threaten Asia with military and political pressures; and (3) serious considerations that some form of unity had to be fashioned for the smaller states if they were to maintain their independence and freedom of political action.[37]

The original purpose of ASPAC, as envisaged by its Korean sponsor, was an anti-Communist defense alliance. But, as this idea was canvassed among other Asian and Pacific governments, it was transmuted into something blander. At the Seoul conference, the Japanese and Malaysian governments made it clear that they did not favor a militantly anti-Communist grouping. As a result, ASPAC was not anti-Communist in character, much less military in nature. It was largely a cultural and economic association.

ASPAC was a loose grouping and had no permanent headquarters. It held its plenary session in Bangkok in 1967, and thereafter met annually in the capitals of the other countries alternately. After the June 1972 conference in Seoul, serious doubts emerged concerning ASPAC's viability. In the wake of the Sino-U.S. detente resulting from U.S. President Richard Nixon's visit to Peking in February 1972 and later the Tokyo-Peking agreement to normalize relations, strong voices were raised to its dissolution. On March 12, 1973, Malaysia announced withdrawal from ASPAC on the ground that "there is no point in belonging to an organization which has done nothing" and Malaysia wanted "to concentrate on cooperation in the Association of Southeast Asian Nations." Then the 1973 conference scheduled for Bangkok was postponed indefinitely,[38] and ASPAC was in fact disbanded.

ASPAC was committed only to political, economic, and social cooperation. By not taking on an anti-Communist military character, the group left the door open to other countries, particularly neutrals. In fact, there were more talks of increasing the membership of the Council, to include such countries as Burma, Singapore, Cambodia, and Laos.[39] Throughout the entire period of its existence, however, Laos attended the council meetings only as an observer, and no new member was added to the organization. Burma certainly was not interested in joining ASPAC, chiefly because of the ideology of member countries and Peking's hostile attitude toward the council. All the nine member nations were Western-leaning and opposed communism in varying degrees. And the P.R.C. had attacked ASPAC as an apparatus for support of U.S. and Japanese national objectives.[40]

ASEAN

ASEAN (Association of Southeast Asian Nations) was born at a time when London had announced plans to pull out east of Suez, the U.S. electorate was showing an increasing disenchantment with its government's military involvement in Vietnam, and Peking was exporting its cultural revolution to Hong Kong, Cambodia, and Burma. Formed by Thailand, Malaysia, Singapore, Indonesia, and the Philippines under the Bangkok Declaration on August 8, 1967, ASEAN was an expansion of ASA with the addition of Indonesia and Singapore and made possible by the end of the former's confrontation against Malaysia in June 1966 and the separation of the latter from Malaysia in August 1965. Despite the fact that security was a matter of major concern to the founding members, the declaration only referred obliquely to the issue, stating that ASEAN would aim to "promote regional peace and stability." The new grouping would confine itself to economic, social, and cultural cooperation and not be a military alliance.[41]

During the first several years ASEAN had achieved considerable success in eliminating mutual suspicion and containing political rivalries among the member countries, but cooperation in economic, social, and cultural fields had made little progress. Rapidly changing events—China's reentry into world affairs in 1969, the announcement of the Nixon Doctrine at Guam to reduce the U.S. military role in Southeast Asia, the Soviet Union's attempt to move into the region to fill the political vacuum by proposing an Asian collective security system, and the clashes between Soviet and Chinese troops along the Ussuri River in Manchuria—created the fear that Southeast Asia would become an arena for Sino-Soviet struggles. Therefore, in September 1970 Malaysian Prime Minister Tun

Razak announced that Malaysia would work for a neutralized Southeast Asia guaranteed by the United States, the Soviet Union, and China. In November 1971 the ASEAN foreign ministers, meeting in Kuala Lumpur, agreed that the neutralization of Southeast Asia was a desirable objective. They called for joint action to secure the recognition of the region as "a zone of peace, freedom and neutrality," free from any form or manner of interference by outside powers.[42] As such ASEAN had assumed political functions.

In 1975 ASEAN states were highly alarmed by the fall of Saigon into Hanoi's hands, and the installation of Communist regimes in Cambodia and Laos. In response to the new situation, they held the first summit meeting in Bali, Indonesia in February 1976. The meeting decided, among other things, to establish a central secretariat, to strengthen economic cooperation, and to take a concerted stance toward the Communist states of Indochina.[43]

Vietnam's invasion of Cambodia and its overthrow of the Khmer Rouge regime in January 1979 as well as the growth of Soviet political influence in Indochina has become a serious concern to ASEAN. The situation has further strengthened political cooperation within ASEAN. Over the past many years ASEAN has spearheaded the diplomatic crusade in the United Nations to denounce Hanoi's occupation of Cambodia. The group also succeeded in engineering the formation of a Cambodian coalition government-in-exile to oppose the Hanoi-backed regime in Phnom Penh in 1982.

There have been talks to turn ASEAN into a military alliance in view of Communist subversion and the Indochina conflict. However, it is generally agreed that a militarized ASEAN would betray the principles of establishing a zone of peace, freedom, and neutrality. It also might provoke Vietnam and increase regional insecurity. Most members still prefer bilateral military cooperation. In recent years bilateral exercises among neighbors in ASEAN have become commonplace.

ASEAN has obtained recognition from all the major developed countries. It has engaged in formal dialogue with the European Economic Community (EEC) since 1972 and with Japan, Australia, New Zealand, and the United States since 1976. The three Communist giants—the P.R.C., the Soviet Union, and Vietnam—also have shifted their attitudes toward ASEAN from negative to affirmative in the 1970s for wooing ASEAN's friendship and cooperation in order to expand their influence in the region.

The Bangkok Declaration of 1967 and the Treaty of Amity of 1976 leave ASEAN open for accession by other states in the Southeast Asian region which subscribe to the organization's aims and principles. Brunei became the sixth member in January 1984, just one week after its independence from British rule. The neutral Burma, whose membership is valued by the ASEAN leaders to enhance the association's image and prestige as a nonideological organization, has consistently stood aloof from the grouping. In mid-April 1967, about four months prior to the formation of ASEAN, Indonesian Foreign Minister Adam Malik reportedly expressed Indonesia's and Thailand's desire to invite Burma as well as Cambodia and Singapore to join the proposed association.[44] Burmese Foreign Minister Thi Han, however, told a visiting *New York Times* correspondent in early May that in the present context it would be quite a while before Burma could even consider regional associations.[45] On May 24 and 25, Malik paid an official visit to Rangoon in an unsuccessful effort to sound out Burmese leaders about the prospective ASEAN. Philippine Foreign Secretary Narciso Ramos brought up the matter of Burma's ASEAN membership again in his talks with General Ne Win while attending the meeting of the Colombo Plan Consultative Committee in Rangoon in December 1967. On returning to Manila, Ramos said that Burma was not ready to join ASEAN.[46]

In April 1968 General Ne Win made his first state visit to Singapore and Malaysia, both ASEAN members, breaking "monastic seclusion" following domestic troubles caused by Maoist Red Guards. His trip had been interpreted by some observers as a signal of Burma's interest in joining the non-Communist ASEAN. In his speech at a Singapore banquet, however, the general clearly reaffirmed Burma's intention to maintain strict neutrality in international affairs.[47] Obviously, the objective of Ne Win's journey was to improve Burma's bilateral relations with the neighboring countries, with possible effect of diminishing Peking's pressure on Burma.

Concerned mainly over the new regional situation after signing the Vietnam cease-fire agrement in Paris in early 1973, Ne Win visited Thailand, Malaysia, and Indonesia in the summer of that year. Talks held with Malaysian and Indonesian leaders gave rise to speculation that Burma was about to join ASEAN. The speculation seemed justified, for Burma had stated at the United Nations General Assembly session in New York in October 1972 that it "fully recognizes ASEAN's objective of making the area a zone of peace."[48] Yet at a reception in Jakarta, the Burmese leader merely advocated a conference of the nations in Southeast Asia to discuss ways of achieving regional peace and stability when circumstances were favorable—not participation of these nations in ASEAN or in its effort to secure neutralization of the region with big-power guarantees.[49] While visiting Rangoon, Australian Prime Minister Gough Whitlam asked Ne Win outright if Burma intended to joint ASEAN. Ne Win replied that Burma could not join ASEAN until all of the organization's members recognized China, and all U.S. bases were removed from Thailand.[50] Undoubtedly, Burma's decision was totally compatible with the principles of its foreign policy in view of ASEAN's pro-Western and anti-Communist orientation as well as Peking's hostile attitude toward the organization.

China's friendly attitude toward ASEAN since the mid-1970s has removed an obstacle for Burma to joint the organization, but other considerations continue to prevent Burma from being associated with it. In reference to ASEAN, the Political Report of the Central Committee of the Burma Socialist Programme Party in February 1977 had this to say:

It [ASEAN] is also trying to get the remaining countries in the region [to] join it and give it their support. Although the goal they have set is good in principle, Burma considers that there is need not only for the countries in the region to take part in the endeavor with a common objective and will, but also countries themselves to be independent and to be free of foreign armies and foreign military bases.[51]

Nevertheless, ASEAN has not given up on Burma. Because of the recent Cambodian war, Burma's association with ASEAN has become increasingly important. In the views of ASEAN leaders Burmese membership would strengthen the organization's diplomatic position in dealing with Vietnam and help restore regional peace and stability. Malaysian Deputy Prime Minister Musa Hitam was said to have made the same effort during his visit to Rangoon in 1982, but Burma again declined to join.[52] Certainly Burma did not want to compromise its neutral policy and become involved in the quarrel between the Communist Indochina and the non-Communist ASEAN.

THE COLOMBO PLAN

The Colombo Plan for Cooperative Economic Development in South and South East Asia, which was renamed the Colombo Plan for Cooperative Economic and Social Development in Asia and the Pacific in December 1977, was established in May 1950, following a proposal put forward by a meeting of Commonwealth foreign ministers in January 1950 at Colombo, Sri Lanka. It came into force on July 1, 1951. The plan was initially set for a period of six years. Subsequent action by consultative committee, the highest review and deliberate body of the Colombo Plan, had extended it successively for additional terms of five years until 1981. At its twenty-eighth meeting in Jakarta in November 1980, the consultative committee gave the plan an indefinite lease of life; its need and relevance will henceforth be examined only if considered necessary.[53]

The purposes of the plan are to promote interest in support for the economic and social development of Asia and the region; keep under review economic and social progress in the region, and the flow of development assistance, with a view to accelerating development through cooperative effort; and facilitate development assistance to and within the region. The plan includes technical assistance and capital assistance, the former given in the form of service of experts and technicians, facilities for study abroad, supply of equipment for research and training, and the latter in the form of grants and loans.

The membership of the Colombo Plan had grown from the original seven countries in 1950 to twenty-six countries as of 1987, extending from the Philippines in the East to Iran in the West, from the Republic of Korea in the North to Indonesia in the South.[54] Burma was invited by Britain to join the plan. In response, Prime Minister U Nu said that Burma would accept it "if we can get some advantage or benefit." He added that Burma needed technical help more than material for the rehabilitation of the country and "if we get that help we are likely to join."[55] Burma attended the 1950 and 1951 Colombo plan conferences as an observer. After very careful and prolonged consideration it decided to become a full member of the plan in March 1952. In doing so, however, it was made clear that participation could only be on the basis of ad hoc plans and not of a six-year plan development, and that Burma's participation did not prevent its claims to other sources of foreign aid.[56]

Burma has since then continued to take part in the Colombo Plan evidently because it receives benefits from that organization. Kyaw Nyunt, leader of the Burmese delegation to the Eighteenth Colombo Plan consultative committee meeting and chairman of the officials' meeting held in Rangoon in November 1967, had this to say: "Burma has sent many of her citizens to absorb knowledge and skills from developed countries. This flow of knowledge has been a source of much progress. For some time to come, people of developing countries must continue to learn pure science and advanced industrial technology from developed countries."[57]

From the time it joined the Colombo Plan in 1952 to 1986 Burma had received from member countries almost 7,000 student and trainee awards and over 2,000 experts in various fields, with a total of $139,146,300 in technical assistance. In addition, the developed member countries had

Table 13.2
Assistance to Burma by Member Countries Under the Colombo Plan
(in Thousands of US dollars), 1952–86

Donor Country	Technical Assistance					Capital Assistance		
	Number of Students Sent	Number of Trainees Sent	Number of Experts Received	Equipment	Total Expenditure	Grant	Loan	Total
Australia	461	940	265	$ 31.0	$ 14,038.9	$ 87,600		$ 87,600
Canada	67	230	54	$ 176.7	$ 3,799.2	$ 26,700	$ 7,600	$ 34,300
Japan	235	1,936	1,942	$ 1,087.7	$ 61,895.8	$335,400	$1,125,000	$ 1,460,400
New Zealand	17	142	16		$ 886.4	$ 710		$ 710
United Kingdom	800	832	209	$ 120.8	$ 21,322.2	$ 44,200		$ 44,200
United States	71	196	130		$ 30,867.0	$ 20,000		$ 20,000
India	5	349	27		$ 5,438.6			
Malaysia	3	73			$ 99.5			
Pakistan	55	53			$ 50.9			
Philippines	9	5			$ 11.9			
Singapore	34	234			$ 381.5			
Sri Lanka		19			$ 12.3			
Thailand		42			$ 75.3			
Indonesia		20						
South Korea		44			$ 266.8			
TOTAL	1,757	5,115	2,643	$ 1,416.2	$ 139,146.3	$514,610	$1,132,600	$ 1,559,610

Notes: Up to 1967 no distinction was made between students and trainees; all fellowship awards were classified as training awards. From 1968 onward students and trainees have been separately classified.
Expenditure for equipment is shown for 1986 only. Data for all other years of equipment are not available.
Capital investment covers only the period of 1971–1986. Japan's capital investment of $258.5 million for 1986 made no division of grant and loan, and it is entirely placed in the column of loan.

Source: Based on data provided to the author by the Colombo Plan Bureau.

extended to Burma capital assistance of $1,559,610,000 from 1971 to 1986. A breakdown of the assistance to Burma by donor countries is shown in Table 13.2.

Like many other developing member countries, Burma which joined the Colombo Plan as recipient of aid has itself become a donor over the years. Burma contributed a total of $5,700 in technical assistance from 1970 to 1977, including one trainee in agriculture in 1970 and three students in medical science in 1975 for Nepal and one trainee in education in 1974 and one student in humanities in 1976 for Australia.[58]

THE ASIAN DEVELOPMENT BANK (ADB)

The Asian Development Bank was established in Manila on August 22, 1966 and commenced operations on December 19 of that year. The purpose of the bank is to foster economic growth and contribute to the acceleration of economic development of the developing member countries in Asia, collectively and individually.

Bank operations are financed from two main sources: ordinary capital resources and special funds. ADB's special funds constitute the "soft loan" window at low rates of interest to meet the needs of the smaller and poorer member countries. In June 1974, the bank set up the Asian Development Fund (ADF) to consolidate special fund resources on an organized and regular basis. A Technical Assistance Special Fund (TASF) is maintained to finance technical assistance operations. The bank lends at near-market rates through its ordinary capital window and on highly concessional terms to the region's poorer nations through the Asian Development Fund. In responding to requests from member governments for loans, the Bank's staff assesses the financial and economic viability of projects and the way in which they fit into the economic framework and development priorities of the country concerned.

Membership in ADB is open to members and associated members of the United Nations Economic and Social Commission for Asia and the Pacific (ESCAP) and other regional countries and nonregional developed countries that are members of the United Nations or of any of its specialized agencies. It had forty-seven members in 1987, of which eighteen are developed countries and twenty-nine are developing nations in the Asia-Pacific region.[59]

For many years Burma was disinclined to join ADB both because of its self-reliance policy against outside assistance and the apprehension of offending the P.R.C., which had criticized the bank. With the national economy worsening in 1973 and China's new favorable posture toward this UN-sponsored financial institution after being admitted to the United Nations in 1971, Burma applied for the membership of ADB on April 9, 1973 and received its approval on the 28th of the same month.

Despite its late arrival Burma has been given much special attention by the ADB. As of July 31, 1988, the ADB had provided thirty-two loans to Burma totaling $530.86 million, including two loans amounting to $6.6 million from ordinary capital resources (OCR) and thirty loans totaling

$524.3 million from the Asian Development Fund (ADF). Technical assistance totaling $10.716 million had been provided for thirty-eight projects, of which $4.961 million were from the bank and $5.755 million from EEC and UNDP with the bank acting as executing agency.[60]

CONCLUSION:
RETROSPECT AND PROSPECT
OF BURMA'S FOREIGN RELATIONS

Bogyoke Aung San, the father of modern Burma, spoke of the importance of alliance for Burma's national security in his presidential address to the AFPFL in May 1946. A small nation, he said, with a defense force and determination can hold off a conventional attack, but it cannot stand alone for long.

Without allies it cannot expect to meet more powerful antagonists in the field of battle with any hope of success. It must therefore put its trust primarily in any regional organization that may be found in the East for the maintenance of peace. . . . Its own forces can be little more than an insurance against sudden invasion.[1]

U Nu also stated the need of his country for good allies on the eve of Burma's independence:

To prevent the destruction of our liberties . . . we need good allies. In a world where the battle is to the strong, our country cannot stand alone. . . . Furthermore, it would be no happy state for us to hang on the skirts of a powerful ally. We must be in a position to take a leading part, a decisive party, in any war in which we may be engaged. We must seek good allies, but we must also strive to be strong ourselves.[2]

After independence the tremendous tasks of economic development, of insurgency suppression, and national defense made foreign assistance and good alliances particularly imperative. During the first two years Burma's foreign policy focused on seeking a beneficial alliance with the West. However, no such alliance with the United States or Britain resulted. While the latter provided limited financial and military assistance to Burma, Rangoon received virtually no help from the former. After the decided ascent of the Communists to power in China in the fall of 1949, the Burmese government had to reassess its pro-Western stance. Before long, a neutralist policy in foreign relations was formally adopted. The policy declares nonalignment with power blocs, friendly relations with all countries, acceptance of aid with no strings attached, and making independent judgment of international issues. Essentially, Burma opposes war, imperialism, colonialism, racial discrimination, and domination of one nation by another; it stands for peaceful coexistence based on the principles of complete equality, independence, noninterference in each other's internal affairs, mutual respect and mutual benefit.

Neutralism, initially shaped by outside circumstances and events, was suited to the internal politics, in which pro-West rightists conflicted with pro-East Leftists. Neutralism was further confirmed and solidified by Burma's history, geography, and culture. Consequently, changes in leadership left Burma a neutral country as firmly as ever.

Burma has diplomatic and consular relations with some sixty countries. There are twenty-five Burmese embassies abroad, one diplomatic mission to the United Nations in New York and another one to the international organization in Geneva, Switzerland, as well as a consulate general in Hong Kong. Fifty-nine countries have embassies in Rangoon.[3] The scope of Burma's foreign relations is guided by four considerations: national security; trade; economic and technical assistance; and geographical location, cultural, and historical ties.

The neutralist policy has changed its patterns since its adoption in 1950 because of shifts in leadership, domestic policies, and the international situation. Four patterns may be classified for descriptions: positive neutralism and balancing relations between the East and the West, 1950–61; negative neutralism and balancing relations between the United States, the Soviet Union, and the People's Republic of China, 1962–72; semipositive neutralism and balancing relations between the Soviet Union and the People's Republic of China, 1973–77; and semipositive neutralism and balancing relations between the U.S.S.R./Vietnam and the People's Republic of China, 1978 to the present. Throughout the entire neutralism period Burma has been most mindful of the P.R.C., due to its size, traditional claims to Burmese territory, geographic contiguity, the existence of a motherland-minded Chinese community in Burma, and an active pro-Peking BCP. U Nu once said: "Our circumstances demand that we follow an independent course and not ally ourselves with any power bloc. . . . Be friendly with all foreign countries. Our tiny nation cannot have the effrontery to quarrel with any power. And least, among these, could Burma afford to quarrel with the new China."[4] Accordingly, to develop and maintain peaceful and neighborly relations with the P.R.C. has always been Burma's top foreign relations priority. Not surprisingly, U Nu had visited China six times between 1954 and 1960, Ne Win twelve times between 1960 and 1985, and San Yu also made a journey to Peking in 1984.

POSITIVE NEUTRALISM AND BALANCING RELATIONS BETWEEN THE EAST AND THE WEST, 1950–61

During the Cold War Burma tried to maintain neutrality to the East and West blocs and act by judging each issue on its merits. The Burmese government condemned equally the Anglo-French-Israeli aggression in Egypt and the Soviet armed intervention in Hungary in 1956. Rangoon voted for the U.S.-sponsored resolution at the United Nations in calling for a halt to North Korea's aggression against the South in 1950, but it publicly deplored the violations of the UN Charter implicit in the ill-fated U.S.-backed 1961 invasion of Cuba. In some issues, however, Burma evidently favored the Communist camp. It opposed the U.S.-sponsored UN resolution branding China as aggressor in Korea in 1951, and abstained from another resolution that requested an embargo by members on strategic items to North Korea and the P.R.C. The Burmese government reacted indifferently to the brutal Chinese suppression of the Tibetan revolt in 1950 and 1959. When Burma rejected Chinese Communist charges in 1952 that the United States had been using germ warfare in Korea, Burmese Ambassador Barrington even took time at the UN to explain Burma's action as maintaining its neutral character in international relations, in order to seek Peking's understanding on this matter. The Burmese government also prevented the rector of Rangoon University from attending a SEATO-sponsored cultural meeting in Bangkok for fear Peking would object. In order to court the P.R.C.'s friendship, U Nu asked New Delhi to delay its recognition of the new Chinese regime, thus letting Burma be the first non-Communist nation to do so. U Nu repeatedly campaigned for the P.R.C.'s UN membership, and insisted that the P.R.C. be invited to participate in the Asian-African Conference in 1955 at the Bogor Preparatory Conference in 1954. Burma opposed the 1961 Belgrade nonaligned conference to condemn the Soviet Union for its resumption of nuclear tests in the official declaration.

Following his 1954 visit to China, Burmese Prime Minister U Nu assumed a more active role in foreign relations. He made extensive world tours, including Britain, the Soviet Union, the United States, Japan, South and North Vietnam, Sweden, Norway, Denmark, Poland, Israel, and Yugoslavia. Rangoon for a time became a major cosmopolitan center in Southeast Asia by being the site of international meetings and visits by foreign leaders and experts. Burma was very active in conference diplomacy. It sponsored the First Asian Socialist Conference in January 1953 and participated in the New Delhi Conference on Indonesia in January 1949, the First Colombo Conference in April 1954, the Bogor Conference in December 1954, the Asian-African Conference in Bandung in April 1955, the Second Asian Socialist Conference in Bombay and the Colombo Powers Conference in New Delhi in November 1956, the Cairo-preparatory Conference for Belgrade Conference in June 1961, and the First Nonaligned Conference in Belgrade in September 1961. U Nu also listed one of the features of Burmese foreign policy as "Our endeavors to bridge the gulf between the two opposing blocs with a view to promote world peace."[5] At the Bandung Conference the Burmese prime minister acted as a behind-the-scenes conciliator. He personally arranged many of the meetings between Chinese Prime Minister Chou En-lai and non-Communist delegates who were seeing him for the first time.[6] U Nu also tried to mediate the conflicts between the P.R.C. and the United States during his visits to Peking and Washington in 1954 and 1955, which might have contributed to the subsequent talks between the representatives of the two countries in Geneva. But he met with total failure in his other effort to bring Egypt and Israel together.[7]

Burma entered close relations with the Soviets and their East European satellites as well as China in 1954 chiefly through barter trade agreements to dispose of its surplus rice. To meet the needs of national development Burma welcomed foreign aid from all countries, East and West, without discrimination provided such aid had no strings attached. U Nu had this to say:

The whole Union is now one vast plain of devastation due to the ravages of World War II and the general insurrection. To rebuild and rehabilitate the strength of the Union, physical, intellectual, moral and economic, we need foreign aid. When we consider the pros and cons of its acceptance, we need to take into account the source from which the aid is coming. What should be seriously taken into account is the fact whether aid has been rendered in good faith or not, whether the conditions of aid are just and equitable and whether they are likely to restrict or affect the sovereignty of the Union.

Leaving aside these aspects, it is not the path of wisdom to consider the source from which aid is forthcoming, whether it be from Russia or Britain or the United States. Such considerations based on the names of aid-giving countries are not conducive to the country's welfare. This is what I would call the method of "longing for the aunt at the expense of one's mother."[8]

Burma began to accept U.S. aid in 1950, terminated it in June 1953, and restored it in February 1956. The United Kingdom, Burma's former colonial power, had extended aid to Burma even before its formal independence in January 1948. Burma and the U.S.S.R. concluded an economic agreement in December 1955. Burma and the P.R.C. signed an agreement of economic and technical cooperation in 1961. Japan, a former enemy, became a friend when its reparations provided a most important ingredient for Burmese economic development. Burma disregarded its principle of nonrecognition of a divided country and established diplomatic relations with the Federal Republic of Germany in 1956 because of Bonn's important economic and technical assistance.

NEGATIVE NEUTRALISM AND BALANCING RELATIONS BETWEEN THE UNITED STATES, THE U.S.S.R., AND THE P.R.C., 1962–72

General Ne Win, a xenophobic type of nationalist, started to eliminate foreign economic and cultural influence in Burma and foster a new ideology, the Burmese Way to Socialism, after coming to power through a military coup in March 1962. All existing foreign cultural programs and activities were ordered to stop, and across-the-board expropriation of private business, banking, commerce, trade, and industry was put into operation. Emphasizing self-reliance and unwilling to play an active role in international affairs, the Ne Win government actually adopted a policy of negative neutralism in foreign relations, reducing the country's contacts with other countries to the barest minimum during this period.[9] The year 1960 saw the Sino-Soviet split and the transformation of a bipolar world into a multipolar world. Burma now sought to maintain balance between the United States, the U.S.S.R., and the P.R.C., the three protagonists in the Asian theater.

Burma's xenophobic measures affected the U.S. interests the most because its influence was dominant in Burma at that time. However, the

Burmese government continued to maintain good relations with the United States. When the United States sent troops near the Burmese-Thailand border following Pathet Lao military victories in Laos in 1962, Rangoon refused to allow protest demonstrations against the U.S. action lest these be interpreted as an unneutral act that would jeopardize Burma's nonalignment policy. In 1963 Burma accepted the continued delivery of small arms from the United States that began in 1958. But on the insistence of General Ne Win, according to a report of the *New York Times*, the military assistance program was kept secret to avoid provoking Communist China.[10] In 1964 an $84 million United States-financed Rangoon-Mandalay highway project was scrapped, presumably at Peking's suggestion, since Chinese Foreign Minister Marshal Chen Yi had just visited Rangoon before the decision. However, Burma did not publicly denounce the U.S. policy in Vietnam, and Ne Win went on his visit to Washington in September 1966 to counterbalance his visits to Peking and Moscow, against Chinese advice which Chinese President Liu Shao-chi and Foreign Minister Chen Yi especially put forward during their journey to Rangoon in the spring of 1966. Early in the year Burma helped arrange a Rangoon meeting between the representatives of North Vietnam and the United States for talks on peace in Vietnam. After the breach with China in mid-1967, Burma accepted an invitation from the United States to send a defense team to a Tokyo military exhibit to select what it wanted. A number of U.S. pilot instructors were enlisted to train crews to operate several new F-86 fighter aircraft.[11] The U.S. military assistance program to Burma ended in 1971 following the normalization of Sino-Burmese relations. One reason for this Burmese decision was that Ne Win regarded Chou En-lai's assurance about the good behavior of Burma's Chinese community more valuable than shiploads of U.S. arms.[12]

Ne Win's relations with the Soviet Union, which had been far from friendly during his caretaker regime, improved noticeably after 1963. The Soviet Union had few economic and cultural interests in Burma when the xenophobic measures were enforced and therefore suffered little. In fear of a nuclear war, Rangoon signed the Nuclear Test Ban Treaty in 1963 that Moscow endorsed and Peking opposed. In 1965 Ne Win paid a good will visit to Moscow. A large number of students, scientists, and technicians were sent to the Soviet Union and East European countries for study and training. The Soviets, in particular, were permitted to serve on the faculty of the Burmese Technical Institute built primarily with Soviet funds. Toward the end of 1967, as a part of its reaction to the Chinese troubles in the middle of the year, Burma received aid from the Soviet Union in the form of arms. The Soviet Union, desiring to strengthen its presence in states close to the southern flank of China, or at least to diminish Peking's influence in such areas, had taken advantage of the Sino-Burmese rift to establish a decent foothold in Burma. It extravagantly praised Burma's "socialist-oriented political system" and rigorously accused Peking of "a two-faced policy" toward Burma—professing friendly relations with the government while providing financial aid for the rebels. But Burma was extremely cautious in its dealings with Moscow as it did not want to irritate the Chinese. Burma expressed no interest in Moscow's 1969 proposal for an Asian Collective Security System, which was regarded as too anti-China and too closely associated with the Soviet Union. It also rejected a bilateral security arrangement with the U.S.S.R. that Soviet President Podgorny presented during his visit to Rangoon in 1971.[13]

Burma's new policies also reduced Chinese influence in the country. Rangoon nationalized two Chinese banks that expanded the P.R.C.'s influence through their loans to Burma's Chinese. Pro-Peking Chinese-run schools were first ordered to follow an official curriculum, being prohibited to offer indoctrination courses in Marxism-Leninism or the teachings of Mao Tse-tung, and then were taken over by the government. Since the measures were applicable to all foreign countries, Burma was not exposed to charges from China of discrimination or partisanship. The Ne Win government made great efforts to assure the Chinese of Burma's friendship. In April 1967 Rangoon went out of its way to placate Peking by repatriating some 500 refugees who fled to Burma to escape the Cultural Revolution.[14] The relations between Burma and China suddenly deteriorated in June 1967 when the Chinese cultural revolution spilled over to Rangoon, resulting in riots and bloodshed. Then Peking denounced the Ne Win government as reactionary and fascist and increased its support to the BCP. However, Ne Win urged the public to exercise restraint and sought to restore the previous friendship by treating the incident as a purely local phenomenon rather than one instigated by China. His patient diplomacy, coupled with the change of Chinese policy internally and externally, brought the Sino-Burmese ties back to normal in late 1970 when Burma returned its ambassador to Peking. Ne Win's visit to China in August 1971 marked a high point of repairing the "wound" and restored the "paukhpaw" relationship between the two countries. Burma, a persistent campaigner for the P.R.C.'s UN membership, voted to admit the P.R.C. to the world organization, which was finally accomplished. Burma also gave China support during the course of the East Pakistan crisis of 1971, in which India and the Soviet Union were involved.

During this period, the effect of rigid socialism on the economy caused a general decline of foreign trade, particularly in rice exports. Good relations existed with Malaysia, Singapore, and Ceylon, which were markets for Burmese rice. Foreign aid was limited to those accorded on a government-to-government basis or following some kind of established international pattern. Aid from the World Bank was suspended. Burma continued its special relationship with Japan and West Germany, which remained Burma's big aid donors. Burma did not utilize a $3 million interest-free agricultural loan offered by the P.R.C. in order to avoid the entry of Chinese experts to implement the projects. Two-thirds of the $84 million Chinese aid loan of 1961 were unused when suspended in 1967, but these funds were reactivated under a new Sino-Burmese economic and technical cooperation agreement in October 1971.

Burma declined to be associated with any regional organizations in the 1960s, including the Asian Development Bank and the Association of Southeast Asian Nations. General Ne Win attended the six-nation Colombo Conference on the Sino-Indian border dispute, but he stayed strictly neutral and evenhanded toward the two quarreling parties. Burma maintained a low profile in the nonaligned movement. The foreign minister was sent to represent Burma at the nonaligned summit conference. At the Consultative Conference of Nonaligned Nations in Belgrade in July 1969, the Burmese delegation, instead of presenting any constructive suggestions, warned the group not to form a Third World bloc, which could cause bloc conflicts and increase world tension.

SEMIPOSITIVE NEUTRALISM AND BALANCING RELATIONS BETWEEN THE U.S.S.R. AND THE P.R.C., 1973–77

In 1973 Burma relaxed the isolationist posture it had adopted in the name of neutrality since 1962 and took a cautiously positive approach to regional and international affairs. The change may be attributed to several factors, some internally and some externally. First, the doctrinaire socialism had not made any economic progress in the first decade. Indeed, the situation seemed to be worse. Outside aid was needed to revive the failing economy and to promote development. Second, Peking's rapprochement with Washington in 1972 had opened opportunities for Rangoon to increase contacts with the West. Finally, Burma expected the emergence of a peaceful and cooperative regional community in Southeast Asia after the Vietnam cease-fire in early 1973. On January 26, 1973, the Burmese government issued a statement welcoming the cease-fire agreement and urging nations of Southeast Asia to come together to work out the means to establish durable peace in the entire region.[15]

The shift in the power relationships in the early 1970s added new dimensions to Burma's traditional neutralist policy. Now Rangoon had to maintain a balance between China and the Soviet Union while still leaning to the former. The United States, no longer an enemy of China, could be dealt with more flexibly. The Soviets continued to compete with China for influence in Burma, particularly by discrediting China for its special ties with the Burmese rebels. The Burmese government preferred to keep silent on Soviet criticism of China to avoid causing the latter's misunderstandings. Ne Win visited Peking in 1975 and twice in 1977, presumably to ask the Chinese government to withdraw or reduce its crucial support to the Burmese Communists. On the eve of his second visit in 1977, Ne Win dismissed two pro-Soviet ministers, which was interpreted as a good will gesture to China in order to win its cooperation in the insurgent case. Burma maintained cultural and educational connections with the United States. Some high-ranking officials had been sent to the United States to study under the Burma-U.S. educational exchange program. In 1974 the two countries signed an agreement under which the United States would provide Burma with helicopters, transport aircraft, and communications equipment to help suppress illicit narcotics production and trafficking.

As regards outside aid, Burma joined the Asian Development Bank in April 1973 and resumed borrowing from the World Bank after eleven years of suspension. The Rangoon authorities were anxious to receive economic and technical assistance from international organizations and the developed countries. The United Nations specialized agencies became a major source of such assistance. Japan and West Germany continued to be the big aid donors to Burma. At the request of the Burmese government, a Burmese Aid Consultative Group was formed in November 1976 under the auspices of the World Bank that comprised Australia, Canada, France, Japan, Britain, West Germany, and the United States.

In 1973 Ne Win began a series of trips to Thailand, Indonesia, Malaysia, and Japan. In 1974 Ne Win made another series of good will missions. In April he visited India, Pakistan, and Bangladesh. Later in May and June, he visited Malaysia, Australia, New Zealand, Indonesia, and Singapore. Apparently, through such personal diplomacy the Burmese leader sought to improve or strengthen bilateral relations between his country and the countries in the region, especially the neighboring countries, which had become increasingly important in view of the new internal and international situation.

SEMIPOSITIVE NEUTRALISM AND BALANCING RELATIONS BETWEEN VIETNAM/SOVIET UNION AND THE P.R.C., 1978 TO THE PRESENT

Burmese foreign relations have shifted to a new orientation since 1978 following the official alliance between Vietnam and the Soviet Union through signing a treaty of peace and friendship; and Sino-Vietnamese hostility resulting from Vietnamese expulsion of overseas Chinese from that country, the Vietnamese invasion of Cambodia—China's only client state—and Chinese attacks against Vietnam. Rangoon has adroitly managed to maintain a balancing act between Peking and Moscow while keeping studiously neutral in the Sino-Vietnamese conflict. But preferential friendship is continuously extended to China.

The Soviet Union continued to play on the Burmese fear of Peking's interference in internal unity. On June 6, 1978, *Pravda* accused the Chinese of sowing discord among various Burmese ethnic groups and providing nationalistic opposition groups with arms. It said that Chinese leaders from time to time declared they wanted to live in friendship with Burma, but in reality pursued a policy "which cannot be assessed as anything but crude interference," and that "Fanning up strife in Burma between ethnic groups, encouraging separations, providing nationalist opposition groupings with arms, the Maoists are seeking to impose their diktat upon Burma and made it carry out a foreign policy line which is to China's liking."[16] But the Soviets have made little headway with the Burmese. Burma was reported to have declined a Soviet loan offered in 1978 and 1979. Burma withdrew from the nonaligned movement at the Havana meeting in September 1979 when the movement became closely aligned with the Soviet Union. Burma implicitly condemned the Soviet invasion of Afghanistan in December 1979 and expressed its subtle opposition to this action by not competing in the Moscow Olympics in 1980. However, Burma refrained from criticizing the brutal destruction of a South Korean airliner by the Soviet Union on September 1, 1983. Formal relations with the Soviet Union remained polite and friendly.

In 1978 Vietnam courted Burma's friendship as part of its efforts to garner support of the non-Communist states in Southeast Asia for its position in relation to its old ally and new rival, China. On the occasion of the thirtieth anniversary of Burmese independence, *Nhan Dan*, the official newspaper, stated: "Burma pursues a policy of positive neutrality and is opposed to imperialism, old and neo-colonialism and racism. It has established economic and cultural relations with the socialist and developing countries and supports the forces of genuine peace, independence and neutrality in Southeast Asia."[17] But by observing the principle of noninterference Burma denounced the Vietnamese invasion of Cambodia and has voted for UN resolutions calling for complete withdrawal of all foreign forces from Cambodia. Burma also withheld recognition of the Hanoi-installed Heng Samrin regime in Phnom Penh and supported the resolution to seat the Pol Pot regime's representative at the UN General Assembly in 1979, which was sponsored by the ASEAN states and backed by the P.R.C. At the 1980 session of the UN General Assembly that voted on the same issue of Cambodian representation, however, Burma was absent from the meeting. Thus Burma took a neutral and independent course to avoid public support for the ASEAN and China position and at the same time did not back the stance of Vietnam and the Soviet Union.

Since 1978, Sino-Burmese relations have become closer and more cordial because of Peking's need of Rangoon's cooperation in its anti-Moscow/Hanoi strategy and Rangoon's continued efforts to court Peking's friendship. The year 1978 saw the significant visit of Chinese Vice Premier Teng Hsiao-ping, the virtually supreme leader of China, to Burma. In 1979 China modified its dual policy toward Burma with the subordination of party-to-party relations to state-to-state relations by curtailing or stopping financial and military assistance to the BCP. China now maintains nominal ties with this antigovernment group but not disowns it, which may serve as a constant reminder to Burma of China's interests, including interest in a certain Burmese political distance from Moscow and Hanoi. The visit of chairman of the Burma Socialist Programme Party Ne Win to China in 1985 at the invitation of the Chinese authorities signifies the special affinity between the two countries beyond government level.

Burma's openness to the West remains unchanged. In 1980 Burma and the United States resumed economic cooperation after a lapse of nearly two decades. U.S. military aid to Burma was also renewed in October 1981. Relations between Rangoon and Washington have been warm in recent years. Japan and West Germany continuously top other countries in bilateral aid to Burma. Close relations exist between Burma and international institutions, from which Burma receives substantial aid for development needs.

Neutralism in foreign relations has been regarded by Burmese leaders as an effective policy and most suitable to their country because it has preserved Burma's independence and helped maintain its friendly relations with all the countries in the world. Burmese first Prime Minister U Nu had this to say:

Because of our neutral stand, we are in a position to be on friendly terms with all countries of both blocs. It may perhaps be difficult to understand that our friendly dealings with all countries are important for the stability of our independence. But, a perusal of the world map and the geographical position occupied by our country and a close study of various countries will convince us, beyond a shadow of a doubt, how far our friendly relations with all countries based on our neutral foreign policy have contributed toward the stability of our independence.[18]

Neutralism's success seems to be attributable less to the efforts of the Burmese government than to outside circumstances and the policies of other nations, especially the major contestants in international politics. The Cold War between East and West after World War II made its way to Asia at the turn of the 1950s. There were also two hot wars: one in Vietnam and the other in Korea. These bloody battles subsequently came to an end by compromise agreements between the two blocs. The shift of Soviet support of armed revolution to peaceful coexistence after Stalin's death and the development of hydrogen weapons by the Soviet Union and the United States decreased the possibility of military conflicts between East and West. However, the Cold War between the two blocs, especially between the United States and the P.R.C., persisted; both sides competed with each other for political and diplomatic support of the region's neutral states, which emerged as a force on the world scene after the Korean War and played a significant role at the Bandung Conference.

The 1960s saw a new international situation in Asia. For a time China offended some of its southern neighbors by Red Guard diplomacy and anti-Soviet strategy. Concerned chiefly with the Chinese threat to their continued existence, some non-Communist states of the region formed a variety of regional organizations such as ASA, ASPAC, and ASEAN in an attempt to strengthen their national resilience. But the Soviet Union tried to fill the vacuum when the United States started to disengage from the area following the failure of its massive military intervention in Vietnam. Consequently, a triangular nonmilitary power struggle for sphere of influence developed among the United States, the Soviet Union, and the P.R.C. The fighting was confined to Vietnam or Indochina.

In the 1970s, the Sino-Soviet rivalry was intensified following the Sino-American rapprochement, the Vietnamese cease-fire, and subsequent Communist victories in Indochina. The Vietnamese invasion of Cambodia and the ensuing Chinese attacks against Vietnam drew Vietnam into close alliance with the Soviet Union and added a new dimension to the power relationships among the three Communist giants. The P.R.C. has since sought to check not only Soviet but also Vietnamese hegemonism and expansionism in Southeast Asia. The United States, a traditional enemy of the Soviet Union and a new friend of China, prefers to work with China in an effort to confront Soviet and Vietnamese designs in the area. The detente between the United States and the P.R.C. enhanced Peking's rising international stature and facilitated the establishment of formal diplomatic relations between China and three ASEAN member states, which in the past had strongly feared Chinese intentions. ASEAN, which maintained neutrality in the conflicts among the Communist countries from the beginning, has changed its stance because of events in Indochina in 1978–79. The organization has emerged as the leading spokesman against Hanoi's occupation of Cambodia. Without the power to confront the Vietnam-Soviet Union combination, ASEAN seems compelled to rely upon U.S. and Chinese diplomatic or military support to force a Vietnamese withdrawal from Cambodia and to promote self-determination for the Khmer people. In the 1980s the P.R.C. has moved to improve relations with the Soviet Union, but Chinese leaders continue their struggle against Soviet and Vietnamese power and influence in Southeast Asia. Under all circumstances in the past, Burma, a non-Communist and solely neutral state in the region, has often been courted by the rival contestants.

Burma has benefited not only from the international situation but also by the policies of the three major rival powers in Asia—the P.R.C., the U.S.S.R., and the United States. The P.R.C. first condemned the Burmese government as a puppet of the imperialists and called for armed struggle to overthrow it. Preoccupied with domestic problems, however, China virtually offered no assistance beyond moral support to its Burmese Communist comrades. China changed its hostile policy to peaceful coexistence with the "bourgeois nationalist" governments of Asia after the Korean War in order to break U.S. containment. Peking sought to establish cordial relations with Rangoon and used Burma as a model for an international united front with a ring of states around it against the United States. For this purpose Peking had taken advantage of some actually or potentially disputed matters with Rangoon to court the latter's friendship. Burma was assured by Chinese Prime Minister Chou En-lai of China's noninterference in the Kuomintang troops in Burmese territory though his previous warning that "any government which offers refuge to the Kuomintang reactionary armed forces shall bear the responsibility for handling this matter and all its ensuing consequences."[19] Chou-En-lai urged overseas Chinese in Burma to obey native law and order, an act to assuage Burmese apprehension of their subversion to serve as Peking's "fifth columnists." To Burma's great relief, Peking signed a border accord under which China even made a considerable concession of its previous territorial claims. Nevertheless, the bait of a border settlement had brought about a nonaggression treaty that would prohibit the United States from using Burma as a base to attack China, thus removing the most dreadful threat to its security. To China, furthermore, such accords would also serve as precedents for border negotiations with India as well as for friendly ties with other Asian countries. Chou clearly referred to this point when he said: "These agreements were eloquent proof that reasonable solutions could be found to complex questions left over from history, and that these arrangements were now examples of the friendly solidarity of Asian countries and important victories for the Five Principles of Peaceful Coexistence."[20] As to the Burmese Communist Party, the P.R.C. has used it as a lever in its relations with the Burmese government, particularly Peking's desire to influence Rangoon foreign policy. The P.R.C. has always made great efforts to bring Burma within its own sphere of influence and to prevent the military presence and eliminate or minimize the influence of hostile powers in Burma (the United States during the 1950s and 1960s, the Soviet Union since 1960, and Vietnam since later 1978). Skillful diplomacy has been usually employed to carry out such policy (Chou En-lai made use of personal diplomacy and visited Rangoon thirteen times between 1954 and 1966). Peking's exportation of its Cultural Revolution to Burma in the mid-1960s, which had caused a Sino-Burmese rift, may be treated as an abnormal approach.

The Soviet Union had actually ignored Southeast Asia before 1954 because of Stalin's belief that the newly independent nations of the area were imperialist puppets who were too strong to allow any positive relationship to develop. As well, Moscow was preoccupied with events in Europe and with the Korean War, and the Kremlin recognized the paramountcy of Peking's interests in the area. After Stalin's death, the new Soviet leadership adopted a policy of peaceful coexistence with the established governments in Asia in an effort to harass the West. The

Burmese rice crisis of 1953–54 afforded the Soviet Union an opportunity to introduce its presence in Burma through the signing of a barter trade agreement. A Soviet aid program was also set up following the Khrushchev and Bulganin tour of Burma in 1955. The Sino-Soviet split since 1960 has made China a Soviet rival for influence in that country. Moscow tries to discredit Peking by propagandizing China's support for antigovernment groups and to note with high approbation the policies of the Burmese government and the BSPP. Nevertheless, history, geography, and culture give Peking the edge in a Sino-Soviet contest in Burma. Rangoon's fear of China further hinders the Soviet Union's efforts. The Burmese Communist Party also has cast its lot with China rather than the Soviet Union. Moscow has to maintain a low profile in Burma, being content with a proper presence in the small Buddhist nation.

U.S. involvement in Asia after the Second World War was prompted by the Communist victory in China and the outbreak of the Korean War. The United States built an alliance system to contain the expansion of Chinese Communists. It also provided aid to non-Communist countries in the area to help their economic development and political stability in strengthening their resistance to communism. Washington began sending aid to Rangoon under a bilateral agreement in September 1950. Though Eisenhower's secretary of state, John Foster Dulles, denounced the neutrals as immoral, the Eisenhower administration was reluctant to have them drawn into the Communist orbit, so U.S. aid to Burma continued. During the early years of the Ne Win military government, cultural and economic contacts with the United States were severely curtailed. Relations between Rangoon and Washington improved after Ne Win visited the United States in 1966. In recent years U.S. interest in Burma has been confined to fighting drug trafficking and maintaining modest economic and military programs. Burma has never been a major object of U.S. attention since the establishment of formal diplomatic relations between the two countries in 1948.

Undoubtedly, outside circumstances and the policies of the major powers have mainly contributed to the success of Burmese neutralism in preserving national independence. Nevertheless, the neutralist foreign policy creates some actual and potential problems for Burma. Since it has not been truly neutral in practice but leaning to the P.R.C., Rangoon may be susceptible to Peking's influence in the future. Furthermore, Burma has increasingly become economically dependent on Japan, which has persistently been Rangoon's foremost aid donor and leading trading partner. Undeniably, the continuous economic support provided by Japan is the essential ingredient in Burma's economic cement and growth; however, such lopsided economic dependence may lead to Japanese domination of the Burmese economy. The neutralist foreign policy is also partly responsible for Burma's economic backwardness, political instability, and national disunity. Burma was listed by the World Bank as the world's sixth poorest nation in 1982, and its per capita income was only $180 in early 1988. The deteriorating foreign economic relations resulting from the self-imposed isolation could hardly lead to a great improvement in the economy, and the weak economy definitely strengthens the rebellions.

Regardless of its merits or demerits, a neutral foreign policy has been pursued by the Burmese government for over three decades. And the Burmese public have raised no important voice against it. U Nu said in 1955: "It is a political fact of life today that any government of Burma which aligned itself with a big power bloc would at once lose the confidence and support of the people."[21] U Ne Win's neutralism was also designed to maintain the regime's survival.[22] The Maung Maung government has promised to take a liberal approach in national affairs. In foreign policy it will certainly open up Burma for positively diplomatic intercourse with other countries while still adhering to neutralism. Negative and isolationist policy, that has proved to be unfeasible, will hardly be favored again. It seems clear that Burma will remain a poor developing and disunited nation unless a new foreign policy is employed as part of government's efforts for national modernization.

Postscript: The Military Coup

On September 18, 1988, just two days after the announcement of Burmese authorities to sever the armed forces and civil servants from the Burma Socialist Programme Party (BSPP), the military ousted President Maung Maung and took over the government to "halt the deteriorating conditions all over the country and for the sake of the interests of the people." It abolished all existing state apparatus, including the People's Assembly, the Council of State, the Councils of Ministers, Justice, Attorneys and Inspectors, and all local governments; imposed a dusk to dawn curfew on Rangoon; and banned demonstrations and public gathering of more than five people. A State Law and Order Restoration Council was formed to rule the country, which was headed by Defense Minister and Chief of Staff General Saw Maung, a henchman of Ne Win and Sein Lwin, and consisted of eighteen other high-ranking military officers.

The State Law and Order Restoration Council

Chairman: General Saw Maung
Members: Lt. General Than Shwe
            Rear Admiral Maung Maung Khin
            Maj. General Tin Tun

Brig. General Aung Ye Kyaw

Maj. General Phone Myint

Maj. General Sein Aung

Maj. General Chit Swe

Brig. General Kyaw Ba

Colonel Maung Thint

Brig. General Maung Aye

Brig. General Nyan Lin

Brig. General Myint Aung

Brig. General Mya Thin

Brig. General Tun Kyi

Brig. General Aye Thaung

Brig. General Myo Nyung

Secretary I: Brig. General Khin Nyunt

Secretary II: Colonel Tin Oo

A nine-member cabinet was soon named, with Saw Maung as prime minister, defense minister, and foreign minister; one civilian, Pe Thein, as health minister; and seven senior armed forces officers to head the various other ministries. The commanders of the nine military regions would administer government in their areas, and towns would be run by their local commanders.

The Cabinet of the Military Government

General Saw Maung   Prime Minister
                    Minister of Defense
                    Minister of Foreign Affairs

Rear Admiral   Minister of Planning and Finance
Maung Maung Khin   Minister of Energy
                    Minister of Mines

Major General   Minister of Transportation & Communications
Tin Tun   Minister of Construction

Major General   Minister of Home and Religious Affairs
Phone Myint   Minister of Information and Culture

Major General   Minister of Education
Aung Ye Kyaw   Minister of Social Welfare and Labor

Major General   Minister of Industry I
Sing A   Minister of Industry II

Major General	Minister of Cooperatives
Chit Swe	Minister of Livestock Breeding and Fisheries
	Minister of Agriculture and Forests
Colonel Able	Minister of Trade
Dr. Pe Thein	Minister of Health

The military takeover, widely believed to be the handiwork of Ne Win, was apparently designed to cope with the mounting political crisis and reasserted BSPP's control over the country. Not surprisingly, opposition leaders greeted the coup with defiance. Former defense minister Tin U, former brigadier general Aung Gyi, and Aung San Suu Kyi, daughter of Burma's found father Aung San, issued a joint statement vowing to "continue our struggle for democracy by various means until the goal is achieved." Former prime minister U Nu claimed that his unofficial government was the only legal one in Burma and asked for international recognition.

After several days of military crackdown—killing hundreds of protesters and forcing thousands of dissident students to flee to areas along the Thai border controlled by ethnic rebels—mass demonstrations were successfully halted. The general strike, which began on August 8, 1988, formally ended on October 3, the deadline set by the military government for civil servants and laborers to return to work with a promise of repayment of September salaries if they returned and a threat of dismissal if they didn't. The military leadership then had the nation in a firm grip.

The junta committed itself to four main tasks: ensuring law and order; facilitating transport and communications; alleviating the shortage of food, clothing, and shelter; and holding general multiparty elections. It has been maintaining tight control over antigovernment activities, including military actions against insurgent organizations. With the aim of carrying out the fourth task, it revoked the 1964 Law to Protect National Unity, which banned all political parties except the BSPP, and a 1974 law designed to protect the ruling party and its organs of power. A five-man elections commission appointed by former president Maung Maung was retained by the military government, and a Political Parties Registration Law was decreed on September 27, 1988.

The BSPP renamed itself the National Unity Party (NUP) on September 29, transforming itself into a regular political party. Aung Gyi, Tin U, and Aung San Suu Kyi formed the National Democratic United League, later renamed the National League for Democracy (NLD), with Aung Gyi as chairman, Tin U as vice chairman, and Aung San Suu Kyi as secretary general, with the aim of uniting the prodemocracy forces in the country. But soon afterward Aung Gyi accused his associates of harboring communists and resigned from the NLD. He then formed the rival Union National Democracy Party (UNDP), and Tin U became the chairman of the NLD. Former premier U Nu led the League for Peace and Democracy Party (LPDP). NUP, NLD, UNDP, LPDP, and an additional 231 political parties were registered with the Elections Commission, but 105 of them were later deregistered, either on their own request or for not being in compliance with the Political Parties Registration Law.

On November 10, 1989, the Elections Commission announced that it would hold multiparty elections on May 27, 1990, and set December 28, 1989 to January 3, 1990 as the period for submitting People's Assembly candidature lists for the various constituencies. According to the ruling council's election campaign order issued on February 23, 1990, a total of 2,412 persons had applied to contest the 492 seats in the national legislature. After the withdrawal, disqualification, and death of several candidates, there remained 2,311 candidates who were allowed to run; of these, 88 were independent candidates, while the 2,223 others belonged to some 93 political parties.

In the economic area, the military regime has liberalized Burma's economic system. A 1965 law on the establishment of a socialist economic system was abolished and a Foreign Investment Law was decreed on November 30, 1988. Rangoon has been actively courting foreign investors. It has granted timber and fishing concessions to Thai firms, signed petroleum lease contracts with Japanese and other foreign oil companies, and opened border trade with China as well. However, the living conditions of the people have shown no improvement. There is a serious inflation problem, among other things. The price of rice, Burma's main food staple, has soared 400 percent. With regard to foreign affairs, the government pledges to continue an independent foreign policy.

The ruling council dropped the term "Socialist Republic" from the country's name and simply renamed the country "The Union of Burma" shortly after the coup, apparently in an attempt to disassociate itself from the previous government, whose ruinous socialist policies of a quarter century had alienated the populace and provoked the 1988 mass protests. On June 18, 1989, it again changed the country's name in English, this time to "The Union of Myanmar," thus supposedly embracing all the racial groups who are residents of the union. Given the stubborn nature of the minority insurgencies, however, it will take much more than a name change to achieve national unity.

The international reaction to Burma's military coup is generally negative. The United States and other major Western nations have suspended aid to Burma since then and, while refraining from cutting off diplomatic relations, have avoided official contacts with Rangoon leaders. On May 8, 1990, the U.S. government also declared that it would continue to suspend economic assistance to Burma until a government broadly acceptable to the Burmese people comes into being. Condemnations of Burma's military regime for human rights abuses have repeatedly been made by the United States, the twelve members of the European Community, Canada, and India. Japan, Burma's foremost aid donor, has also cut off aid to Burma. But it formally recognized the Saw Maung government in March 1989 and promised resumption of aid if the military authorities lived up to their commitment of holding free and fair multiparty elections in May 1990.

The multiparty elections which were held on May 27, 1990, as scheduled, were generally considered free and fair, with remarkably few complaints. To the surprise of the military authorities, the National League for Democracy, the main opposition party, scored a landslide victory, winning nearly 400 of the 485 contested seats in the 492-member national assembly—elections were postponed in seven constituencies. The NLD did so in spite of many disadvantages, including that its chairman, Tin U, who has been imprisoned for sedition since December 1989, and secretary general, Aung San Suu Kyi, who has been under house arrest for alleged contacts with unlawful organizations since July 1989, were barred from running, and that there were stringent restrictions on campaigning. By contrast, the military-backed National Unity Party made a notably poor showing and won no more than ten seats. Even Thi Gyaw, the head of the NUP, was defeated by a NLD candidate. Aung Gyi, the Union National Democracy Party chief, also lost to his NLD opponent. (U Nu, the leader of the League for Peace and Democracy, was disqualified from standing in the polls because of his refusal to dissolve his declared interim government.) The outcome of the elections, the first of this kind in Burma in thirty years, clearly reflected the popular dislike for the military dictatorship; and the "winds of change" toward democracy emanating recently from Eastern Europe may also have influenced the decision of the Burmese voters. The final results of the elections have not officially been announced; nor has the timetable for a transfer of power been set. On May 30, three days after the elections, General Saw Maung, the leader of the military regime, said that "Our duties will not be over until a government has been formed in accordance with the law." The military will doubtless remain in power for some time until a new constitution is adopted and a civilian government formed. In light of foreign and domestic pressures, it seems most unlikely that Rangoon will ignore the people's mandate and indefinitely put off the transfer of power. However, given the obstinacy of U Ne Win, who still has the final voice in the decisions of the Rangoon regime, the future is hardly predictable.

NOTES

CHAPTER 1

1. Milton W. Meyer, *Southeast Asia: A Brief History* (Totowa, N.J.: Littlefield, Adams and Co., 1965), pp. 29–30.

2. D. G. E. Hall, *A History of Southeast Asia*, 4th ed. (New York: St. Martin's Press, 1981), pp. 176–77.

3. Frederic M. Bunge, ed., *Burma: A Country Study* (Washington, D.C.: The American University Foreign Area Studies, 1983), p. 12.

4. Maung Htin Aung, *A History of Burma* (New York: Columbia University Press, 1967), p. 6.

5. Godfrey Eric Harvey, *History of Burma from the Earlier Time to March 10, 1824, the Beginning of the English Conquest*, new impression (London: Frank Cass and Co., 1967), pp. 29–30, 47–48.

6. Hall, *History of Southeast Asia*, pp. 147, 200.

7. Ibid., pp. 433–34.

8. J. S. Furnivall, *Colonial Policy and Practice: A Comparative Study of Burma and Netherland India* (Cambridge, England: University Press, 1948), p. 70.

9. John F. Cady, *A History of Modern Burma* (Ithaca, N.Y.: Cornell University Press, 1958), pp. 104–5.

CHAPTER 2

1. John W. Henderson et al., *Area Handbook for Burma* (Washington, D.C.: The American University Foreign Area Studies, 1971), p. 44.

2. *Burma's Fight for Freedom* (Rangoon: Government of the Union of Burma, Department of Information, 1948), p. 11.

3. Maung Maung, *Burma's Constitution* (The Hague: Martinus Nijhoff, 1959), pp. 259–308.

4. Frank N. Trager, *Burma—From Kingdom to Republic: A Historical and Political Analysis* (London: Pall Mall Press, 1966), pp. 119–39.

5. *Far Eastern Economic Review* (FEER) (Hong Kong), "A Twelve-Year Chapter and a New Start," March 17, 1960, p. 52.

6. Josef Silverstein, "Burma," in George McTurnan Kahin, ed., *Governments and Politics of Southeast Asia* (Ithaca, N.Y.: Cornell University Press, 1964), p. 127.

7. Trager, *Burma*, p. 200.

8. According to Richard Butwell, the coup reflected the failure of Burma under U Nu's leadership to register sufficient progress toward a solution of its main economic and social problems, to operate a delicately balanced constitutional structure linking the majority Burman race and a variety of ethnic minorities, to effect a meaningful synthesis between traditional Buddhist value and the though and practices of twentieth century socialism, and to make democratic institutions work in Burma. See Richard Butwell, "The Four Failure of U Nu's Second Premiership," *Asian Survey*, March 1962, pp. 3–11.

9. *Keesing's Contemporary Archives*, March 31–April 7, 1962, p. 18,675.

10. *The Burmese Way to Socialism*, Manifesto of Burma Revolutionary Council, Rangoon, April 30, 1962.

11. Frederic M. Bunge, ed., *Burma: A Country Study* (Washington, D.C.: The American University Foreign Area Studies, 1983), p. 59; *The Guardian* (Rangoon), February 14, 1964.

12. David I. Steinberg, "Burma: Ne Win After Two Decades," *Current History 79*, no. 461 (December 1980), pp. 180–84.

13. Ibid., pp. 182–83.

14. See M. C. Tun, "Civilian Face," FEER, May 27, 1972, P. 22.

15. FEER, Asia 1972 Yearbook, p. 113.

16. FEER, Asia 1974 Yearbook, p. 105; 1975 Yearbook, p. 135.

CHAPTER 3

1. For the full text of the Constitution of the Socialist Republic of the Union of Burma, see Albert P. Blaustein and Gisbert H. Flanz, eds., *Constitutions of the Countries of World*, vol. III (Dobbs Ferry, N.Y.: Oceane, 1982). A constitutional amendment adopted in 1985 creates a new position of vice chairman of the Council of State and vice president of the Republic.

2. *Asian Recorder*, October 15–21, 1974, p. 12,243; FEER, Asia 1975 Yearbook, p. 136.

3. Frederic M. Bunge, ed., *Burma: A Country Study* (Washington, D.C.: The American University Foreign Area Studies, 1983), pp. 195, 199.

4. *Forward*, April 1, 1974, p. 2.

5. Edwin W. Martin, "The Socialist Republic of the Union of Burma: How Much Change?" *Asian Survey*, February 1975, p. 129.

6. *Forward*, April 1, 1974, p. 3. The military background of members of the State Council and the Council of Ministers is based on this author's knowledge; there may be some omissions or errors.

7. Minutes of the second Pyiyhu Hluttaw Meeting, March 2–10, 1978. The military background of members of the State Council and the Council of Ministers is based on this author's knowledge; there may be some omissions or errors.

8. Pleading ill health and old age, Ne Win told the Fourth Congress of the BSPP in August 1981 that he would remain as president until October, when elections for the People's Assembly are held. "It is best to effect a smooth transition at the time of your own choosing than to let circumstances force you," he said. It was his wish, he added, "to create a precedent by handing over power at the most suitable and opportune moment." See *Asiaweek* (Hong Kong), August 21, 1981, p. 23.

9. Yearbook (Burma)—1982, November 9, 1981. The military background of members of the State Council and the Council of Ministers is based on this author's knowledge; there may be some omissions or errors.

10. Hugh C. MacDougall and Jon A. Wiant, "Burma in 1985, Consolidation Triumphs Over Innovation," *Asian Survey*, February 1986, p. 187; *Asiaweek*, August 5, 1983, p. 10.

11. *Forward*, December 1, 1985, pp. 14–15. The military background of members of the State Council and the Council of Ministers is based on this author's knowledge; there may be some omissions and errors.

12. David I. Steinberg, "Burma: Ne Win After Two Decades," *Current History* 79, no. 461 (December 1980), p. 182.

13. MacDougall and Wiant, "Burma in 1985," p. 187.

14. Steinberg, "Burma: Ne Win After Two Decades," p. 181.

15. MacDougall and Wiant, "Burma in 1985," p. 187. The seventeen members of the Central Executive Committee elected in 1985 are Chairman U Ne Win (retired general), Vice Chairman U San Yu (retired general), General Secretary U Aye Ko (retired lieutenant general), Joint General Secretary Sein Lwin (retired brigadier-general), General Kyaw Htin (present deputy prime minister and minister for defense), Lieutenant General Saw Maung (present deputy minister for defense and chief of staff of the armed forces), U Chit Hlaing (retired commodore, navy), U Saw Pyu (retired chief of staff, air), U Sein Tu (retired colonel), U Tint Swe (retired brigadier-general), U Tun Tin (retired colonel), U Tun Yi (retired major-general), U Min Gaung (retired general), U Maung Maung Kha (retired colonel), U Ye Goung (retired lt. colonel), U Than Tin (retired colonel), and U Hla Tun (retired brigadier-general). See *Forward*, September 1, 1985, p. 15. The military background of the members is based on this author's knowledge.

16. Bunge, *Burma: A Country Study*, p. 248.

17. See lists of members of the State Council and the Council of Ministers in the above section of elections and formation of government.

18. *New York Times*, September 27, 1981.

19. FEER, August 4, 1988, p. 12.

20. *Asian Recorder*, February 5–11, 1975, p. 12,424.

21. *U.S. News & World Report*, March 19, 1984, p. 65; Maung Maung Gyi, "Foreign Policy of Burma since 1962: Negative Neutralism for Group Survival," in F. K. Lehman, ed., *Military Rule in Burma since 1962* (Singapore: Maruzen Asia, 1981), p. 24.

22. *Asiaweek*, March 28, 1985, pp. 37–40.

23. Ibid., July 4, 1980, pp. 32–33; FEER, Asia 1982 Yearbook, p. 122.

24. *Asiaweek*, May 29, 1981, p. 6.

25. Raja Segaran Arumgam, "Burma: A Political and Economic Background," *Southeast Asian Affairs 1975* (Singapore: The Institute of Southeast Asian Studies, 1976), p. 43.

26. *Asian Recorder*, February 5–11, 1975, p. 12,424.

27. John B. Haseman, "Burma in 1987: Change in the Air?" *Asian Survey*, February 1988, pp. 102–3.

28. *New York Times*, July 2, 1988; FBIS-EAS, June 22, 1988, p. 16.

29. *New York Times*, September 2, 1988.

30. FEER, Asia 1978 Yearbook, pp. 146–47.

31. *U.S. News & World Report*, March 9, 1984, p. 65.

32. *Asiaweek*, July 15, 1983, p. 18.

33. Ibid., April 28, 1978, pp. 44–45.

34. *Asian Recorder*, November 19–25, 1977, p. 14,033.

35. MacDougall and Wiant, "Burma in 1985," pp. 188–89; Josef Silverstein, "Burma in 1985: A Nation on Hold," *Southeast Asian Affairs*, 1986, p. 58; FEER, March 31, 1988, p. 35, and April 21, 1988, p. 35.

36. *The Guardian*, August 11, 1987.

37. Haseman, "Burma in 1987," pp. 101–3.

38. *Asiaweek*, August 5, 1988, p. 11; *New York Times*, August 23, 1988.

39. Quoted in Mya Than, "Burma in 1986, the Year of the Snake," *Southeast Asian Affairs*, 1987, p. 115.

40. Haseman, "Burma in 1987," p. 102.

41. Bunge, *Burma: A Country Study*, pp. 224–25; Josef Silverstein, "Burma in 1981: The Changing of the Guardians," *Asian Survey*, February 1982, pp. 183–84; FEER, Asia 1982 Yearbook, p. 123.

42. Nine antigovernment movements are: the Karen National Union, the Karenni National Progressive Party, the Kachin Independent Organization, the Shan State Progress Party, the Palaung State Liberation Organization, the Pa-O National Organization, the New Mon State Party, the Wa National Organization, and the Araken State Liberation Party.

43. *Keesing's Volume 33*, March 1987, p. 35,004; *Asiaweek*, August 16, 1985, p. 25.

44. FEER, April 16, 1987, pp. 28–29.

45. *Asiaweek*, August 16, 1985, pp. 28, 30; FEER, June 18, 1987, p. 36.

46. *Asiaweek*, August 16, 1985, p. 30.

47. Ibid.

48. Ibid., July 4, 1980, p. 33.

49. Ibid., August 16, 1985, p. 20.

50. Steinberg, "Burma: Ne Win After Two Decades," p. 183.

51. *New York Times*, July 24, 1988.

52. FBIS-EAS, July 28, 1988, p. 57.

53. *New York Times*, August 20, 1988.

54. Ibid., August 21, 1988.

55. Ibid., August 25, 1988; *Chronicle* (San Francisco), August 26, 1988.

56. *New York Times*, August 30, 1988.

57. Ibid., September 11–14, 1988.

CHAPTER 4

1. *Burma Weekly Bulletin*, April 17, 1960.

2. U Nu's speech on Korea, delivered in Parliament on September 5, 1950. See *From*

Peace to Stability (Rangoon: Government of the Union of Burma, Ministry of Information, 1951), p. 99.

3. Frank N. Trager, *Burma—From Kingdom to Republic* (London: Pall Mall Press, 1966), pp. 218–19.

4. See *Toward Peace and Democracy* (Rangoon: Government of the Union of Burma, Ministry of Information, 1949), p. 209.

5. Quoted in Richard Butwell, *U Nu of Burma* (Stanford, Calif.: Stanford University Press, 1963), p. 172.

6. John Seabury Thomson, "Burmese Neutralism," *Political Science Quarterly* 72, no. 2 (June 1957), p. 271.

7. William C. Johnstone, *Burma's Foreign Policy: A Study in Neutralism* (Cambridge, Mass.: Harvard University Press, 1963), p. 43.

8. *From Peace to Stability*, p. 22.

9. U Nu, "Insurrection: An Analysis and a Remedy," speech in Rangoon, December 11, 1949. See *From Peace to Stability*, pp. 51–53.

10. *The Nation* (Rangoon), March 7, 1950.

11. *From Peace to Stability*, p. 86.

12. Ibid., p. 101.

13. U Nu, "Internal and External Problems," speech before Parliament on March 8, 1951, in *From Peace to Stability*, pp. 195–96.

14. *New York Times*, June 26, 1951.

15. U Nu, "Towards a Welfare State," speech at the First Union Welfare Conference. See *Burma Looks Ahead* (Rangoon: Government of the Union of Burma, Ministry of Information, 1953), pp. 98, 103.

16. U Nu, "Advice to University Students," Convocation Address, Rangoon University. See *Forward with the People* (Rangoon: Government of the Union of Burma, Ministry of Information, 1955), pp. 88–89.

17. U Nu's speech on Korea, *From Peace to Stability*, p. 101.

18. U Nu, "War and Its Consequences," *Burma Weekly Bulletin*, September 22, 1954, p. 188.

19. According to Maung Maung Gyi, the neutralist policy is a product of the tension between the Leftist and Centrist forces. The contradiction between the two political forces with different ideological persuasions could be synthesized or reconciled only by a policy that stays clear of the pull from the West and the lure from the East. Neutralism may not provide a focus for domestic cohesion, but it precludes opposition to and criticism against the ruling government of partiality toward one power bloc or the other. See Maung Maung Gyi, "The Crucial Third Dialectic of Burma's Neutralism under Ne Win," in Josef Silverstein, ed., *The Future of Burma in Perspective: A Symposium* (Athens, Ohio: Ohio University Center for International Studies, 1974), pp. 24–41.

20. *Burma Weekly Bulletin*, June 21, 1956, p. 74.

21. Ne Win's speech to Chamber of Deputies, October 31, 1958. See William C. Johnstone et al., *A Chronology of Burma's International Relations 1945–58* (Rangoon: Rangoon University, 1959), p. 95.

22. *The Nation* (Rangoon), March 3, 1962.

23. Albert P. Blaustein and Gisbert H. Flanz, eds., *Constitutions of the Countries of World*, Vol. III (Dobbs Ferry, N.Y.: Oceane, 1982).

CHAPTER 5

1. Quoted by U Ba Swe in Martyr's Day Speech, July 19, 1953. *Burma* 4 (October 1953), p. 4.

2. FEER, March 3, 1966, p. 405.

3. Reuters dispatch to *The Nation*, Rangoon, December 3, 1949.

4. Translation of speech delivered by Premier U Nu in Parliament on September 27, 1957 (Rangoon: Government of the Union of Burma, Ministry of Information, 1958), p. 35.

5. John W. Henderson et al., *Area Handbook for Burma* (Washington, D.C.: The American University Foreign Area Studies, 1971), p. 189.

6. *From Peace to Stability* (Rangoon: Government of the Union of Burma, Ministry of Information, 1951), pp. 51–53.

7. Michael Leifer, *The Foreign Relations of the New States* (London: Longman, 1974), pp. 12, 14.

8. New China News Agency (NCNA) (Peking), November 23, 1949.

9. William C. Johnstone, *Burma's Foreign Policy: A Study of Neutralism* (Cambridge, Mass.: Harvard University Press, 1963), p. 171.

10. Oliver E. Clubb, *The Effects of Chinese Nationalist Military Activities on Burmese Foreign Policy*, Hopkins Center Monograph (Rangoon: 1959), pp. 2–15.

11. William C. Johnstone et al., *A Chronology of Burma's International Relations 1945–58* (Rangoon: Rangoon University, 1959), pp. 24, 31; John H. Badgley, "Burma and China," in A. M. Halpern, ed., *Policies Toward China* (New York: McGraw-Hill, 1965), p. 306.

12. Richard Butwell, *U Nu of Burma* (Stanford, Calif.: Stanford University Press, 1963), pp. 181–82.

13. *From Peace to Stability*, pp. 197–98.

14. *The Nation*, July 31, 1956.

15. *Chung Hua Jen-Min Hung-Ho Kuo fen-sheng ti-tu* (Provincial atlas of the People's Republic of China) (Shanghai: 1953), notes to map, no. 46.

16. See Liao Cheng-chih, vice chairman of the P.R.C. Chinese Affairs Commission, reported to the First Enlarged Conference of the Overseas Chinese Affairs Commission, *Jen-Min-Jih-Pao* (The People's Daily), July 12, 1951.

17. Quoted in Harold C. Hinton, *China's Relations with Burma and Vietnam: A Brief Survey* (New York: Institute of Pacific Relations, 1958), p. 46.

18. Johnstone, *Burma's Foreign Policy*, pp. 220, 233.

19. *The Nation*, November 8, 1950.

20. Robert Trumbell's Report, *New York Times*, October 24, 1954.

21. "Foreign Policy of Revolutionary Government of the Union of Burma," Burma Socialist Programme Party Central Organization Committee, 1968, Appendix (A), p. 127.

22. Johnstone, *Burma's Foreign Policy*, pp. 175–76.

23. NCNA, December 10, 1954.

24. Johnstone, *Burma's Foreign Policy*, p. 172.

25. Chou En-lai, "On the Present International Situation: China's Foreign Policy and the Liberation of Taiwan," June 28, 1956, p. 95. Quoted in Kuo-kang Shao, "Chou En-lai's Diplomatic Approach to Non-aligned States in Asia, 1953–60," *China Quarterly*, June 1979, p. 331.

26. See *From World Peace to Progress* (Rangoon: Government of the Union of Burma, Ministry of Information, 1954).

27. Ralph Pattman, *China in Burma's Foreign Policy* (Canberra: Australian National University Press, 1973), p. 18.

28. Badgley, "Burma and China," p. 308.

29. Joint communique by Chou En-lai and U Nu, *Jen-Min Jih-Pao* (The People's Daily), Peking, December 13, 1954.

30. Chou En-lai, "Speech Delivered to the Political Committee of the Asian-African Countries at Bandung," *Jen-Min Jih-Pao*, April 23, 1955.

31. The Sino-Indonesian negotiations culminated in the signing of the Dual Nationality Treaty between the two countries in April 1955. The instruments of ratification were not exchanged until January 1960. From China's point of view, the treaty had failed to provide a quick solution to the problem of dual nationality, it had tended to disrupt rather than improve relations with the Indonesian government, and in Indonesia there was continued discrimination against all Chinese, whether nationals, dual nationals, or Indonesians of Chinese descent. See Stephen Fitzgerald, *China and Overseas Chinese: A Study of Peking's Changing Policy 1949–1970* (Cambridge, England: University Press, 1972), p. 107.

32. *Jen-Min Jih-Pao*, December 13, 1954.

33. Johnstone, *Burma's Foreign Policy*, p. 193.

34. Hinton, *China's Relations with Burma*, p. 54.

35. Johnstone, *Burma's Foreign Policy*, p. 21.

36. Johnstone et al., *A Chronology of Burma's International Relations*, p. 73.

37. Badgley, "Burma and China," pp. 310–11.

38. Frank N. Trager, "Burma's Foreign Policy, 1948–56," *Journal of Asian Studies* 17, no. 2 (1958), p. 101.

39. *The Nation* (Rangoon), April 6, 1955.

40. Richard J. Kojicki, "The Sino-Burmese Frontier Problem," *Far Eastern Survey* (March 1957), p. 37.

41. Harold C. Hinton, *Communist China in World Politics* (New York: Houghton Mifflin Company, 1966), p. 37.

42. *The Nation*, January 24 and October 15, 1958; Johnstone, *Burma's Foreign Policy*, pp. 184–85.

43. Badgley, "Burma and China," p. 132.

44. Maung Maung, *Burma and General Ne Win* (London: Asia Publishing House, 1969), p. 268.

45. For the full text of the treaty, see *Jen-Min Jih-Pao*, October 2, 1960, p. 3.

46. *Jen-Min Jih-Pao*, editorial, February 1, 1960.

47. *Peking Review* 5 (February 2, 1960), p. 13.

48. *Jen-Min Jih-Pao*, editorial, February 1, 1960.

49. Johnstone, *Burma's Foreign Policy*, p. 196.

50. *Peking Review* 2 (January 13, 1961), pp. 6–8.

51. *Asian Recorder*, November 19–25, 1960, p. 3,643.

52. Vidya Prakash Dutt, *China and the World: An Analysis of Communist China's Foreign Policy* (New York: Praeger, 1964), p. 173.

53. Johnstone, *Burma's Foreign Policy*, p. 198.

54. *Peking Review* 16 (April 21, 1961); *Asiaweek*, May 29, 1981, p. 30.

55. *New York Times*, December 30, 1963.

56. Harold Munthe-Kaas, "Tiger Unleashed," FEER, July 20, 1967, p. 155.

57. NCNA, March 7, 1962.

58. Robert A. Holmes, "Burmese Domestic Policy: The Politics of Burmanization," *Asian Survey*, March 1967, pp. 188–97.

59. Johnstone, *Burma's Foreign Policy*, pp. 198–99.

60. *Forward*, August 1, 1962, p. 3.

61. Ibid., May 7, 1963, pp. 3–4.

62. Robert A. Holmes, "The Sino-Burmese Rift: A Failure for China," *Orbis* 16, no. 1 (Spring 1972), pp. 215–16.

63. "Foreign Policy of the Revolutionary Government of the Union of Burma," pp. 79–80.

64. *Forward*, August 15, 1965, p. 6.

65. Robert A. Holmes, "Burma's Foreign Policy toward China since 1962," *Pacific Affairs* 45, no. 2 (Summer 1972), p. 245.

66. "Foreign Policy of the Revolutionary Government of the Union of Burma," pp. 33, 89.

67. According to Robert A. Holmes, Burma safeguarded its nonaligned policy and refused to become closely identified with the Chinese position on major international issues. Rangoon signed the Nuclear Test Ban Treaty of 1963, Peking opposed it; Burma had recognized as Indian territory land claimed by China in the Sino-Indian dispute; Burma favored the formation of Malaysia while China attacked it as a neocolonialist plot and supported Indonesia's "Confrontation Policy"; Burma had maintained neutrality in the Vietnam war whereas China had been vehemently anti-U.S. and pro-NLF and North Vietnam; Rangoon maintains cordial relations with Moscow with which Peking is engaged in a bitter ideological dispute; finally Burma has maintained neutrality on the Laotian issue, while China supports the Pathet Lao. All these have contributed to Peking's hostility toward Rangoon. See Holmes, "The Sino-Burmese Rift: A Failure for China," pp. 211–36.

68. *Asian Recorder*, August 13–19, 1967, pp. 7,855–56.

69. Ibid., p. 7,855.

70. NCNA, November 1, 1967.

71. Frank N. Trager, "Burma: 1967—A Better Ending than Beginning," *Asian Survey*, February 1968, p. 113.

72. *Asian Recorder*, November 19–25, 1967, p. 8,012.

73. Quoted in Trager, "Burma: 1967," p. 114.

74. *Working People's Daily* (Rangoon), July 17, 1968.

75. Ne Win's speech at the annual conference of the BSPP, *Working People's Daily*, November 7, 1969.

76. Ibid.

77. *The Guardian*, editorial, July 10, 1967.

78. Holmes, "Burma's Foreign Policy toward China since 1962," p. 247.

79. Rangoon Domestic Service, August 18, 1969; April 18, 1968; and March 24, 1969.

80. Holmes, "Burma's Foreign Policy toward China since 1962," pp. 245–46.

81. *New York Times*, March 19, 1968.

82. FEER, February 20, 1969, p. 311.

83. *Working People's Daily*, November 7, 1969.

84. Robert A. Holmes, "China-Burma Relations since the Rift," *Asian Survey*, August

1970, p. 695; Robert C. Horn, "Changing Soviet Policies and Sino-Soviet Competition in Southeast Asia," *Orbis* 17, no. 1 (Spring 1973), p. 506.

85. *Asian Recorder*, October 29–November 4, 1971, p. 10,431; November 12–18, 1971, p. 10,453.

86. FEER, Asia 1972 Yearbook, p. 114.

87. Holmes, "China-Burma Relations since the Rift," p. 698.

88. *The Economic Review* (London), no. 1, 1976, p. 12.

89. *Asian Recorder*, March 5–11, 1978, p. 14,197.

90. *New York Times*, August 18, 1971; *Peking Review* 30 (July 30, 1971), pp. 14–16.

91. Edwin W. Martin, "The Socialist Republic of the Union of Burma: How Much Change?" *Asian Survey*, February 1975, p. 134.

92. *The Working People's Daily*, June 7, 1978.

93. *Asiaweek*, August 7, 1981, p. 34; Aung Kin, "Burma in 1982, On the Road to Recovery," *Southeast Asian Affairs*, 1983, p. 98; FEER, Asia 1982 Yearbook, p. 123.

94. *South China Morning Post* (Hong Kong), May 13, 1985.

95. David I. Steinberg, "Burma Under the Military: Toward a Chronology," *Contemporary Southeast Asia* 3, no. 3 (December 1981), p. 281; *Business Times* (Hong Kong), November 29, 1985; FBIS-EAS, November 16, 1987, p. 22.

96. International Monetary Fund, *Direction of Trade Statistics Yearbook, 1977*, p. 89; *1984*, p. 107; *1986*, p. 120; *1988*, p. 119.

CHAPTER 6

1. Prime Minister U Nu referred to this point in his report to the Parliament on September 27, 1957. He said, "The history of Thai-Burmese relations was not a very happy one. Whenever the Burmese were strong enough, they took it out of the Thais, and whenever the Thais were strong enough, they returned the compliment. Although the flames had died down with the passage of time, the embers remained smouldering under the ashes. This was the situation when we regained our independence in 1948." See U Nu's speech to Parliament on September 27, 1957 (Rangoon: Government of the Union of Burma, Ministry of Information, 1958), p. 35.

2. *Forward*, December 22, 1962, pp. 3–4.

3. *Forward*, August 7, 1963, p. 3; *Asian Recorder*, July 30–August 7, 1963, p. 5,328.

4. Josef Silverstein, "Burma," in George Kahin, ed., *Governments and Politics of Southeast Asia* (Ithaca, N.Y.: Cornell University Press, 1964), p. 166.

5. John Henderson et al., *Area Handbook for Burma* (Washington, D.C.: The American University Foreign Area Studies, 1971), p. 196; Evelign Colbert, *Southeast Asia in International Politics, 1941–1956* (Ithaca, N.Y.: Cornell University Press, 1977), p. 185.

6. Corrine Phuanykasen, *Thailand's Foreign Relations, 1964–80* (Singapore: Institute of Southeast Asian Studies, 1984), p. 22.

7. *The Economic Review*, no. 1, 1973, p. 14; Jon A. Wiant, "Burma in 1973: New Turn in the Burmese Way to Socialism," *Asian Survey*, February 1974, p. 175.

8. *New Nation* (Bangkok), October 20, 1978.

9. *Asiaweek*, May 26, 1978, p. 8.

10. M. C. Tun, "Scuttling Hopes of Friendship," FEER, July 1, 1977, p. 20.

11. William L. Scully and Frank N. Trager, "Burma 1978: The Thirtieth Year of

Independence," *Asian Survey*, February 1979, p. 154; *Straits Times* (Singapore), May 13, 1978.

12. *New Straits Times* (Kuala Lumpur), July 26, 1980.

13. Robert H. Taylor, "Burma's Foreign Relations since the Third Indochina Conflict," *Southeast Asian Affairs*, 1983, p. 105.

14. *Asiaweek*, August 16, 1985, p. 28.

15. Suthichal Yoon, "Political Realities Move Thailand, Burma Closer," *Nation* (Bangkok), March 4, 1986.

16. Frederic Bunge, ed., *Burma: A Country Study* (Washington, D.C.: The American University Foreign Area Studies, 1983), pp. 228–29; M. C. Tun, "Cleaning up the Opium Kingdoms," FEER, February 16, 1979, p. 31.

17. *Asiaweek*, July 22, 1977, p. 14.

18. *Straits Times*, May 13, 1978.

19. Yoon, "Political Realities Move Thailand, Burma Closer."

20. Aung Kin, "Burma in 1979, Socialism with Foreign Aid and Strict Neutrality," *Southeast Asian Affairs*, 1980, p. 104.

21. *Straits Times*, April 14, 1979.

22. *The Guardian* (Rangoon), March 29, 1982.

23. *Asiaweek*, July 30, 1982, p. 16.

24. *Straits Times*, April 14, 1979; FEER, September 20, 1974, p. 35.

25. Albert D. Moscotti, "Current Burmese and Southeast Asian Relations," *Southeast Asian Affairs*, 1978, p. 90.

26. *Bangkok Post*, May 8, 1978.

27. Kin, *Burma in 1979*, p. 105.

28. FEER, Asia 1970 Yearbook, p. 81.

29. FEER, December 31, 1976, p. 16.

30. *Straits Times*, May 13, 1978.

31. *The Economic Review*, no. 2, 1985, p. 27.

32. International Monetary Fund, *Direction of Trade Annual, 1958–62*, p. 330; *1963–67*, p. 138; *1968–72*, p. 247. *Direction of Trade Statistics Yearbook, 1979*, p. 89; *1986*, p. 120; *1988*, p. 119.

33. Hugh Tinker, *The Union of Burma: A Study of the First Years of Independence*, 4th ed. (New York: Oxford University Press, 1967), p. 343.

34. *Keesing's Contemporary Archives*, March 31–April 7, 1951, p. 11,373.

35. U Nu's speech to Parliament on September 27, 1957, p. 35.

36. Edward M. Law Yone and David G. Mendelbaum, "The New Nation of Burma," *Far Eastern Survey*, October 25, 1950, p. 193.

37. *Economic Survey of Asia and the Far East* (Hong Kong), 1965, p. 176.

38. William C. Johnstone et al., *A Chronology of Burma's International Relations, 1945–58* (Rangoon: Rangoon University, 1959), p. 74.

39. *Asian Recorder*, February 1–7, 1958, p. 1,877.

40. Moscotti, "Current Burmese and Southeast Asian Relations," pp. 91–92.

41. M. C. Tun, "Burma's Oil Deal," FEER, May 13, 1974, p. 8.

42. *Working People's Daily*, editorial, September 29, 1978.

43. FEER, Asia 1965 Yearbook, pp. 98–99; 1968 Yearbook, p. 118; International Monetary Fund.

44. *Straits Times*, April 22, 1968.

45. *Siaran Akhbar*, April 24, 1968.

46. K. E. Rafferty, *Burma and Southeast Asian Regionalism* (Washington, D.C.: Research Analysis Corporation, 1969), p. 10.

47. *New Straits Times* (Kuala Lumpur), November 15, 1982.

48. Ibid., July 3, 1975.

49. International Monetary Fund.

50. *New Straits Times*, November 15, 1982; Bunge, *Burma*, p. 163.

51. *Straits Times*, editorial, April 22, 1968.

52. *Sunday Times* (Singapore), April 21, 1968; FEER, Asia 1969 Yearbook, p. 114.

53. *Straits Times*, October 4, 1980; FEER, August 22, 1980, p. 11.

54. *Straits Times*, January 17, 1986.

55. *Asian Recorder*, February 19–25, 1986, p. 18,761.

56. Ibid.

57. Ibid., November 19–25, 1963, p. 5,519.

58. *Forward*, December 1, 1970, p. 2.

59. International Monetary Fund.

60. Direction of the Rice Export Trade of Burma, Central Statistical and Economic Department, the Revolutionary Government of the Union of Burma, 1970, Table III, pp. 53–55.

CHAPTER 7

1. Frank N. Trager, *Burma—From Kingdom to Republic* (London: Pall Mall Press, 1966), p. 262.

2. William C. Johnstone, *Burma's Foreign Policy* (Cambridge, Mass.: Harvard University Press, 1963), p. 152.

3. Translation of speech delivered by Premier U Nu in Parliament on September 27, 1957 (Rangoon: Government of the Union of Burma, Ministry of Information, 1958), p. 38.

4. Russell H. Fifield, *The Diplomacy of Southeast Asia: 1945–1958* (New York: Harper and Brothers, 1958), p. 218.

5. *President Ho Chi Minh's Visit to the Republic of India and the Union of Burma* (Hanoi: Hanoi's Foreign Languages Publishing House, 1958), pp. 123–25.

6. Fifield, *Diplomacy of Southeast Asia*, p. 218.

7. *The Nation* (Rangoon), November 10, 1954.

8. Harvey H. Smith et al., *Area Handbook for North Vietnam* (Washington, D.C.: The American University Foreign Area Studies, 1967), p. 218.

9. "Foreign Policy of the Revolutionary Government of the Union of Burma," Burma Socialist Programme Party Central Organization Committee, 1968, pp. 88–89.

10. *Asian Recorder*, October 15–21, 1966, p. 7,335.

11. *Straits Times*, July 22, 1976.

12. *The Economic Review*, No. 2, 1977, p. 16.

13. FEER, Asia 1981 Yearbook, p. 116.

14. *The Guardian* (Rangoon), October 1, 1980.

15. *Straits Times*, July 24, August 5, 1982; FEER, Asia 1983 Yearbook, p. 124; *New Straits Times*, August 5, 1982.

16. International Monetary Fund, *Direction of Trade Annual, 1958–62*, p. 330; *1963–67*, p. 138; *1968–72*, p. 247. *Direction of Trade Statistics Yearbook, 1979*, p. 89; *1986*, p. 120; *1988*, p. 119.

17. *Burma Weekly Bulletin*, November 24, 1954.

18. Quoted in Roger M. Smith, *Cambodia's Foreign Policy* (Ithaca, N.Y.: Cornell University Press, 1965), p. 73.

19. Donald P. Whitaker et al., *Area Handbook for the Khmer Republic* (Washington, D.C.: The American University Foreign Area Studies, 1967), p. 206.

20. *Sunday Times* (Singapore), November 27, 1977; Albert D. Moscotti, "Current Burmese and Southeast Asian Relations," *Southeast Asian Affairs*, 1978, pp. 93–94.

21. Trager, *Burma—From Kingdom to Republic*, pp. 263–64.

22. "Foreign Policy of the Revolutionary Government of the Union of Burma," pp. 41, 72, 107.

23. *Working People's Daily*, editorial, January 25, 1977.

24. *Asiaweek*, July 8, 1977, p. 22.

25. *The Guardian*, October 23, 1979.

26. Ibid.

CHAPTER 8

1. *Burma Weekly Bulletin*, September 29, 1955.

2. Kyaw Win, ed., *U Nu Saturday's Son: Memoirs of the Former Prime Minister of Burma* (New Haven: Yale University Press, 1975), p. 227.

3. For the text of the Treaty of Peace and Friendship between Burma and India, see Maung Maung, *Burma in the Family of Nations*, 2d. ed. (Amsterdam: Djambatan, 1957), pp. 226–27.

4. *The Nation*, July 8, 1951.

5. The debt amounted to £54 million including the capital and interest. Under the Indian-Pakistani arrangement upon the partition of the Indian Empire of Great Britain, Pakistan was entitled to 17 and a half percent of the debt and India 82 and a half percent. See Russell Fifield, *The Diplomacy of Southeast Asia: 1945–58* (New York: Harper and Brothers, 1958), p. 213.

6. *Asian Recorder*, July 14–20, 1956, p. 929.

7. Shangkar Singh, *Burma and India, 1948–1962* (New Delhi: Oxford and IBH Publishing Co., 1979), pp. 64–65.

8. M. S. Rajan, *India in World Affairs, 1954–56* (New York: Asia Publishing House, 1964), p. 568.

9. Hugh Tinker, *The Union of Burma*, 4th ed. (New York: Oxford University Press, 1967), p. 350; Singh, *Burma and India*, pp. 70–71.

10. W. F. Van Eekelen, *Indian Foreign Policy and the Border Dispute with China* (The Hague: Martinus Nijhoff, 1964), p. 51.

11. Ibid., pp. 56–62.

12. *The Nation*, January 28, 1962.

13. Quoted in Richard Butwell, *U Nu of Burma* (Stanford, Calif.: Stanford University Press, 1963), p. 192.

14. Foreign Affairs Record, *India, Vol. 6*, 1960, p. 296.

15. *From Peace to Stability* (Rangoon: Government of the Union of Burma, Ministry of Information, 1951), pp. 1–2.

16. *The Nation*, June 6, 1956.

17. Win, *U Nu Saturday's Son*, pp. 225–26.

18. K. M. Panikkar, *In Two Chinas: Memoirs of a Diplomat* (London, 1956), p. 68.

19. *The Nation*, October 22, 24, and 25, 1951.

20. See Singh, *Burma and India*, pp. 67–68.

21. Butwell, *U Nu of Burma*, pp. 235–36.

22. See Singh, *Burma and India*, pp. 77–78.

23. *Forward*, December 22, 1962, pp. 2–3.

24. *Asian Recorder*, September 30–October 6, 1964, p. 6,064.

25. "Foreign Policy of the Revolutionary Government of the Union of Burma," Burma Socialist Programme Party Central Organization Committee, 1968, p. 49.

26. *Asian Recorder*, January 15–21, 1966, p. 6822.

27. Frederic M. Bunge, ed., *Burma: A Country Study* (Washington, D.C.: The American University Foreign Area Studies, 1983), p. 211; John W. Henderson et al., *Area Handbook for Burma* (Washington, D.C.: The American University Foreign Area Studies, 1971), p. 195.

28. *Asian Recorder*, May 7–13, 1969, p. 8,907.

29. FEER, Asia 1970 Yearbook, p. 81.

30. *Statist* (London), September 10, 1965, p. 677.

31. *Asian Recorder*, January 15–21, 1966, pp. 6,871–72.

32. Ibid., June 4–10, 1973, p. 11,420.

33. Ibid., August 27–September 2, 1977, p. 13,901.

34. Josef Silverstein, "Burma in 1980: An Uncertain Balance Sheet," *Asian Survey*, February 1981, p. 221.

35. *The Economic Review*, no. 3, 1984, p. 24; FEER, Asia 1985 Yearbook, p. 127.

36. *Asian Recorder*, November 25–December 1, 1968, p. 8,635; *Forward*, November 1, 1967, p. 4.

37. Statistics provided by the Colombo Plan Bureau at the request of this author.

38. International Monetary Fund, *Direction of Trade Annual, 1958–62*, p. 330; *1963–67*, p. 138; *1968–72*, p. 247. *Direction of Trade Statistics Yearbook, 1979*, p. 89; *1986*, p. 120; *1988*, p. 119.

39. *Asiaweek*, Min Thu's correspondence (mimeograph), April 30, 1984.

40. Mujtaba Razvi, *The Frontiers of Pakistan: A Study of Frontier Problem in Pakistan's Foreign Policy* (Karachi: National Publishing House, 1971), p. 200; William C. Johnstone et al., *A Chronology of Burma's International Relations 1945–58* (Rangoon: Rangoon University, 1959), p. 24.

41. *Asian Recorder*, February 5–11, 1964, p. 5,651.

42. "Foreign Policy of the Revolutionary Government of the Union of Burma," p. 53.

43. *Forward*, June 1, 1966, p. 2.

44. "Foreign Policy of the Revolutionary Government of the Union of Burma," p. 53.

45. *Keesing's Contemporary Archives*, February 19–26, p. 25,113.

46. M. C. Tun, "Burma Taking a New Stand," FEER, May 20, 1974, p. 34.

47. *Asian Recorder*, June 18–24, 1985, p. 18,367.

48. Ibid., p. 18,368.

49. International Monetary Fund, *Direction of Trade Annual, 1958–62*, p. 330; *1963–67*, p. 138; *1968–72*, p. 247. *Direction of Trade Statistics Yearbook, 1979*, p. 89; *1986*, p. 120; *1988*, p. 119.

50. *Bangkok Post*, May 10, 1973.

51. FEER, May 11, 1972, p. 18.

52. Ibid., May 20, 1974, p. 34.

53. *Asian Recorder*, August 13–19, 1977, p. 13,877.

54. *Keesing's Contemporary Archives*, October 6, 1978, p. 29, 238.

55. Aung Kin, "Burma in 1982, On the Road to Recovery," *Southeast Asian Affairs*, 1983, p. 99; *Asiaweek*, March 23, 1979, p. 18.

56. *Working People's Daily*, May 25, 1979.

57. FEER, Asia 1980 Yearbook, p. 149.

58. *Working People's Daily*, February 24, 1982.

59. Tin Maung Maung Than, "Burma in 1983: From Recovery to Growth?" *Southeast Asian Affairs*, 1984, p. 120; Asia 1985 Yearbook, p. 127.

60. *Forward*, December 1, 1986, pp. 10–11, 28.

61. International Monetary Fund, *Direction of Trade Statistics Yearbook, 1979*, p. 89; *1986*, p. 120; *1988*, p. 119.

62. Frank N. Trager, *Burma—From Kingdom to Republic* (London: Pall Mall Press, 1966), pp. 259–60.

63. *Forward*, March 1, 1966, p. 2.

64. Ibid.

65. See Chapter 13, Table 13.2: Assistance to Burma by Member Countries under Colombo Plan, 1952–86.

66. International Monetary Fund, *Direction of Trade Annual, 1958–62*, p. 330; *1963–67*, p. 138; *1968–72*, p. 247. *Direction of Trade Statistics Yearbook, 1979*, p. 89; *1986*, p. 120; *1988*, p. 119.

67. *Asian Recorder*, April 2–8, 1960, p. 3,241.

68. *Forward*, December 15, 1966, pp. 2–3.

69. Ibid., November 15, 1969, pp. 3–4.

70. Fellowship awards granted by Burma to Member Countries under the Colombo Plan, data provided by the Colombo Plan Bureau in response to this author's request.

CHAPTER 9

1. Translation of speech delivered by Premier U Nu in Parliament on September 27, 1957 (Rangoon: Government of the Union of Burma, Ministry of Information, 1958), pp. 36–37.

2. William C. Johnstone et al., *A Chronology of Burma's International Relations, 1945–58* (Rangoon: Rangoon University, 1959), pp. 24, 39.

3. For the full text of the Reparations and Economic Cooperation Agreement and the Treaty of Peace and Friendship between Burma and Japan, see *Keesing's Contemporary Archives*, December 4–11, 1954, p. 13,921.

4. Lawrence A. Olson, *Japan in Postwar Asia* (New York: Praeger Publishers, 1970), pp. 25–26; FEER, January 14, 1960, p. 50.

5. *Forward*, April 7, 1963, p. 3.

6. *Bangkok Post*, July 20, 1955.

7. *Asian Recorder*, January 1–7, 1962, p. 4,343.

8. *Forward*, October 15, 1966, p. 4.

9. *Asian Recorder*, November 5–11, 1967, p. 7,999.

10. FEER, Asia 1985 Yearbook, p. 126.

11. Albert D. Moscotti, "Current Burmese and Southeast Asian Relations," *Southeast Asian Affairs*, 1978, p. 83.

12. *Asian Recorder*, February 19–25, 1981, p. 15,891.

13. FEER, Asia 1985 Yearbook, p. 126.

14. OECD (Paris), *Geographical Distribution of Financial Flows to Developing*

Countries, 1966, pp. 138–39; *1967*, pp. 147–48; *1978*, pp. 38–39; *1983*, pp. 46–47; *1986*, pp. 64–65; *1988*, pp. 64–65.

15. International Monetary Fund, *Direction of Trade Annual, 1958–62*, p. 330; *1963–67*, p. 138; *1968–72*, p. 247. *Direction of Trade Statistics Yearbook, 1979*, p. 89; *1986*, p. 120; *1988*, p. 119.

16. See Chapter 13, Table 13.2: Assistance to Burma by Member Countries under the Colombo Plan, 1952–86.

17. International Monetary Fund.

18. See Chapter 13, Table 13.2: Assistance to Burma by Member Countries under the Colombo Plan, 1952–86.

19. International Monetary Fund.

20. William C. Johnstone, *Burma's Foreign Policy* (Cambridge, Mass.: Harvard University Press, 1963), p. 210.

21. Ibid., p. 224.

22. Translation of speech delivered by Premier U Nu in Parliament on September 27, 1957, pp. 38–39.

23. *Asiaweek*, October 21, 1983, pp. 10–15; John McBeth, "The Verdict is Guilty," FEER, November 17, 1983, pp. 18–19.

24. International Monetary Fund, *Direction of Trade Annual 1958–62*, p. 152; *1963–67*, p.–138; *1968–72*, p. 247. *Direction of Trade Statistics Yearbook 1979*, p. 89; *1986*, p. 120; *1988*, p. 119.

25. *Asian Recorder*, June 18–24, 1961, p. 4,007.

26. *Working People's Daily*, editorial, September 25, 1977.

27. See McBeth, "Verdict is Guilty," p. 18; Tin Maung Maung Than, "Burma in 1983: From Recovery to Growth?" *Southeast Asian Affairs*, 1984, p. 119; Rodney Tasker, "Strained Neutrality," FEER, January 5, 1984, p. 20.

28. *Korea Herald*, September 3, 1985.

29. International Monetary Fund, *Direction of Trade Annual, 1968–72*, p. 248; *Direction of Trade Statistics Yearbook, 1979*, p. 288; *1986*, p. 121; *1988*, p. 120.

CHAPTER 10

1. U.S. Department of State Bulletin, 17 (July 13, 1947), p. 101.

2. Ibid., 17 (January 12, 1948), p. 61.

3. *New Times of Burma* (Rangoon), March 3, 1953.

4. William C. Johnstone et al., *A Chronology of Burma's International Relations 1945–58* (Rangoon: Rangoon University, 1959), p. 38.

5. *New Times of Burma*, July 2, 1953.

6. *New York Times*, February 27, 1955.

7. FEER, Asia 1964 Yearbook, p. 95.

8. *New York Times*, editorial, April 23, 1962.

9. Ibid., February 27, 1955.

10. U Nu, Martyr's Day Speech, July 19, 1954 (Rangoon: Government of the Union of Burma, Ministry of Information, 1954), p. 1.

11. *New York Times*, July 3, 1955.

12. William C. Johnstone, *Burma's Foreign Policy* (Cambridge, Mass.: Harvard University Press, 1963), p. 95.

13. Excerpt from the statement issued by Ne Win on his arrival at Washington on

September 6, 1966, "Foreign Policy of the Revolutionary Government of the Union of Burma," Burma Socialist Programme Party Central Organization Committee, 1968, p. 67.

14. *Asian Recorder*, October 15–22, 1966, p. 7,335.

15. FEER, Asia 1976 Yearbook, p. 126.

16. Aung Kin, "Burma in 1979," *Southeast Asian Affairs*, 1980, p. 67.

17. Frank N. Trager, *Burma—From Kingdom to Republic* (London: Pall Mall Press, 1966), pp. 297–303.

18. *The Nation* (Rangoon), May 5, 1950.

19. *New York Times*, March 29, 1953.

20. Trager, *Burma—From Kingdom to Republic*, p. 313.

21. U Nu, "Report to Parliament on International Situation on September 20, 1960," *Burma Weekly Bulletin*, September 29, 1960.

22. See Trager, *Burma—From Kingdom to Republic*, pp. 310–20.

23. Johnstone et al., *A Chronology of Burma's International Relations*, p. 45; Richard Butwell, *U Nu of Burma* (Stanford, Calif.: Stanford University Press, 1963), p. 173.

24. Trager, *Burma—From Kingdom to Republic*, pp. 322–23.

25. John W. Henderson et al., *Area Handbook for Burma* (Washington, D.C.: The American University Foreign Area Studies, 1971), p. 203.

26. Josef Silverstein, "Problems in Burma: Economic, Political and Diplomatic," *Asian Survey*, February 1967, p. 124n.

27. FEER, Asia 1971 Yearbook, p. 109.

28. International Monetary Fund, *Direction of Trade Annual, 1958–62*, p. 329; *1963–67*, p. 137; *1968–72*, p. 247. *Direction of Trade Statistics Yearbook, 1979*, p. 89; *1988*, p. 119.

29. For the full text of the treaty, see Maung Maung, *Burma in the Family of Nations* (Amsterdam: Djambatan, 1957), Appendix IX, pp. 192–95.

30. Johnstone, *Burma's Foreign Policy*, p. 27.

31. Butwell, *U Nu of Burma*, p. 171.

32. Johnstone, *Burma's Foreign Policy*, pp. 49–50.

33. Trager, *Burma—From Kingdom to Republic*, p. 220.

34. U Nu, "Review of the General Situation," speech delivered in Parliament, February 1, 1949, in *Toward Peace and Democracy* (Rangoon: Government of the Union of Burma, Ministry of Information, 1949), p. 177.

35. *Forward*, October 1, 1979, p. 3.

36. Johnstone et al., *A Chronology of Burma's International Relations*, pp. 13, 38.

37. The data were provided by the Colombo Plan Bureau in response to this author's request.

38. FEER, Asia 1961 Yearbook, p. 45.

39. International Monetary Fund.

40. OECD (Paris), *Geographical Distribution of Financial Flows to Developing Countries, 1966*, pp. 138–39; *1967*, pp. 147–48; *1978*, pp. 38–39; *1983*, pp. 46–47; *1986*, pp. 64–65; *1988*, pp. 64–65.

41. International Monetary Fund.

42. FEER, December 18, 1984, pp. 30–31.

43. OECD (Paris), *Geographical Distribution of Financial Flows to Developing Countries*.

44. International Monetary Fund.

45. The data were provided by the Colombo Plan Bureau in response to this author's request.

46. International Monetary Fund.

47. OECD (Paris), *Geographical Distribution of Financial Flows to Developing Countries.*

48. International Monetary Fund.

CHAPTER 11

1. See Russell H. Fifield, *The Diplomacy of Southeast Asia, 1945–1958* (New York: Harper and Brothers, 1958), p. 225.

2. William C. Johnstone, *Burma's Foreign Policy* (Cambridge, Mass.: Harvard University Press, 1963), p. 82.

3. Alvin Z. Rubinstein, "Soviet Policy in South and Southeast Asia," *Current History* 36, no. 209 (January 1959), p. 26.

4. *New York Times*, May 9, 1956.

5. *Keesing's Contemporary Archives*, December 10–17, 1955, pp. 14,585–86.

6. Ibid., December 24–31, 1955, p. 14,605.

7. Ibid., June 2–9, 1956, p. 14,908.

8. Frank N. Trager, *Burma—From Kingdom to Republic* (London: Pall Mall Press, 1966), p. 335.

9. For a detailed account of these events, see Johnstone, *Burma's Foreign Policy*, pp. 185–87.

10. FEER, July 19, 1962, p. 110.

11. FEER, Asia 1963 Yearbook, p. 54.

12. *Forward*, April 22, 1963, pp. 2–4.

13. FEER, Asia 1966 Yearbook, p. 97; *Forward*, October 15, 1965, pp. 2–4.

14. For an excerpt from the communique, see "Foreign Policy of the Revolutionary Government of the Union of Burma," Burma Socialist Programme Party Central Organization Committee, 1968, pp. 57, 85.

15. Quoted in *Asian Notes*, July 13, 1967.

16. Robert C. Horn, "Soviet Influence in Southeast Asia: Opportunities and Obstacles," *Asian Survey*, August 1975, p. 658.

17. *Asian Recorder*, November 12–18, 1971, p. 10,453.

18. Horn, "Soviet Influence in Southeast Asia," p. 658.

19. *The Guardian*, October 1, 1980.

20. FEER, Asia 1963 Yearbooks, p. 62; International Monetary Fund, *Direction of Trade Annual, 1958–62*, p. 152; *1963–67*, p. 138; *1968–72*, p. 248. *Direction of Trade Statistics Yearbook, 1979*, p. 288; *1986*, p. 121; *1988*, p. 120.

21. *Straits Times*, July 28, 1980.

22. William C. Johnstone et al., *A Chronology of Burma's International Relations 1945–58* (Rangoon: Rangoon University, 1959), p. 53.

23. *Asian Recorder*, January 1–7, 1955, pp. 1–2.

24. For the full text of joint communique, see *Tito Speaks in India and Burma* (New Delhi, 1955), pp. 195–97.

25. *Keesing's Contemporary Archives*, December 10–17, p. 14,585.

26. *Asian Recorder*, March 28–April 4, 1959, p. 16,728.

27. FEER, Asia 1964 Yearbook, p. 139.

28. Tin Maung Maung Than, "Burma in 1983, From Recovery to Growth?" *Southeast Asian Affairs*, 1984, p. 120.

29. *Asian Recorder*, March 5–11, 1983, p. 1,761.

30. FEER, Asia 1962 Yearbook, p. 62; International Monetary Fund, *Direction of Trade Annual, 1958–62*, p. 151; *1963–67*, p. 137; *1968–72*, p. 247. *Direction of Trade Statistics Yearbook, 1979*, p. 89; *1986*, p. 120; *1988*, p. 119.

31. *Asian Recorder*, April 23–29, 1963, p. 5,158.

32. FEER, November 16, 1966, pp. 288–89.

33. *Forward*, March 1, 1984, pp. 32–34; December 1, 1984, p. 16.

34. Ibid.

35. Min Thu, "Visit—Czechoslovakia" (February 26, 1984, Mimeographed).

36. *Forward*, November 7, 1962, p. 21.

37. FEER, November 10, 1966, p. 289; *Forward*, August 1, 1966, p. 3.

38. *The Economic Review*, no. 1, 1972, p. 15.

39. FEER, Asia 1984 Yearbook, p. 138; Than, "Burma in 1983," p. 121.

CHAPTER 12

1. William C. Johnstone et al., *A Chronology of Burma's International Relations 1945–58* (Rangoon: Rangoon University, 1959), pp. 16–35.

2. Richard J. Kojechi, "Burma and Israel, A Study in Friendly Asian Relations," *Middle Eastern Affairs* 10, no. 3 (March 1959), p. 112.

3. Quoted in Russell H. Fifield, *The Diplomacy of Southeast Asia, 1945–1958* (New York: Harper and Brothers, 1958), p. 184.

4. Ide Anak Agung Gge Agung, *Twenty Years, Indonesian Foreign Policy 1945–65* (The Hague: Mouton and Co., 1973), p. 215.

5. Richard Butwell, *U Nu of Burma* (Stanford, Calif.: Stanford University Press, 1963), p. 188.

6. Frank N. Trager, *Burma—From Kingdom to Republic* (London: Pall Mall Press, 1966), p. 230.

7. *Keesing's Contemporary Archives*, December 10–17, 1955, p. 14,585.

8. *Asian Recorder*, July 11–17, 1959, p. 2,755.

9. Ibid., January 22–28, 1962, p. 4,379.

10. Translation of speech delivered by Premier U Nu in Parliament on September 27, 1957 (Rangoon: Government of the Union of Burma, Ministry of Information, 1958), p. 40.

11. William C. Johnstone, *Burma's Foreign Policy* (Cambridge, Mass.: Harvard University Press, 1963), p. 144.

12. Ibid., pp. 105, 107–8.

13. *Asian Recorder*, January 1–7, 1963, p. 4,965.

14. Speeches of U Nu (Rangoon: Government of the Union of Burma, Ministry of Information, 1960), pp. 10–11.

15. Diplomatic and Consular List, Political Department, Ministry of Foreign Affairs, Socialist Republic of the Union of Burma, Rangoon, July 1986, pp. 9–90.

16. International Monetary Fund, *Direction of Trade Annual, 1958–62*, p. 151; *1963–67*, p. 137; *1968–72*, p. 247. *Direction of Trade Statistics Yearbook 1979*, p. 89; *1986*, p. 120; *1988*, pp. 119–20.

CHAPTER 13

1. For U Nu's speech on Korea to Parliament on September 5, 1950, see *From Peace to Stability* (Rangoon: Government of the Union of Burma, Ministry of Information, 1951), p. 99.

2. Ibid., p. 100.

3. See William C. Johnstone, *Burma's Foreign Policy* (Cambridge, Mass.: Harvard University Press, 1963), p. 227.

4. *Burma Weekly Bulletin*, May 12, 1955, p. 37.

5. Quoted in Richard Butwell, *U Nu of Burma* (Stanford, Calif.: Stanford University Press, 1963), p. 176.

6. *Forward*, November 1, 1971, p. 9; *UN News Brief* 1, no. 16 (UN Information Centre, Rangoon, October 1975), p. 6.

7. Annual Report on Development Cooperation with the Socialist Republic of the Union of Burma, Annual Reports 1974 to 1987 (UNDP, Burma).

8. Robert A. Mortimer, *The Third World Coalition in International Politics*, 2nd ed. (Boulder: Westview Press, 1984), p. 12.

9. For a detailed description of the nonaligned movement, see William M. LeoGrande, "Evolution of the Nonaligned Movement," in *Problems of Communism*, January-February 1980, pp. 35–52.

10. *Working People's Daily*, October 14, 1964.

11. Ibid., July 26, 1969.

12. Ibid., September 9, 1979.

13. *Asian Recorder*, October 22–28, 1979, p. 15,134.

14. *Keesing's Contemporary Archives*, January 8, 1980, pp. 30,041–42; FEER, October 26, 1979, p. 39.

15. *The Guardian* (Rangoon), September 21, 1979.

16. Ibid., September 12, 1979.

17. *Asian Recorder*, January 8–14, 1980, p. 15,255.

18. *Bangkok Post*, May 19, 1977; *Nation*, June 12, 1977; *Asiaweek*, September 25, 1981, p. 5.

19. Manu Walyapechra, *Regional Security for Southeast Asia: A Political Geographic Assessment* (Bangkok: Thai Watana Panich Co., 1975), p. 80.

20. Quoted in Johnstone, *Burma's Foreign Policy*, p. 99.

21. *The Nation* (Rangoon), September 15, 1954.

22. *An Asian Speaks . . . About Neutrality*, a collection of speeches made by U Nu, Prime Minister of Burma, during a visit to the United States June 29–July 16, 1955 (Washington, D.C.: Embassy of the Union of Burma, 1955), p. 14.

23. Quoted in H. Arthur Steiner, *The International Position of Communist China* (New York: American Institute of Pacific Relations, 1958), p. 22.

24. *New York Times*, March 5, 1955.

25. Bernard K. Gordon, *The Dimension of Conflict in Southeast Asia* (Englewood Cliffs, N.J.: Prentice-Hall, 1966), pp. 165–66.

26. Bernard K. Gordon, "Regionalism in Southeast Asia," in Robert O. Tilman, ed., *Man, State and Society in Contemporary Southeast Asia* (New York: Praeger Publishers, 1969), p. 508n.

27. Vincent K. Pollard, "ASA and ASEAN, 1961–1967; Southeast Asian Regionalism," *Asian Survey*, March 1970, pp. 250–54.

28. Quoted in Gordon, "Regionalism in Southeast Asia," p. 507.

29. According to Vincent K. Pollard, from China's point of view it was difficult or pointless to distinguish ASA activities from SEATO activities, particularly after Peking's denouncement of an abortive prototype of ASA in the proposed Southeast Asian Friendship and Economic Treaty. See Pollard, "ASA and ASEAN," p. 245.

30. Gordon, *The Dimension of Conflict in Southeast Asia*, pp. 167, 171.

31. See Walyapechra, *Regional Security, pp. 100–1; Rene Peritz, Changing Politics of Modern Asia* (New York: D. Van Nostrand Company, 1973), pp. 71–76.

32. FEER, August 15, 1963, p. 371.

33. Ibid., July 1964, p. 10.

34. MAPHILINDO was once suggested by Philippine President Macapagal as a means of harnessing "the unity, resourcefulness and strength of the Malay peoples against the pressing southward drive of China's hordes." According to R. S. Milne, MAPHILINDO might have been conceived of as a long-range bulwark against the ambition of Peking. Alternatively, it might have been the prelude to tougher action, on the Indonesian pattern, against Chinese actually residing in Malaya and the Philippines. Prime Minister Lee Kuan Yew of Singapore, himself of Chinese descent, had criticized MAPHILINDO as a racial concept directed against the Chinese. See R. S. Milne, "Malaysia," *Asian Survey*, February 1964, p. 696; Werner Levi, *The Challenge of World Politics in South and Southeast Asia* (Englewood Cliffs, N.J.: Prentice-Hall, 1968), p. 150n.

35. Indonesian Foreign Minister Adam Malik said in Bangkok in April 1967 that preparations for the new group (ASEAN) are almost complete, and added that it would cover technical, economic, and cultural fields and be more perfect than MAPHILINDO. See Gordon, "Regionalism in Southeast Asia," p. 518n.

36. Walyapechra, *Regional Security*, p. 102; *New York Times*, June 16, 1966.

37. Peritz, *Changing Politics of Modern Asia*, p. 82.

38. "Malaysia," *Facts on File* 33 (March 18–24, 1973), p. 243; Chon-Ki Choi, "Problems Related to Economic Integration in the ASPAC Region," *Asia Quarterly*, no. 2, 1974, p. 84.

39. FEER, August 22, 1968, p. 350.

40. Peritz, *Changing Politics of Modern Asia*, p. 84.

41. For the text of the Bangkok Declaration,, see Han H. Indorf, "ASEAN: Problems and Prospects," Occasional Paper, no. 38, Institute of Southeast Asian Studies (Singapore), 1975, Annex 1, pp. 58–62.

42. J. L. S. Girling, "A Neutral Southeast Asia?" *Australian Outlook*, August 1973, p. 125.

43. Lawrence D. Stifel, "ASEAN Cooperation and Economic Growth in Southeast Asia," *Asian Pacific Community*, no. 4, Spring/Early Summer 1979, pp. 133–36; Harvey Stockwin, "The Bali Postscript: Hands Off, Hanoi," FEER, March 12, 1976, pp. 28–29.

44. *The Guardian*, August 14, 1967.

45. *New York Times*, May 2, 1967.

46. K. E. Rafferty, *Burma and Southeast Asian Regionalism* (Washington, D.C.: Research Analysis Corporation, 1969), p. 8.

47. *Working People's Daily*, editorial, April 22, 1968.

48. FEER, Asia 1974 Yearbook, p. 107.

49. Ibid., July 9, 1973, p. 19.

50. Ibid., March 11, 1974, p. 24.

51. *Working People's Daily*, February 22, 1977.

52. *Asian Recorder*, July 23–29, 1983, p. 17,281.

53. Union of International Associations, *Yearbook of International Organizations, 1986–87*, vol. 1 (New York: K. G. Saur, 1986), p. CC0281.

54. Members of the Colombo Plan are Afghanistan, Australia, Bangladesh, Bhutan, Burma, Canada, Fiji, India, Indonesia, Iran, Japan, Cambodia, Korea (Republic), Laos, Malaysia, Maldives, Nepal, New Zealand, Pakistan, Papua New Guinea, Philippines, Singapore, Sri Lanka, Thailand, United Kingdom, and the United States. See *Europa Yearbook, 1987*, vol. 1 (London: Europa Publications Limited), p. 112.

55. *Bangkok Post*, December 17, 1951.

56. *Burma Weekly Bulletin*, March 15, 1952, p. 6.

57. *Forward*, December 15, 1967, p. 3.

58. The data were provided by the Colombo Plan Bureau in response to this author's request.

59. The above descriptions are taken from *Europa Yearbook, 1987*, p. 101; T. I. Garcia, ed., *Encyclopedia of Banking and Finance*, 8th ed. (Boston: Bankers Publishing Company, 1983), p. 56; Asian Development Bank, Basic Information, November 1986.

60. Asian Development Bank, Loan, Technical Assistance and Private Sector Operations Approvals, no. 8817, July 1988, pp. 1, 11–12, 23.

CHAPTER 14

1. Quoted in Maung Kyaw Thet, "Some Burmese Views on the Neutralization of Southeast Asia," in *New Directions in the International Relations of Southeast Asia: The Great Powers and Southeast Asia* (Singapore: The Institute of Southeast Asian Studies, 1973), p. 151.

2. Quoted in Hugh Tinker, *The Union of Burma*, 4th ed. (New York: Oxford University Press, 1967), p. 342.

3. The twenty-five countries in which Burma has an embassy are Australia, United States, Bangladesh, People's Republic of China, Czechoslovakia, Egypt, France, Federal Republic of Germany, India, Indonesia, Israel, Italy, Japan, United Kingdom, Lao People's Democratic Republic, Malaysia, Nepal, Pakistan, Philippines, Union of Soviet Socialist Republics, Singapore, Sri Lanka, Thailand, Socialist Republic of Vietnam, Yugoslavia. See *Burma Trade Guide*, Socialist Republic of the Union of Burma, Ministry of Trade, p. 90. In addition to the aforementioned countries, other countries that have established an embassy in Rangoon are Albania, Algeria, Argentina, Belgium, Brazil, Bulgaria, Canada, Chile, Cuba, Cyprus, Denmark, Finland, German Democratic Republic, Greece, Hungary, Iran, Iraq, Republic of Korea, Mauritius, Mongolia, Morocco, New Zealand, Nigeria, Norway, Poland, Portugal, Romania, Spain, Sweden, Switzerland, Syria, Turkey, Austria, and the Netherlands. See *Diplomatic and Consular List*, Political Dept., Ministry of Foreign Affairs, Socialist Republic of the Union of Burma, Rangoon, July 1986, pp. 9–90.

4. *From Peace to Stability* (Rangoon: Government of the Union of Burma, Ministry of Information, 1951), pp. 51–53.

5. U Nu's address at Martyr's Day Mass Rally on July 20, 1956, *Burma Weekly Bulletin*, July 26, 1956.

6. John Seabury Thomson, "Burmese Neutralism," *Political Science Quarterly* 72, no. 2 (June 1957), p. 276.

7. William C. Johnstone, *Burma's Foreign Policy* (Cambridge, Mass.: Harvard University Press, 1963), p. 144.

8. U Nu's address at Martyr's Day Rally on July 19, 1950, in *From Peace to Stability*, pp. 90–91.

9. Maung Maung Gyi characterizes the neutralism of the Burmese government since 1962 as "negative neutralism" which refers to a policy that (1) is inward-looking, xenophobic, and immature in its weltanschaug, (2) fails to infuse dynamism into the nation's economy, and (3) lacks courage to pursue an active and leading role in regional matters. It is more than isolation and noninvolvement; it is closed and self-serving, only responding selectively to inputs from abroad. See Maung Maung Gyi, "Foreign Policy of Burma since 1962: Negative Neutralism for Group Survival," in F. K. Lehman, ed., *Military Rule in Burma since 1962* (Singapore: Maruzen Asia, 1981), p. 10.

10. *New York Times*, December 30, 1963.

11. John F. Cady, *The United States and Burma* (Cambridge, Mass.: Harvard University Press, 1976), p. 259.

12. *The Guardian*, November 8, 1971.

13. FEER, February 18, 1974, p. 32.

14. F. S. B. Donnison, *Burma* (New York: Praeger Publishers, 1970), p. 234.

15. FEER, Asia 1974 Yearbook, p. 106.

16. *Asian Recorder*, July 23–29, 1978, p. 14,418.

17. *Asiaweek*, January 20, 1978, p. 14.

18. *The Nation* (Rangoon), November 20, 1954.

19. Evelign Colbert, *Southeast Asia in International Politics, 1941–1956* (Ithaca, N.Y.: Cornell University Press, 1977), p. 133.

20. NCNA, April 10, 1960.

21. *An Asian Speaks . . . About Neutrality*, a collection of speeches made by U Nu, Prime Minister of Burma, during a visit to the United States, June 29–July 16, 1955 (Washington, D.C.: Embassy of the Union of Burma, 1955), p. 14.

22. According to Maung Maung Gyi, Ne Win's negative neutralism in foreign policy is for group (Ne Win's regime) survival; see Maung Maung Gyi, "Foreign Policy of Burma since 1962."

BIBLIOGRAPHY

BOOKS

Agung Gde Agung, Ide Anak. *Twenty Years, Indonesian Foreign Policy: 1945–65*. The Hague: Mouton and Co., 1973.

Blaustein, Albert P., and Gisbert H. Flanz, eds. *Constitutions of the Countries of the World*, Vol. III: *The Constitution of the Socialist Republic of the Union of Burma*. Dobbs Ferry, N.Y.: Oceane, 1982.

Bunge, Frederic M., ed. *Burma: A Country Study*. Washington, D.C.: The American University Foreign Area Studies, 1983.

Burma Socialist Programme Party Central Organization Committee. *Foreign Policy of the Revolutionary Government of the Union of Burma*. Rangoon: 1968.

Butwell, Richard. *U Nu of Burma*. Stanford, Calif.: Stanford University Press, 1963.

Cady, John F. *A History of Modern Burma*. Ithaca, N.Y.: Cornell University Press, 1958.

———. *The United States and Burma*. Cambridge, Mass.: Harvard University Press, 1976.

Clubb, Oliver E. *The Effects of Chinese Nationalist Military Activities on Burmese Foreign Policy*. Hopkins Center Monograph. Rangoon: 1959.

Colbert, Evelign. *Southeast Asia in International Politics, 1941–1956*. Ithaca, N.Y.: Cornell University Press, 1977.

Donnison, F. S. B. *Burma*. New York: Praeger, 1970.

Dutt, Vidya Prakash. *China and the World: An Analysis of Communist China's Foreign Policy*. New York: Praeger, 1964.

Fifield, Russell H. *The Diplomacy of Southeast Asia, 1945–1958*. New York: Harper and Brothers, 1958.

Fitzgerald, Stephen. *China and Overseas Chinese: A Study of Peking's Changing Policy, 1949–1970.* Cambridge, England: University Press, 1972.

Furnivall, J. S. *Colonial Policy and Practice: A Comparative study of Burma and Netherland India.* Cambridge, England: University Press, 1948.

Gordon, Bernard K. *The Dimension of Conflict in Southeast Asia.* Englewood Cliffs, N.J.: Prentice-Hall, 1966.

Government of the Union of Burma, Ministry of Information. *Toward Peace and Democracy.* Rangoon: 1949.

———. *From Peace to Stability.* Rangoon: 1951.

———. *Burma Looks Ahead.* Rangoon: 1953.

———. *From World Peace to Progress.* Rangoon: 1954.

———. *Forward with the People.* Rangoon: 1955.

Hall, D. G. E. *A History of Southeast Asia,* 4th ed. New York: St. Martin's Press, 1981.

Halpern, A. M., ed. *Politics Toward China.* New York: McGraw-Hill, 1965.

Harvey, Godfrey Eric. *History of Burma from the Earlier Time to March 10, 1824, the Beginning of the England Conquest.* New impression. London: Frank Cass and Co., 1967.

Henderson, John W., et al. *Area Handbook for Burma.* Washington, D.C.: The American University Foreign Area Studies, 1971.

Hinton, Harold C. *China's Relations with Burma and Vietnam: A Brief Survey.* New York: Institute of Pacific Relations, 1958.

———. *Communist China in World Politics.* New York: Houghton Mifflin Company, 1966.

Htin, Aung Maung. *A History of Burma.* New York: Columbia University Press, 1967.

Indorf, Han H. "ASEAN: Problems and Prospects." Occasional Paper, no. 38. Singapore: Institute of Southeast Asian Studies, 1975.

Johnstone, William C. *Burma's Foreign Policy: A Study in Neutralism.* Cambridge, Mass.: Harvard University Press, 1963.

———, et al. *A Chronology of Burma's International Relations 1945–58.* Rangoon: Rangoon University, 1959.

Kahin, George McTurnan, ed. *Governments and Politics of Southeast Asia,* 1st and 2nd editions. Ithaca, N.Y.: Cornell University Press, 1959 and 1964.

Lehman, F. K., ed. *Military Rule in Burma Since 1962.* Singapore: Maruzen Asia, 1981.

Leifer, Michael. *The Foreign Relations of the New States.* London: Longman, 1974.

Levi, Werner. *The Challenge of World Policies in South and Southeast Asia.* Englewood Cliffs, N.J.: Prentice-Hall, 1968.

Maung Maung. *Burma's Constitution.* The Hague: Martinus Nijhoff, 1959.

———. *Burma and General Ne Win.* London: Asia Publishing House, 1969.

———. *Burma in the Family of Nations.* Amsterdam: Djambatan, 1957.

Meyer, Milton W. *Southeast Asia: A Brief History.* Totowa, N.J.: Littlefield, Adams and Co., 1965.

Mortimer, Robert A. *The Third World Coalition in International Politics,* 2d ed. Boulder, Colo.: Westview Press, 1984.

Olson, Lawrence A.. *Japan in Postwar Asia.* New York: Praeger, 1970.

Panikkar, K. M. *In Two Chinas: Memoirs of a Diplomat.* London: 1956.

Pattman, Ralph. *China in Burma's Foreign Policy.* Canberra: Australian National University Press, 1973.

Peritz, Rene. *Changing Politics of Modern Asia.* New York: D. Van Nostrand Company, 1973.

Phuanykasen, Corrine. *Thailand's Foreign Relations, 1964–80*. Singapore: Institute of Southeast Asian Studies, 1984.

Rafferty, K. E. *Burma and Southeast Asian Regionalism.* Washington, D.C.: Research Analysis Corporation, 1969.

Rajan, M. S. *India in World Affairs, 1954–56.* New York: Asia Publishing House, 1964.

Razui, Mujtaba. *The Frontiers of Pakistan: A Study of Frontier Problem in Pakistan's Foreign Policy.* Karachi: National Publishing House, 1971.

Silverstein, Josef. *Burma: Military Rule and Politics of Stagnation.* Ithaca, N.Y.: Cornell University Press, 1977.

———, ed. *The Future of Burma in Perspective: A Symposium.* Athens, Ohio: Ohio University Center for International Studies, 1974.

Singh, UMA Shangkar. *Burma and India, 1948–1962.* New Delhi: Oxford and IBH Publishing Co., 1979.

Smith, Harvey H., et al. *Area Handbook for North Vietnam.* Washington, D.C.: The American University Foreign Area Studies, 1967.

Smith, Roger M. *Cambodia's Foreign Policy.* Ithaca, N.Y.: Cornell University Press, 1965.

Socialist Republic of the Union of Burma, Ministry of Foreign Affairs. *Diplomatic and Consular List.* Rangoon: 1986.

Steiner, H. Arthur. *The International Position of Communist China.* New York: American Institute of Pacific Relations, 1966.

Tilman, Robert O., ed. *Man, State and Society in Contemporary Southeast Asia.* New York: Praeger, 1969.

Tinker, Hugh. *The Union of Burma: A Study of the First Years of Independence*, 4th ed. New York: Oxford University Press, 1967.

Trager, Frank N. *Burma—From Kingdom to Republic: A Historical and Political Analysis.* London: Pall Mall Press, 1966.

Van Eekelen, W. F. *Indian Foreign Policy and the Border Dispute with China.* The Hague: Martinus Nijhoff, 1964.

Walyapechra, Manu. *Regional Security for Southeast Asia: A Political Geographic Assessment.* Bangkok: Thai Watana Panich Co., 1975.

Whitaker, Donald P., et al. *Area Handbook for the Khmer Republic.* Washington, D.C.: The American University Foreign Area Studies, 1967.

Win, Kyaw, ed. *U Nu Saturday's Son: Memoirs of the Former Prime Minister of Burma.* New Haven: Yale University Press, 1975.

NEWSPAPERS

Bangkok Post.
Guardian (Rangoon).
Jen Min Jih Pao
Nation (Rangoon).
New China News Agency.
New Nation (Bangkok).
New Straits Times (Kuala Lumpur).
New York Times.
South China Morning Post (Hong Kong).
Straits Times (Singapore).
Working People's Daily (Rangoon).

PERIODICALS

Asia Quarterly.
Asia Yearbook.
Asian Development Bank. *Loan, Technical Assistance and Private Sectors Operations Approvals.*
Asian Pacific Community.
Asian Recorder.
Asian Survey.
Asiaweek.
Australian Outlook.
Burma Weekly Bulletin.
China Quarterly.
Contemporary Southeast Asia.
Current History.
Economic Review (London).
Far Eastern Economic Review.
Far Eastern Survey.
Foreign Broadcast Information Services, Daily Report, East Asia.
Forward (Rangoon).
International Monetary Fund. *Direction of Trade Annual* and *Direction of Trade Statistics Yearbook.*
Journal of Asian Studies.
Keesing's Contemporary Archives.
Middle Eastern Affairs.
OECD. *Geographical Distribution of Financial Flows to Developing Countries.*
Orbis.
Pacific Affairs.
Peking Review.
Political Science Quarterly.
Problems of Communism.
Southeast Asian Affairs.
UNDP, Burma. *Annual Report on Development Cooperation with the Socialist Republic of the Union of Burma.*
U.S. News & World Report.

INDEX

ABOUT THE AUTHOR

CHI-SHAD LIANG received his Ph.D. from New York University and has taught political science at universities in the United States, Singapore, and Taiwan. His interests, originally focused on Western governments and politics, turned to Southeast Asian affairs after he joined the faculty of Nanyang University in 1975. He is the author of numerous articles on Southeast Asian politics, including "Thailand's Foreign Policy" and most recently "The Normalization of Diplomatic Relations between Indonesia and the People's Republic of China." He is presently engaged in a study of the foreign policies of all the countries of Southeast Asia.

DATE DUE

		NOV 0 0 2001	
			Printed in USA